CENSORSHIP IN SOUTH ASIA

CENSORSHIP IN SOUTH ASIA
CULTURAL REGULATION FROM SEDITION TO SEDUCTION

EDITED BY

Raminder Kaur
William Mazzarella

INDIANA UNIVERSITY PRESS
Bloomington and Indianapolis

This book is a publication of

Indiana University Press
601 North Morton Street
Bloomington, IN 47404-3797 USA

http://iupress.indiana.edu

Telephone orders: 800-842-6796
Fax orders: 812-855-7931
Orders by e-mail: iuporder@indiana.edu

The paper used in this publication meets the minimum requirements
of the American National Standard for Information Sciences—Permanence
of Paper for Printed Library Materials, ANSI Z39.48-1992.

Manufactured in the United States of America

Library of Congress Cataloging-in-Publication Data

Censorship in South Asia : cultural regulation from sedition to
seduction / edited by Raminder Kaur and William Mazzarella.
p. cm.
Includes bibliographical references and index.
ISBN 978-0-253-35335-1 (alk. paper) — ISBN 978-0-253-22093-6 (pbk. : alk. paper)
1. Censorship—India. 2. Censorship—South Asia.
I. Kaur, Raminder. II. Mazzarella, William, date–
Z658.I4C46 2009
363.310954—dc22

2008052447

1 2 3 4 5 14 13 12 11 10 09

Contents

Acknowledgments

T he origins of this volume are shrouded in the mists of the distant past— November 2002, to be precise, when some of the contributors to the present volume assembled at the annual meeting of the American Anthropological Association in New Orleans to participate in a panel on censorship in South Asia. That so much time has passed between those initial conversations and the publication of this book makes the editors all the more grateful for the work, patience, and trust that the contributors and the splendid people at Indiana University Press—especially Rebecca Tolen—have put into the project. Acknowledgment is also overdue to Nayanika Mookherjee and Monika Mehta for their input during earlier stages of this project. Raminder Kaur would like to thank the British Academy for its Small Research Grant (SG-35512) to begin research on public perceptions and representations of nuclear issues in 2003, and the Economic and Social Research Council for its grant (RES-000-23-1312) to develop the work and bring it to fruition. William Mazzarella is indebted to the Law and Society Program of the National Science Foundation, whose generous support allowed him to begin investigating issues of censorship.

CENSORSHIP IN SOUTH ASIA

Between Sedition and Seduction
Thinking Censorship in South Asia

William Mazzarella and Raminder Kaur

C ensorship has been getting a lot of publicity in South Asia recently. The mid-1990s alone saw a veritable carnival of controversies over the line between the acceptable and the unacceptable in public culture. By way of example, one might point to the uproar in 1994 over the alleged obscenity of Madhuri Dixit's song-and-dance sequence "Choli ke peeche kya hai?" (What lies behind the blouse?) in Subhash Ghai's film *Khalnayak* (The Villain); to Shekhar Kapur's *Bandit Queen* (1994), which ran afoul of caste sentiment, the film censor board, and its real-life protagonist, outlaw-turned-parliamentarian Phoolan Devi; to Mani Ratnam's feature *Bombay*, whose dramatization of the Bombay riots of 1992–93 managed to offend Hindu groups, Muslim groups, and secular intellectuals alike; to the extraordinary intensity of protest (including one self-immolation) and policing that surrounded the Miss World 1996 pageant in Bangalore; to the Bombay ban on Salman Rushdie's *The Moor's Last Sigh* (1995), which, in the wake of the national ban on *The Satanic Verses* (1989), desecrated Indian political idols old and new by featuring a dog named Jawaharlal Nehru and an unflattering, thinly veiled portrait of Maharashtrian strongman Bal Thackeray; to Mira Nair's feature adaptation of the *Kamasutra*, whose Hindi version was in 1997 subjected to more stringent cuts than its English-language equivalent; to the public burning of a scholarly article, printed by the *Illustrated Weekly of India* in 1994, that dared to call into question elements of the mythical narratives surrounding both the seventeenth-century Maratha ruler Shivaji and the nineteenth-century proto-nationalist heroine the Rani of Jhansi, and to the cinema smashing, legal challenges, and extra-legal harassment that greeted Deepa Mehta's *Fire* in 1998, not to mention the direct physical violence that ended the first attempt at filming its successor, *Water*, in Banaras in 2000, before it had even properly begun.[1]

And that is just India. In November 2007, Pakistani President Pervez Musharraf declared a state of emergency and suspended the country's 1973 constitution for a third time. Independent news stations were forced off the air, hundreds of protesting journalists and lawyers were arrested, and the Supreme

Court was stacked with clients of the regime. But this relatively dramatic move—in some ways reminiscent of the much more extended Emergency imposed by Indira Gandhi in India in 1975–77—was not Musharraf's first experiment with censorship. Sporadic official interference with the media, as well as "disappearances," had marked his rule since its beginnings in a "bloodless" coup in 1999. As in other parts of the world, the Internet presents wholly new challenges to official regulation in Pakistan. "Cyber-cops" working for the Pakistan Internet Exchange assiduously filter pornography, blasphemy, and "anti-Islamic" content from online networks. More generally, as Asad Ahmed's contribution to this volume shows, Islamic orthodoxy is regularly asserted in the form of blasphemy accusations. Popular culture is by no means immune: Islamist parties have been involved in incidents such as the 2003 provincial banning of music by the pop band Junoon. And in the wake of the murder of three journalists in October of that year, the press has censored itself more stringently.

Bangladesh emerged onto the international map of censorship when Taslima Nasreen's novel *Lajja* was banned in 1993. Like that of Salman Rushdie's *The Satanic Verses*, the banning of *Lajja* only heightened the adulation with which it was greeted in the "liberal" West. Nasreen's more recent books, *Ka* and *Dwikhandita*, personal memoirs that identify the author's sexual partners in both Bangladesh and West Bengal, have provoked lawsuits and bans in both cross-border regions. In Nepal, two major incidents since 1990 stand out (prior to that year, under the Panchayat regime, press censorship was strictly enforced). First, there was the deafening silence consequent upon the Narayanhiti massacre of 2001, when the editor in chief, general manager, and publisher of *Kantipur* were arrested for publishing an editorial by Baburam Bhattarai, the second in command of the Maoists, alleging that the king's brother Gyanendra was implicated in the deaths (see Genevieve Lakier, this volume). Second, there was the more dispersed regime of press censorship imposed along with the state of emergency from November 2001 until August 2002. While not as brutal as other emergencies in the region, it involved comparable restrictions on the press: all pro-Maoist publications were raided and shut down the day before the emergency was declared. As for Sri Lanka, censorship in that country has generally been a function of the ongoing battle between the state and the Liberation Tigers of Tamil Eelam. While some aspects of President Chandrika Kumaratunga's media censorship have now been revoked, it is still illegal to report on any proposed operations or military activity by the security forces, or on the acquisition of arms, ammunition, or other equipment by the armed forces or the police.

The incidents we have listed here are only some of the best known, most publicized controversies of recent years. By no means a comprehensive list, they nevertheless give some indication of the terrain with which we are concerned in this book. Our intention in bringing them together under the rubric "South Asia" is to explore the commonalities that result from their shared history of colonial subjugation, to account for their different locations in distinct national polities, and finally to examine the more recent connections and contestations brought about by regional liberalization in the 1990s and beyond. Even though the primary emphasis of this volume is on Indian materials, our underlying ambition is comparative.

The very fact that these and other similar controversies were taken up and circulated by the cosmopolitan media establishment in South Asia (and often beyond) is itself an important social fact. Superficially, part of what made them compelling as public dramas was the way that they seemed to stage the contradictions of South Asian public culture in an age of globalization, a period that combined effervescent consumerism with surging religious nationalism. From the mid-1980s, and especially after 1991, the deregulation of consumer goods markets joined hands with an explosion in new commercial media. In the 1980s, India saw the spread of color television (already established in the rest of South Asia) and the coming of video and cable; in the 1990s, South Asians began being influenced by transnational satellite broadcasting and the Internet.

In this context, the relationship between the public interest and the interests of publicity inevitably became more complicated. Marketers, politicians, cultural producers, and social movements all sought to establish a presence and a profile, to realize the value-creating possibilities of these new affect-intensive fields of public identification, as well as to proclaim their dangers (Brosius and Butcher 1999; Kaur 2003; Mankekar 1999; Mazzarella 2003; Rajagopal 2001). Structurally, the lure of what one might call "profitable provocation" meant that the boundaries of public civility and decorum were constantly being challenged. Key areas included the public representation of sex, the supposed irrationality of religious appeals in an ostensibly secular democracy, and the line between legal and illegal forms of political action—this last paradigmatically represented by the popular rise of hypermasculinized, often violent political organizations like Bombay's Shiv Sena (Eckert 2003; D. Gupta 1982; T. Hansen 2001; Katzenstein 1979).

With so much publicity, many of these controversies actually became less rather than more intelligible. The media reportage quickly imposed a kind of discursive hardening, a sort of dramaturgical standardization. It was the prescripted urban drama of cultural globalization, the overdetermined clash between the cosmopolitans and the localists, between modernity and tradition, iconically fungible and ready-made for nightly summary on CNN. At the same time, it would certainly be a mistake to suggest that we might reach the "truth" of these events by stripping away the "distortions" and "biases" imposed upon them by the media. These were struggles that, in a very fundamental way, lived and breathed in the media, found their distinctive forms and their conditions of possibility in the space provided by a particular configuration of media and publics.

On the one hand, then, the essays in this book represent a collective attempt to step back from the clamor, the relentless repetition of assertions and counterassertions. On the other hand, we recognize, and indeed theorize, the inseparability of medium and message. In part, this means placing the contemporary moment in historical and regional context. To what extent do the contemporary discourses, practices, and conditions of censorship echo or reconfigure those of the colonial period? The essays by William Mazzarella on the 1920s and Tejaswini Ganti on the 1990s, for instance, suggest striking continuities in the social dynamics of film censorship. Meanwhile, Asad Ahmed describes the present-day adaptation in Pakistan of colonial legal precedents regarding the management of blasphemy. Historical and comparative contextualizations also require us, in turn, to rethink the very category of censorship. To what extent is it an adequate or relevant descriptor for the kinds of public cultural controversies that we invoked above? In what ways might we retheorize censorship to gain a fuller understanding of the cultural politics of publicity in South Asia?

From Censorship to Cultural Regulation

As with many social phenomena, the harder one looks at censorship, the stranger it becomes. At the most elementary level, it quickly becomes clear that the common understanding of censorship as the repressive action of states and state-sanctioned institutions will not get us very far. One might even say that there seems to be something of a correlation between the regulation of cultural production and the proliferation of provocative forms.

Repression first: by considering censorship only as a matter of silencing and of denial, we risk missing what several scholars have identified as its productive aspects. On one level, we are referring here to the relatively obvious point that any kind of utterance or discourse, indeed the very possibility of language, depends upon a kind of constitutive foreclosure (Bourdieu 1991; Butler 1997, 1998). This foreclosure is, as Judith Butler argues, "a kind of unofficial censorship or primary restriction in speech that constitutes the possibility of agency in speech" (Butler 1997, 41). In this sense, censorship does not act upon a sovereign subject from "outside"; rather, it is one of the very preconditions of subjectivity itself.

In practice, the relation between explicit and implicit forms of censorship is often ambiguous. Genevieve Lakier's contribution to this volume demonstrates this through an analysis of the self-censorship at work in the (lack of) representations of the massacre of Nepal's royal family in the indigenous media. And Tejaswini Ganti shows how, in the world of Mumbai film production, self-censorship is inextricable from personal dispositions toward controversial themes. An open question—both empirically and theoretically—is the extent to which the positive meanings allowed or encouraged by a certain linguistic or semiotic configuration are "haunted" by the possibilities that they must disavow, but which remain crucial to their intelligibility. By attending to the particular politics of disavowal that structure particular events or sites we may well understand something important about the dialectic of fascination and loathing that seems to characterize so much in the realm of censorship.

On another level, some have theorized censorship as productive according to a Foucauldian schema. Classically, we imagine the censor, as Dominic Boyer (2003) reminds us, as the very embodiment of the anti-intellectual. The endangered word (lively, inventive, poetic) confronts the complacent philistinism of the censor (sluggish, pedantic, literal-minded). But censorship may also be understood as a generative technology of truth. Far from only silencing, censorship can be read as a relentless proliferation of discourses on normative modes of desiring, of acting, of being in the world. Censorship, then, would be not so much a desperate rearguard action as a productive part of the apparatus of modern governmentality (Foucault 1977, 1981, 1985; Burchell, Gordon, and Miller 1991). We find, for example, that the discourses on Indian women's sexuality that emerge out of censorship practices are internally contradictory in interesting ways (Mehta 2001a, 2001b). Moreover, as many recent public controversies over obscenity in the media have demonstrated, these discourses are routinely brought up against equally normalizing but quite different narratives of Indian sexuality—the compulsory invocation, by "cosmopolitan" critics of censorship, of Vatsyayana's *Kamasutra* and the erotic temple carvings at Khajuraho and Konarak as an integral part of the South Asian civilizational heritage is a case in point (Mazzarella 2003).

Then there is the issue of censorship as the action of states or state-sanctioned institutions. This raises two questions. The first is one of location: where is censorship? What are its sites? Where should we look for its logic and its motivation? Should we be examining the utterances and ideologies of those individuals authorized by states to intervene in the public field? To what extent does it makes sense to say that the person who enacts censorship is better placed to comment on it than the person who is subjected to it? The Foucauldian commandment would of course encourage us, at the very least, to situate the deliberate utterances of practitioners within a wider institutional field. But what is the best way to discern the play of censorship in the textual traces left by its operation? How should we read the relationship between the carapace of case law and the relatively ephemeral rhythms of public debate?

The second question is: what counts as censorship? Are we stretching the term too far if we force it to accommodate not only the operations of official regulatory authorities (the courts, the police, censor boards), but also various "extra-legal" or "extra-constitutional" initiatives and interventions? Some, for example, speak of the "silent censorship" that market forces (or, better, the social relations that are reified as such) exert on the contents of the media (Jansen 1988). Does violent action against the screening of a film count as censorship? Or indeed any of the many "nonviolent" tactics by which activists in South Asia often seek to prevent particular events from unfolding—*bandh, hartal, dharna, gherao, morcha,* and so forth?

What about the connections between legal and extra-legal forms of censorship? Does it matter if violent or nonviolent "extra-legal" protests are linked, by either alliance or overt sympathy, to those who in fact do control the official machinery of regulation? Such, for instance, was the case at the time of the Shiv Sena's agitations against Deepa Mehta's *Fire* in Bombay and Delhi in 1998. Only recently ousted from political power in the state of Maharashtra, the Shiv Sena smashed theaters and intimidated actors, and its actions were greeted ambiguously by the national government. National political leaders deplored the "lawlessness" of the violence, but regionally affiliated allies at the center expressed solidarity with the Shiv Sena and approval of its actions. And the Minister for Information and Broadcasting was in fact, to the dismay of many, persuaded to return the film to the Censor Board for recertification (a practice that the Indian Supreme Court declared illegal in December 2000).

On occasion, conversely, the Indian Supreme Court has effectively acknowledged the social force of an unofficial ban. In mid-2006, after Aamir Khan, the lead actor in the feature film *Fanaa*, publicized his support for the rehabilitation of people displaced by the Narmada dam project in Gujarat, cinemas were subjected to violent, government-supported protests in that state (see Ganti, this volume). Constitutionally guaranteed freedom of expression was thus pitted against the repressive practices of a state government claiming to be acting in the interests of the people. The deadlock was only partly resolved when public interest litigation filed in the Supreme Court yielded the verdict that while nothing could be done against the unofficial ban, individual theaters would receive protection if they decided to screen the film. In this way, in the language of the ruling, "any untoward incident" might be avoided. Certainly, "extra-legal" or "extra-constitutional" forms of censorship, particularly when backed by local leaders, often seem to carry more social force than official decrees.

Censorship is not just *in* but also *of* the public sphere. The censor's work is generally figured as semiclandestine, shy of—indeed perhaps structurally opposed to—publicity. We might imagine a nondescript functionary, seated at an anonymous desk in some minor alleyway of the corridors of power, wielding his pen and scissors with smug pedantry (and, yes, it does seem to us that the censor, despite all evidence to the contrary, is generically imagined as a man). But censorship, as we have suggested, often actually courts the full glare of publicity. And its agents are by no means always impersonal bureaucrats. Moreover, the censor's work is, it turns out, curiously dependent upon that which it would silence. Not just structurally—a society without obscenity would no longer require censors—but also sensuously: no one pays the provocative word or image as much careful, detailed, even loving attention as the censor.

We are all familiar with this compulsive dependency from the drama of legal process, in which the forbidden word must be spoken again and again precisely to establish its unspeakability. And we recognize it in marketing strategies that court bans in order to heighten the desirability of a product by marking it as controversial. Official censors will themselves often dismiss the indignant objections of their "victims" as nothing but publicity stunts. Shekhar Kapur in the field of commercial cinema (*Bandit Queen; Elizabeth*) and Anand

Patwardhan in that of political documentary (*Father, Son and Holy War; War and Peace*) have both been accused of this in recent years.[2]

In this age of liberalization and proliferating media, the singular central- ized authority of government film censorship is increasingly coming to be supplemented by self-regulatory councils and professional advisory bodies, such as the Advertising Standards Council of India (see Angad Chowdhry's chapter in this volume) and the Press Council. Such independent organiza- tions respond to and act upon public complaints against already circulating images and texts. But when it comes to the cinema, there has long been a sense that pre-censorship is necessary. The Government of India's Central Board of Film Certification retains the tradition established in 1920 when the first regional film censor boards were founded: moving images are censored before they reach the viewing public.

Richard Burt (1994) points out that censorship sometimes even becomes quite flamboyant, as keen and as media-savvy a participant in the great game of publicity as its ostensible quarry. In this mode, censorship competes vigorously for the conviction and attention of its publics. "Censorship not only legitimates discourses by allowing them to circulate, but is itself part of a performance, a simulation in which censorship can function as a trope to be put on show." Book burning, then, is not simply about getting rid of the books, but equally about "staging an opposition between corrupting and purifying forces and agencies" (xviii). This publicity-seeking side of censorship is evident across the spectrum of regulatory action. Few cultural protests, whether on the left or the right, whether peaceful or incendiary, commence these days before newspaper and television reporters are in place and press releases have been distributed. But the official organs of censorship are equally conscious of the need to perform their efficacy and their relevance. When film actor Anupam Kher took over as chairman of the Central Board of Film Certification in India in the autumn of 2003, the board was quick to promote a new clampdown on indecency in song remixes from Hindi films and in film trailers on television.

All this points to the fact that any claim to authority or power via regu- latory action in the field of public culture necessarily involves some kind of active participation in the poetics and politics of publicity. Calculated inter- ventions into the play of publicity—in the name of protecting the sentiments or cultural integrity of a particular constituency—are a standard feature of contemporary South Asian politics. Such forms of "censorship"—calling for the withdrawal of this or that film, book, or newspaper article—are obvi- ously not just silencing tactics; rather they rely, for their political efficacy, on harnessing and mobilizing the public energy of the very artifacts that they appear to be trying to suppress. That such wagers on mass attention should be a matter of some ambivalence is not surprising. The ideal of communicative rationality in public debate frowns upon the affective, spectacular tactics of publicity—the performance of this distinction becomes particularly evident during elections, when candidates' speeches are closely monitored for potential boundary breachings. Publicity is by definition an affect-intensive game. It touches upon the embodied and the intimate; its mode of persuasion is one of resonance rather than reason. It often seems dangerously close to disorder and chaos, to the nightmare transformation of the enlightened democratic public into the rampaging crowd. But this ambivalent aesthetics is, we are suggesting, the condition of any effective appeal to identification and authority. Public culture may be seen, then, as a field of contest between competing experiments, often improvised and volatile, with the profitable and productive harnessing of this volatile substance. That such experiments, sometimes extraordinarily compelling to their constituencies, are always inconclusive, provisional, and even dangerous goes without saying.

Many of the analyses in this volume deal with the affective intensity of images, that unstable corporeal energy that is captured in Jean-Francois Lyotard's (2004) notion of the "figural." But in other chapters, the censored objects are speech acts or texts, closer, perhaps, to Lyotard's "discourse." Our aim in these pages is not to prejudge the relation between image and text in the work of censorship, but rather to offer a provocative juxtaposition of situations that, taken together, might open up new ways of thinking about the libidinal economies of South Asian public cultures.

From one perspective, censorship seems designed to moderate the excessive force or perceived violence that such experiments in public cultural action may involve, as in the case of "hate speech," "obscenity," or—and this is an important one in India—incitement to communal violence (Butler 1997; Gates 1997; Heumann, Church, and Redlawsk 1997; Strum 1999; Walker 1994). But from another perspective, censorship also seems to routinize transgression. Michael Taussig, developing Elias Canetti's aphorism about the secret at the heart of power (Canetti 1984, 290), argues that social orders are based on "public secrets": that is, forms of knowledge or representation that are generally, even obsessively, known insofar as they must not be overtly acknowledged (Taussig 1999). Everyday social dynamics, then, depend upon the institutionalization or management of transgression, the normalization of a system of taboos and their breaking. In India, this dynamic has recently become particularly evident around the phenomenon of the screen kiss. For the first fifty years of Indian independence, Indian commercial filmmakers rigorously observed an unwritten (but nevertheless incessantly discussed) "ban" on hero-heroine kissing. The prohibition began to be breached with some regularity in the 1990s, but always with a *frisson* that effectively reinstated the power of the prohibition. One film, *Kwahish* (2003), was marketed primarily on the premise that it contained seventeen kissing scenes; meanwhile, critics complained that Indians looked "unnatural" and "awkward" kissing in films, and actresses keen to be seen as respectable made much of their visceral dislike of screen kissing.[3]

Madhava Prasad (1998) has developed an interesting argument that the prohibition on the screen kiss is an index of the impossibility of a bourgeois space of conjugal privacy and intimacy in the context of a social order that continues in large measure to idealize a patriarchal-feudal model of the family and, by extension, of social relations in general. We do think that the question of the intimate and its possible relations to public culture is crucial. But we are also interested in exploring the ways in which the compulsive assertion and foregrounding of a prohibition serves to routinize a pattern of incitement, a relation of desire and transgression. Here, too, censorship is not only or even primarily a mechanism of denial and repression; rather it serves to articulate a language of the hidden and the sacred in which everything is "out in the open" even if it is not "shown." We are, of course, well aware of this dynamic when it comes to marketing or to show business: the strategic deployment of the tease, of provocation as a means of focusing attention, realizing profits, and attracting audiences. However, mainstream politics is no less performative, no less dependent upon a volatile calculus of provocation and respectability, defiance and dignity (T. Hansen 2001, 2004; Kaur 2003).

What we are proposing, then, is to resituate the concept of censorship as a particular (perhaps in some ways privileged) variant of a more general set of practices which we are calling "cultural regulation" (cf. Post 1998; Thompson 1997). Cultural regulation comprises a spectrum of public cultural interventions that would, according to conventional taxonomies, be considered quite distinct and, at the extremes, diametrically opposed—as in the case of "publicity" and "censorship."[4] By placing these practices on an analytic continuum, we hope to make visible the ways in which both rely on specific (more or less conscious) attempts to generate value (commercial or symbolic) out of a delicate balancing of incitement and containment. So whereas the term "censorship" to a greater or lesser extent alludes to the institutionalized frames of a legalistic discourse, the concept of "cultural regulation" points to the performative, the productive, and the affective aspects of public culture.

On one level, then, we are interested in calling into question the too-quick equation of state censorship with cultural regulation per se. At the same time, we believe that it is crucial to recognize the reasons and social effects of this equation. If we began with the figure of formal censorship, we did so because state-sanctioned censorship has become the most consciously and conspicuously formalized institution of cultural regulation. It brings the burden and force of state power to bear on its public cultural interventions, even as it claims, often rather complacently, to be acting in the public interest. No wonder it is reviled; no wonder we are tempted to understand the field of public culture as a relentless struggle between the valor of free expression and the cynicism of repressive power.

The fact that state censorship has become such a paradigmatic figure of regulation enables the complementary institutionalization of the discourse of free speech. But the phenomenon of state censorship is also inevitably compelling because of the seemingly self-evident way in which it expresses a claim to sovereignty in matters of cultural production. One result of this is that almost any would-be authoritative intervention into public cultural controversy at once challenges, and is more or less covertly covetous of, this sovereignty (cf. Das 1995). We are certainly not advocating that the differences between state-sponsored and non-state-sponsored regulatory initiatives be downplayed. That would obviously be both politically and analytically indefensible. But we are suggesting that it may be analytically productive to examine the extent to which non-state interventions remain entangled in a state-based model of sovereignty and, conversely, the extent to which the state depends on discursive and performative devices whose efficacy is anything but "empty and homogenous." In this volume, Raminder Kaur, for example, explores how the performance of nuclear politics in India struggles with a tension between authoritarian efficacy and the appearance, at least, of democratic accountability. In a zone such as this, censorship is not so much a matter of outright prohibition or the absence of transparency. Rather, it may take the form of an anxiously measured public revelation of information, narratives, and images within the spectacular, performative space of publicity.

Although we are inspired by questions of general theoretical significance, the method we are proposing is one of concrete historical and ethnographic engagement. At the same time, taking cultural regulation as an ethnographic object means grappling with discourses and practices that themselves almost invariably at once make universalizing claims (in relation to rights or duties) and particularizing assertions (often in the name of culture or tradition). We see this combination articulated today all over the world in the name of multiculturalism. But it was forged in the crucible of colonization, and the happy hybridity of the multicultural ideal continues to look rather more problematic from a postcolonial vantage point.

Private Lives, Public Affairs

The distinction between reasoned debate and affective excitability easily gets mapped onto a supposedly constitutive difference between Western and non-Western publics. This understanding has deep colonial roots, of course, but it persists to this day in the self-understandings of South Asian elites (cf. Haynes 1992; Varma 1998). Foreign scholars of cultural regulation in India will often be told something like "In theory I am all for freedom of speech and expression. But in a society like ours . . ." Those who staff the formal institutions of cultural regulation (the courts, the censor boards) lean on this combination of cosmopolitan idealism and apparently "pragmatic" particularist vigilance in order to protect an excitable, indiscriminate, and ignorant majority from its own worst tendencies.

So far, so familiar. It is hardly necessary to point to the myriad ways in which this is a flagrantly ideological, self-serving, and elitist discourse. Instead, we would like to push the inquiry in a slightly different direction. When is public affective agitation "good" and when is it "bad"? When, for example, does it promise commitment or patriotism and when does it threaten unrest and chaos? What are the mediations and the forms of social action that harness agitation to given social projects, reactionary and revolutionary alike? What are the imagined locations of the affective as opposed to the deliberative in given public formations? How, in South Asian contexts, have these formations changed from colonial to postcolonial times, and what regulatory strategies have been mobilized to manage them?

We are reminded of Partha Chatterjee's (1993, 6) famous proposition that Indian publics under colonialism were predicated on a constitutive split: between an "outer" or "material" domain of instrumental politics, and an "inner" or "spiritual" domain of cultural identity and sentiment. This split, Chatterjee argues, allowed for the formation of a distinctively Indian modernity under colonialism: one in which Indians could participate in the public game of power politics, as defined by British conventions and institutions, and yet nurture the sanctity of a civilizational self-identity away from the predations of power. And indeed it was around the time when this inner domain started becoming an important resource for Indian projects of cultural renewal that the British started losing touch with it. As C. A. Bayly points out, after about 1800 the British were on shaky ground when it came to "affective knowledge" of Indian life; they were "weakest in regard to music and dance, the popular poetry of sacred erotics, dress and food, though such concerns are near the heart of any civilization" (1996, 55).

Bayly suggests that the kind of model of colonial public life that Chatterjee espouses is flawed in that it misses the existence of precolonial spaces of public debate and deliberation. And Sandria Freitag, for her part, argues that we would profit from exploring the debt that contemporary public culture on the subcontinent owes to the meeting between new media technologies and long-standing indigenous practices of display, ritual, and performance pertaining to the public life of royal courts, devotional observance, and theatrical spectacle (Freitag 1996, 2001). It is clear that such performative idioms are crucial not only to an understanding of the colonial period but also to contemporary South Asian public cultures. And yet it seems to us that this line of argument risks overlooking some of the important implications of Chatterjee's model.

First, Chatterjee is careful to specify that his outer/inner division does not in fact correspond to the European categories of "public" and "private" (see also Kaviraj 1997). For one thing, the content of the inner domain in colonial India was much more than a private concern: it was the very substance of a shared cultural heritage. Second, while Bayly is right to point to the precolonial existence of deliberative publics and elaborate systems of news reporting, the colonial period introduced a normative concept of publicness that was quite new, in that it rested on the characteristically modern assumption of the abstract equality of all participants in public debate. The fact that Indian colonial publics obviously did not even approximately approach such a state did not, as Jürgen Habermas might argue, invalidate the normative force of the ideal. Instead, it introduced a new and ambivalent political field, which, in its doubleness, mirrored that of the inner and outer domains. Claims to justice and recognition could now refer both to the specifics of cultural identity and to the universalizing ideal of human dignity.

As has been extensively documented, British policy grappled at every step with this contradiction—and several of the papers in this volume explore the regulatory antinomies that it generated. But what we want to stress here is that the very fact that the inner domain of cultural substance was, by definition, much more than a private concern meant that the split became unstable as soon as it had been imagined. Insofar as "Indianness" (the content of the inner domain) would become a resource for public mobilizations in the nineteenth century and beyond—whether reformist, traditionalist, or nationalist—this inner domain would, as it were, have to be "outed." In other words, Chatterjee's model foregrounds a problem that is crucial to our project: the ambiguity of identifications and solidarities whose basic substance is marked as being off-limits to the cut and thrust of political action and that nonetheless, at the same time, inevitably become a crucial basis for the efficacy of emergent forms of publicity.

In fact, the whole colonial problem of asserting and, in that very assertion, protecting Indian identities exhibits, in textbook form, the ambivalent dynamic of cultural regulation. Again and again, one sees the struggle to find acceptable ways to harness deep affect in the service of public agendas, models whereby the volatility and erotics of meaning-that-matters might be legitimated by reference to scientific universality, nationalist transcendence, religious sublimation, or the "natural" truth of aesthetic beauty. Thus, the intensity, the affective density of the "inner" domain might be provisionally connected to the public projects of the "outer" domain without either "polluting" the formal requirements of the outer domain with the intimate excesses of sentiment or—even more fatally—indecently exposing the intimate domain to the impersonal gaze of an anonymous public. Small wonder, then, that woman should have become such a central cipher for this conflicted fusion—woman as nation, woman as embodiment of virtue, woman as aesthetic ideal, woman as locus of dangerous sexual energy (Sangari and Vaid 1990; Thomas 1989; Uberoi 1990). Nor did the end of British rule resolve the tension. Especially with the boom in commercial publicity during the last couple of decades, publicly circulated images of womanhood have become more hotly contested than ever (Bose 2002, 2006; Chanda 2003; John and Nair 2000; Kasbekar 2001; Kishwar 2001; Mankekar 1999).

One might easily be left with the impression that the agonies of ambivalence were the exclusive preserve of the colonized. To be sure, the project of colonialism set up a situation in which, for the colonized, "the *fact of difference* itself is a constitutive moment that structures the experience of modernity" (A. Gupta 1998, 37, emphasis in original). But it is perhaps too easily forgotten that insofar as the colonies were a kind of laboratory for the norms and forms of a European modernity (Rabinow 1989), the colonizers, as regulators and as administrators, were not simply attempting to contain eruptions of native sentiment within an iron cage of universalizing reason. The British in India also fitfully and ambivalently understood the importance of mobilizing local "affective knowledge" in the service of empire; theirs was also a complex game of incitement and containment, a constant reaching back and forth across the line that divided the intimate and the affective from the formal and the rational.[5] One sees how this awkward oscillation pervaded the tactics of colonial rule in the history of Indian censorship, of course, all the way from the first real regulations at the end of the eighteenth century to the elaborate, paranoid machinery of empire's endgame. But it is also, and by the same token, present in all the halting British attempts at once to suppress and to appropriate "native" idioms of performance, ritual, and cultural production for their own ends (Cannadine 2002; Cohn 1983).

The field of cultural regulation, then, emerged at once as a problem of administration and a problem of defiance. From the beginning it was defined by a deeply ambivalent relationship to the tension between the sentimental devices of publicity and the instrumental reason of political strategy. This was the ground out of which the legal apparatus of censorship and containment developed. But this apparatus cannot be understood apart from the publics that it was meant to regulate, and thus inevitably also to affirm.

The Birth of Cultural Regulation

As early as the end of the eighteenth century, the potentials of the nascent mass media—at this point the press—were being registered and regulated. One of the very first newspapers in India, James Hicky's *Bengal Gazette*, was closed down in 1780 after only a few months of operation, on grounds that invoked both the brittleness of decency and the volatility of public discourse. The censoring order cited "several improper paragraphs tending to vilify private characters, and to disturb the peace of the settlement" (quoted in Jones 2001, 1160).

Looking across the period stretching from the late eighteenth century through to Independence in 1947, we might consider the shifting politics of cultural regulation in several ways. Firstly, there is the question of intensity. When was there more and when was there less regulation? What were the spurs and influences on this variation? Secondly, there is the matter of regulatory categories and discourse. Why and when did specific markers of excess such as "obscenity," "sedition," and "blasphemy" come into play in projects of cultural regulation, and what can we learn from their shifting interrelationships?

Thirdly, how should we understand the regulatory politics of the changing importance and availability of particular media, if by "media" we mean not only print (textual and visual), cinema, and radio but also specific idioms of performance and public display? Obviously, we are in no position to "answer" these questions here; each of the papers in this volume represents a set of possible and partial responses. But we do think it is worth developing, in a very preliminary way, some of the implications of asking such questions for the study of cultural regulation in modern South Asia.

British attempts to regulate the press in colonial India waxed and waned to an awkward rhythm, as authorities were caught between immediate administrative concerns "on the ground" and more distant—and sometimes more liberal—parliamentary opinion back in London (Barrier 1974; Bhattacharya 2001; Jones 2001; Kaul 2003). As Gerald Barrier puts it, "Caught between a tradition that favored a free press and anxiety over all but the most innocuous criticism, the British swung back and forth from strict controls to virtual freedom of expression" (1974, 4). A formal system of press censorship was introduced in 1799, in connection with the war to annex Mysore.[6] During the next century and a half, one sees periods of relative liberality, in which the ideal of the freedom of the press was foregrounded, and periods of panic, in which the power of emergent Indian publics appeared as a threat to the foundations of British rule. Important moments here include the rise of a vernacular press starting in the teens of the nineteenth century, the shock of the 1857–58 Rebellion, and waves of militant nationalist activism in the first decade of the twentieth century, the early 1920s, and the early 1930s.

On the basis of a steadily consolidating vernacular press, particularly in North India, the emergent publics of the latter half of the nineteenth century also saw a complex cross-cutting of nationalist, linguistic, communal, and moral-sexual concerns. Publicists, militants, cultural producers, and bureaucrats were all becoming increasingly cognizant of the affective efficacy of sexuality and religion as focal points of political mobilization. It is during this period that "obscenity" formally emerged as a category of regulation, and as a category that was understood as implicated in "sedition," that is, in explicitly political forms of provocation (Bayly 1996; C. Gupta 2002; Sharma 1968; cf. Mazzarella, forthcoming). On one level, the struggle over erotics in the printed matter of this period is a witness to the striking affective power of the press as a mass medium with a rapidly expanding vernacular audience. On another level, printed "erotic" literature also became a site for an internal struggle over the relative acceptability of "popular" versus "high" forms of cultural production. Charu Gupta has, for instance, effectively juxtaposed the movement to establish a *shuddh* (pure) literary Hindi public in the very earliest years of the twentieth century to both the denigration of late medieval, overtly eroticized poetic idioms and a contemporary boom in mass-produced sex manuals (cf. Orsini 2002).

These struggles were further complicated by the increasing significance, from the late nineteenth century, of mass-produced visual media: first, gradual improvements in picture printing, from woodcuts to lithographs, and subsequently the cinema, which came to India with a representative of the Lumière brothers in 1896 and had grown into a thriving domestic industry twenty years later. The political effects of print were certainly not restricted to the literate alone, since it was—and still is—quite common for printed texts to be read or performed for wider audiences. Nevertheless, the forging of "national" and sometimes explicitly "nationalist" image-making vocabularies profoundly changed both the social relations and the aesthetics of Indian public culture. It also brought about a closer, mutually amplifying, and mutually re-mediating relationship between these new "mass media" and older forms of performance or ritual.[7] Here, too, we see a complex struggle over aesthetic distinction. The "high" nationalist painting of the likes of Abanindranath Tagore, developed as part of a literary and scholarly discourse on Indian cultural particularity, is self-consciously opposed to the "vulgarity" of bazaar prints as well as the imitative banality of "company art" (Guha-Thakurta 1992, 1995; cf. Kapur 2000).

But perhaps the most influential outcome of this historical juncture was the consolidation of a mass-produced middlebrow national aesthetic, typified by the "god poster" lithography of a Ravi Varma or, later, a C. Kondiah Raju (Smith 1995; Inglis 1995; Pinney 1997a, 1997b; Jain 2007). These visual conventions were, in turn, definitively influential on the depiction of mythological themes in the nascent Hindi cinema and are still popularly perceived as the "correct" visual rendering of Hindu deities, whether in the comic book nationalist pedagogy of *Amar Chitra Katha* or the sensationally successful television serialization of the *Ramayana* of the late 1980s (Hawley 1995; Lutgendorf 1995; Mankekar 1999; Rajagopal 2001). In India, where the devotional gaze is often understood as a medium of grace, this visual veracity is as much a matter of efficacy as of verisimilitude (Babb 1981; Eck 1998). Although their social and political functions may have shifted, the forceful efficacy potentially residing in divine images has obviously not been reduced by mechanical reproduction or by their translation into calendar art, cinema, and video and television programming (Davis 1997; Little 1995; Smith 1995). As Christopher Pinney argues in this volume, it was precisely the colonial desire to divide the (authentic, customary) religious from the (spurious, seditious) political that gave the sphere of religion such particular potency in the transmission of ideas, campaigns, and agitation against the British.

Consequently, the mobilizing power of such images has also been a constant feature of regulatory anxiety. Although the Indian nationalist leadership was, on the whole, relatively indifferent to the political potential of cinema, the British certainly took it seriously (Chabria and Usai 1994; Chowdhry 2000). The colonial government instituted a comprehensive commission of inquiry into its political economy, its possible social effects, and the adequacy of existing regulatory measures in 1927–28 (Arora 1995; Jaikumar 2003, 2006; Mehta 2001a; Sarkar 1982; Vasudev 1978). In this volume, William Mazzarella explores how the colonial censor tried to manage the "vital energy" of Hollywood cinema in

this early period. Indeed, post-Independence Indian governments have continued this trend. The censorship of film has been rigorously formalized on
the basis of the Cinematograph Act of 1952 and the Cinematograph (Censorship) Rules of 1958; as Girja Kumar (1990) points out, the regulation of other
media may be just as vociferously pursued, but always by means of a much
more haphazard and improvisatory legal infrastructure. Of course, the degree
of legal routinization is not necessarily a useful measure of the practical politics
of any regime of censorship. As Tejaswini Ganti shows in this volume, the relationship between Bollywood and the Indian state is an ambivalent one, neither
dedicatedly adversarial nor straightforwardly complicit.[8]

Independence and Ambivalence

The coming of Indian independence in 1947 was marked by a characteristic
ambivalence vis-à-vis public culture. On the one hand, the very fact of an Indian
nation-state was supposed, by definition, to mark the historical overcoming of
the split between "inner" and "outer" domains. On the other hand, the Nehruvian formula for secularism, convinced of its universal validity, imposed a stringent filter on what kind of affect-intensive, embedded representations and
practices would be allowed to participate in public culture. These two faces
of Nehru are evident in his own writings. There is the Nehru who, with some
eloquence, sought in prison writings like *The Discovery of India* and *Glimpses
of World History* to fuse a world-historical rapprochement between the com-
mandments of modernity and the density of Indian tradition. But then there is
also the Nehru noted by Shashi Tharoor (2003), who exasperatedly writes to a
(Muslim) friend that all Indians should be required to immerse themselves in
the rationalist atheism of Bertrand Russell.

Sandria Freitag (2001) observes that the consolidation of a nationalist visual
repertoire around the turn of the twentieth century made patriotism the new
mediator between the sacred and the profane. This mediation was, as Arvind
Rajagopal (2001) describes, predicated upon a political compromise between the
secular nationalist leadership and the custodians of cultural and religious tradition. Its resolution was projected onto the future, onto the moment of independence. For that reason, the actual achievement of independence brought the leadership of the new nation face to face with the need to make good on the promise
of integrating prosaic policy with the transcendent truth of the nation.

Under Nehru, Republic Day parades, government craft emporia, official
cultural festivals, and other government-staging events and spectacles harnessed
a state-driven and secularized understanding of "Indian tradition" to the great
projects of modernization and development (Appadurai and Breckenridge 1992;
Greenough 1995; Singh 1998; S. Roy 2007). At the same time, Nehru famously
referred to his monuments of modernism, the hydroelectric dams and the steel
mills, as the "temples" of modern India (Deshpande 1993; Khilnani 1998), thus

perhaps also acknowledging the potential for a serious affective deficit at the heart of the developmentalist dispensation.

The question was never simply one of whether secularism should mean a complete evacuation of religious commitments from public life or, alternatively, a pluralistic recognition of religious values in political and legal process (Bharucha 1998; Bilgrami et al. 2006; Nandy 2002). Rather, as a formally empowered cultural regulator, the state after Independence always struggled with the tension between a recognition of the importance of an affective grounding for any successful polity and a fear of what such an affective grounding might mean in practice for a self-consciously "modern" and "developing" nation, particularly vis-à-vis sentiments and commitments that might be defined as "religious." After Nehru's death in 1964, this early dilemma became a justification for both a stream of attacks, from the right, on the supposed cultural inauthenticity and alienation of the Nehruvian model (Nehru as the "last Englishman") and the increasingly assiduous manipulation of communal "vote-banks" by national political leaders.[9]

Much has been written on the stunning expansion of commercial entertainment-based television in India in the 1980s: how it brought together, in a volatile compact around the affect-intensive television image, a range of new middle-class aspirations, the blandishments of consumerism, and a mass acceptance of an overtly and frequently aggressive religious nationalism (S. Kumar 2005; Mankekar 1999; Mazzarella 2003; Rajagopal 2001). From a regulatory point of view, these were, in some ways, peculiar days (Farmer 1996). Through the state television service, Doordarshan, the government retained sole proprietorship over this boisterously mushrooming medium, constantly striving to reconcile its habituated "fear of the image" (Ohm 1999) with highly profitable content that was often lustily corporeal. With programming increasingly farmed out to the private sector but control still centralized in the hands of the government, television in the 1980s became a kind of tug-of-war between state and commercial interests (cf. Appadurai and Breckenridge 1995).

But it also doubled as a laboratory for new experiments in cultural regulation. By this we mean not only the often heavy-handed blackouts that Doordarshan imposed on particular news items or on the doings and sayings of political critics. We are also thinking of experiments in the profitable mass mobilization of affect, whether commercial, religious, or political. Indeed, one of the defining features of this period, as many have noted, was the increasing televisual interpenetration of devotional viewing, political propaganda, and consumer goods advertising.

These developments laid the foundations for the media scandals with which we started this chapter. Today the dawning consumerism and televisual politics of the 1980s are almost invariably read as a prequel to the full-tilt tryst with liberalization that started with the reforms of 1991. In subscribing to this teleology, however, we may miss something equally, if not more, important about the new televisual dispensation: namely, the ways in which it was a response to the failure of Indira Gandhi's experiment with dictatorship during the Emergency of 1975–77. In histories of the media, the Emergency has come to stand as the exception that proves the rule of Indian democratic freedom, and an object lesson in the political dangers of censorship. After all, the story goes, was it not precisely Mrs. Gandhi's totalizing approach to information control that isolated her from "public opinion" to such a degree that she mistakenly believed that she would have no trouble winning the national election in 1977?

The style of information management that prevailed during the Emergency was exceptionally crude. Press materials generally had to be submitted for pre-screening under official categories such as "pre-censorship," "news management," and the starkly simple "banned." As Soli Sorabjee (1977) notes, although overt political critique was of course almost impossible, the restrictions also extended to such topics as strikes, the nuclear program, reports on family planning and vasectomy follow-up centers, and even the arrest of legendary actress Nargis for shoplifting in London. Under the Defense of India Rules and the Maintenance of Internal Security Act, thousands were jailed and silenced, and—in a kind of perfect sovereign recursivity—any reference to censorship in the media was itself banned. Troubling bodies were incarcerated (political opponents, editors, activists) or physically moved (recalcitrant judges), power to newspapers was cut, and a comprehensive range of "directives" was issued to the media from Samachar, the central government news agencies. Mrs. Gandhi's heir apparent, Sanjay, is said to have personally demanded substantial cash "contributions" in return for permission to premiere new films in the capital.

To be sure, although Mrs. Gandhi's second period in office (1980–84) did see some highly controversial blanket bans on media reportage during localized episodes of political turmoil (for example in Punjab and in Assam), the crudely repressive measures of the Emergency were not repeated in India. But by identifying these crude tactics with censorship per se, we risk losing sight of some of the subtler forms of cultural regulation that were developed in tandem with the expansion of the commercial media in the early to mid-1980s. As Shiv Visvanathan puts it, the Emergency was not so much an embarrassing aberration as "a pilot plant, a large scale trial for the totalitarianisms and emergencies that were to come later" (Visvanathan 1998, 45). One could argue that cultural regulation under the sign of liberalization, particularly after Mrs. Gandhi's assassination in late 1984, required a rapid reinterpretation of the kind of state-centric authoritarian populism that the Emergency had come to typify.

Emphatically consigning Mrs. Gandhi to a superseded past, mere months after her death, was of course never going to be an easy or an uncontested process.[10] As a project, it involved something far more comprehensive than the dismissal of the Emergency as a historical anomaly, a dismissal that she herself had already propounded during her last years in office. Rather, what was required was the impression of a more dispersed affective field, one not so tightly cathected onto the singular image of the charismatic leader. The new, liberalized mode of citizenship was one in which the energies of public participation should be seen as coming from below rather than from the "commanding heights" of the Planning Commission. It located the nation's destiny less in the heroic agency of a leader and more in the embodied and embedded impulses of everyday life. The languages of faith and tradition, of consumerist desire, and of regionally chauvinist identifications might still at times trouble the sovereignty of the national project, but they attained, in this period, a new image of authenticity, the dignity of affective truth, as compared to the alienating abstractions, the grand schemes of the Nehru years.

Our point is certainly not to suggest that liberalization in fact brought about some kind of authentically democratic revival. Rather, what is visible in debates over the media from this period is a diffuse consciousness, expressed in many different idioms by many different interest groups, of a tension between sovereignty and control in public communications and an increasingly complex set of claims on representation and recognition in public culture. At times, the government clamped down and silenced dissent in the old, crude way. At others, however, the myriad voices emerging from inside and around the government seemed to be advocating the possibility of a more subtle co-optation, one in which consumer choice, religious assertion, and regional pride might perhaps still be harnessed to a collective national project. By the same token, of course, the legitimacy of the state as the final arbiter in public cultural matters, in matters of value, identity, and desire, was increasingly being called into question. When Hindi movie star Manisha Koirala decided that Shashilal Nair, the director of *Ek Chhoti Si Love Story* (2002), had deceived her by inserting provocative, partially undressed scenes featuring a body double of her, her actions reflected a perfect understanding of the ambiguities of the new dispensation. Hedging her bets, she appealed in quick succession to the Censor Board, the Ministry of Information and Broadcasting, and Shiv Sena chief Bal Thackeray for justice.

We are now in a very different situation from that which prevailed in the 1980s. Strategies of regulation have diversified in proportion to the proliferation of new media. The coming of commercial satellite television in the early 1990s shifted television away from state control. In response, government has sought to reassert its authority. In addition to making regular—if relatively ineffectual—noises about bringing television directly under the authority of the Central Board of Film Certification, authorities have, via a 2006 decision of the Mumbai High Court, made it illegal for any television station broadcasting in India to screen films with A censor certificates (indicating that they are suitable for audiences 18 and over). The liberalization and globalization of consumer markets have intensified competition in the field of visual publicity, requiring Indian advertisers to keep up with international benchmarks in profitable provocation. And the increasing regionalization of both television and the press has allowed a far wider range of local identities to find their aspirations and their reification in the mass media.

When the television version of the *Ramayana* was broadcast in the late 1980s, controversy raged around the fact that Doordarshan, the broadcast medium of a self-avowedly secular state, was both presiding over and profiting from such blatantly "religious" content.[11] In response to this accusation, Philip Lutgendorf (1995) reminds us that recitations and performances of the epics have always enjoyed and depended upon political patronage in India. And one could even add that from a certain perspective, the landscape of the 1990s and after might look like a return to something like a premodern diversity of cultural patrons and publics, each presiding over their own regional turf, their own chosen "traditions." But what such an analysis would miss, in its neoliberal enthusiasm, is the tension that persists between a diversity of claimants to cultural sovereignty and the singular regulatory authority represented by the state and, in particular, by the language and institutions of the law. We are all familiar with this tension as it pertains to the antinomies and limits of liberalism. One thinks, for example, of the Shah Bano case of 1986, which pitted a particularist appeal to Muslim law against the putative universalism of a common civil code.

This is also a question of publics and the forms of media that constitute them. It has become *de rigueur* to insist that we have transcended the age of "the masses," that the diversification of markets and media has consigned the age of standardization and massification to the dustbin of history. But in South Asia, such a diversification continues to coexist with a developmentalist narrative which constitutes precisely "the masses" as the prime beneficiaries of state action, both redistributive and regulatory. It is the masses that are the objects (and intended future subjects) of the process of modernization. And it is the masses that may most typically be injured or misled by provocative, obscene, or seditious public communications. On the one hand, we may sympathize with Ashis Nandy's (1995) call for an approach to Indian politics that captures the messiness, ambiguity, and unpredictability that a more rationalist *Realpolitik* elides. And certainly an ethnographic approach would seem to be ideally suited to such a pursuit. On the other hand, we would suggest that the politics of cultural regulation are played out at the intersection between such a politics of the concrete and the reified terms of administration.

This tension also plays itself out as a crisis of temporality. Against the perpetual "not yet" of Third World time, the permanent deferral of the full realization of modernity, the big movements of the last couple of decades have been premised on a big immediacy, on a sensuous immersion. This dream of immediacy is present in the often violent identitarian politics of regional and religious chauvinism, in the promise of instant consumerist gratification, and in the fullness of devotional absorption upon which contemporary political spectacle is so often premised.

×   ×   ×

We began with the juxtaposition of censorship and publicity, in order to ask what it might mean that practices of cultural regulation seem to have become so central to contemporary South Asian public cultures. We hope to have suggested that this not only concerns what does or does not "go into" public circulation, but also points to the political centrality of discourses on and around practices of regulation. Regulation is self-reflexive: it cannot help but articulate the terms and foundations of its own legitimacy. For this reason, regulation is performative too: the silencing gesture is not only often quite public, but also simultaneously invokes an entire sociocultural dispensation.

The conventional language that attaches to censorship and its refusal—"security," "freedom of speech," "diversity," "choice," and so forth—must itself be read as a political technology that helps to negotiate what we referred to earlier as the tension between the public interest and the interests of publicity. Naturally, in an era of globalization and rapidly exploding commercial media networks, the stakes of profitable provocation are immeasurably heightened. But it is absolutely crucial that we understand the politics of the relationship between a generalized discourse on censorship and the specificities of long-standing local histories of media and performance. This is never simply a matter of "localizing" abstract or universalizing claims. Rather, as the essays in this volume show, in their various ways, cultural regulation is in some sense the attempt to forge an authoritative relationship between the energy of embedded and embodied phenomena and trans-local normative categories.

Typically, mainstream discussions of censorship in South Asia, as elsewhere, are stolidly steadfast in declaring censorship a bad thing. We would agree that the repressive aspects of censorship do need to be noted. It is perfectly possible to acknowledge, in a Foucauldian mode, the perverse productivity of various forms of cultural regulation while still recognizing that censorship does silence even as it speaks. But the interesting question is not *Censored ke peeche kya hai?* (What lies behind the censored?). Rather, what we hope to show with this collection is that there is nothing self-evident about censorship, nor about the worlds it makes. Censorship is not merely a constant forge of discourse nor is it only a ruthless mechanism of silence. As a gamble on publicity, cultural regulation is, for all its apparently routinized banality, an uncertain and open-ended venture. Therein lies its fascination and its importance for cultural analysis. We hope that the papers in this volume, taken together, will encourage readers to dwell with the censors, to look twice, and to refuse to grant them the obviousness to which they aspire.

Notes

1. *Water* was eventually filmed, under the false name *River Moon*, in Sri Lanka in 2003 and released in 2005.

2. However, as shown by the Supreme Court's verdict in 2006 allowing the documentary *Father, Son and Holy War* to be aired on Doordarshan, after a ten-year struggle to get it approved, some of these contestations may simply be cases of government reticence driven by personal politics.

3. Film critic T. G. Vaidyanathan once remarked, in a commentary on Aparna Sen's *Paroma* (1985), that "Indians look far more convincing when they are not making love. When they are, the whole business looks forced, contrived, and bloodless" (1996, 116).

4. Sanford Levinson writes, "*Regulation* is an ambiguous term. We often speak of 'a regulation' in the sense of a mandatory requirement or prohibition. Yet we also refer easily, especially if we have been influenced even in the slightest by Michel Foucault, to an unarticled 'regulation' as a means of defining what is 'regular' or, ultimately, 'normal,' within a given political-cultural order" (1998, 197). We extend this insight to accommodate the performative and the affective consequences of regulation.

5. Bose and Jalal note of the century of "Company Raj" (1757–1857), "since the colonial state could establish a semblance of cultural legitimacy only by appropriating symbols and meanings that commanded authority in indigenous society, the distinction between public and private law was never an easy one to maintain" (Bose and Jalal 1998, 74). And for the post-Company period: "Although in 1858 the colonial power had announced its intention not to interfere in the private realm of 'religion' and 'custom,' its policies in the late nineteenth century ensured that precisely these concerns had to be bandied about in the 'public' arenas of the press and politics" (108).

6. Tapti Roy (1995) sees the 1840s in Bengal as the moment when, under the eagle eye of the Irish missionary James Long, the colonial government began to classify all published materials in a synoptic manner. By 1867, in the wake of the 1857–58 Rebellion, all books in India had to be officially registered.

7. Tapti Roy (1995) notes that this amplification occurred between print and performance as well. In Bengal, the growth of the press did a great deal to expand the popularity of the *kathakata* genre, as well as the burgeoning "modern" theater. Kathryn Hansen (2001) shows how important emergent forms of print publicity—flyers, handbills, newspaper advertising—were to the marketing of the traveling theater troupes (initially predominantly Parsi) that began traversing the subcontinent in the 1850s.

8. In the interests of brevity, we are not taking up the issue of audio-only media here. But much remains to be said on the "official" culture promulgated by All-India Radio (Lelyveld 1995) that doubles as a device to police the borders with Sri Lanka and Pakistan. In addition, cassette technology has of course made possible forms of grass-roots mobilization that few other mass-media technologies can equal (Rajagopal 2001; Manuel 1993).

9. Rajagopal (2001) reminds us of a practice that seems to straddle the Nehruvian and the communal political strategies: during the Emergency, All-India Radio would broadcast readings from the *Ramcharitmanas* on the grounds that it was "folk culture."

10. In some sense, it was of course this tension that eventually sullied Rajiv Gandhi's "Mr. Clean" image—namely, his inability to transcend the compulsions of the party machinery that had been established during his mother's rule. More immediately, the conflict expressed itself in several incidents of sudden censorship. For example, the sudden cancellation, in February 1986, of a Doordarshan screening of Jack Anderson's documentary *Rajiv's India*, which some members of the party old guard apparently felt was insufficiently respectful of Mrs. Gandhi's political legacy.

11. As Rajagopal (2001) points out, contestation of the politics of secularism around the televised epics partly took the form of arguments about whether the material should be understood as "religious" or "cultural."

References

Appadurai, Arjun, and Carol Breckenridge. 1992. "Museums Are Good to Think: Heritage on View in India." In Ivan Karp et al., eds., *Museums and Communications: The Politics of Public Culture*. Washington, D.C.: Smithsonian Institution Press.

———. 1995. "Public Modernity in India." In Carol Breckenridge, ed., *Consuming Modernity: Public Culture in a South Asian World*. Minneapolis: University of Minnesota Press.

Arora, Poonam. 1995. "Imperiling the Prestige of the White Woman: Colonial Anxiety and Film Censorship in British India." *Visual Anthropology Review* 11(2): 36–50.

Babb, Lawrence. 1981. "Glancing: Visual Interaction in Hinduism." *Journal of Anthropological Research* 37(4): 47–64.

Barrier, N. Gerald. 1974. *Banned: Controversial Literature and Political Control in British India, 1907–1947*. Columbus: University of Missouri Press.

Bayly, C. A. 1996. *Empire and Information: Intelligence Gathering and Social Communication in India, 1780–1870*. Cambridge: Cambridge University Press.

Bharucha, Rustom. 1998. *In the Name of the Secular: Contemporary Cultural Activism in India*. New Delhi: Oxford University Press.

Bhattacharya, Sanjoy. 2001. "India: 1900–1947." In Derek Jones, ed., *Censorship: A World Encyclopedia*. Chicago: Fitzroy Dearborn.

Bilgrami, Akeel, et al., eds. 2006. *The Crisis of Secularism in India*. Durham, N.C.: Duke University Press.

Bose, Brinda, ed. 2002. *Translating Desire: The Politics of Gender and Culture in India*. New Delhi: Katha.

———. 2006. *Gender and Censorship*. New Delhi: Women Unlimited.

Bose, Sugata, and Ayesha Jalal. 1998. *Modern South Asia: History, Culture, Political Economy*. New Delhi: Oxford University Press.

Bourdieu, Pierre. 1991. "Censorship and the Imposition of Form." In John Thompson, ed., *Language and Symbolic Power*. Cambridge, Mass.: Harvard University Press.

Boyer, Dominic. 2003. "Censorship as a Vocation: The Institutions, Practices and Cultural Logic of Media Control in the German Democratic Republic." *Comparative Studies in Society and History* 45(3): 511–45.

Brosius, Christiane, and Melissa Butcher, eds. 1999. *Image Journeys: Audio-Visual Media and Cultural Change in India*. New Delhi: Sage.

Burchell, Graham, Colin Gordon, and Peter Miller. 1991. *The Foucault Effect: Studies in Governmentality*. Chicago: University of Chicago Press.

Burt, Richard. 1994. "Introduction: The 'New' Censorship." In Richard Burt, ed., *The Administration of Aesthetics: Censorship, Political Criticism and the Public Sphere*. Minneapolis: University of Minnesota Press.

Butler, Judith. 1997. *Excitable Speech: A Politics of the Performative*. London: Routledge.

———. 1998. "Ruled Out: Vocabularies of the Censor." In Robert C. Post, ed., *Censorship and Silencing: Practices of Cultural Regulation*. Los Angeles: The Getty Research Institute.

Canetti, Elias. 1984. *Crowds and Power*. Trans. Carol Stewart. New York: Farrar, Straus and Giroux.

Cannadine, David. 2002. *Ornamentalism: How the British Saw Their Empire*. New York: Oxford University Press.

Chabria, Suresh, and Paolo Usai, eds. 1994. *Light of Asia: Indian Silent Cinema, 1912–1934*. New Delhi: Wiley Eastern.

Chanda, Ipshita. 2003. *Packaging Freedom: Feminism and Popular Culture*. Kolkata: Stree.

Chatterjee, Partha. 1993. *The Nation and Its Fragments: Colonial and Postcolonial Histories*. Princeton, N.J.: Princeton University Press.

Chowdhry, Prem. 2000. *Colonial India and the Making of Empire Cinema: Image, Ideology and Identity*. Manchester: Manchester University Press.

Cohn, Bernard. 1983. "Representing Authority in Victorian India." In Eric Hobsbawm and Terence Ranger, eds., *The Invention of Tradition*. Cambridge: Cambridge University Press.

Das, Veena. 1995. *Critical Events: An Anthropological Perspective on Contemporary India*. New Delhi: Oxford University Press.

Davis, Richard. 1997. *Lives of Indian Images*. Princeton, N.J.: Princeton University Press.

Deshpande, Satish. 1993. "Imagined Economies: Styles of Nation-Building in Twentieth-Century India." *Journal of Arts and Ideas* 25–26 (December): 5–36.

Eck, Diana. 1998. *Darsan: Seeing the Divine Image in India*. New York: Columbia University Press.

Eckert, Julia. 2003. *The Charisma of Direct Action: Power, Politics and the Shiv Sena*. New Delhi: Oxford University Press.

Farmer, Victoria. 1996. "Mass Media: Images, Mobilization, and Communalism." In David Ludden, ed., *Contesting the Nation: Religion, Community and the Politics of Democracy in India*. Philadelphia: University of Pennsylvania Press.

Foucault, Michel. 1977. *Discipline and Punish: The Birth of the Prison*. Harmondsworth: Penguin.

———. 1981. *Power/Knowledge: Selected Interviews and Other Writing*. New York: Pantheon.

———. 1985. *The History of Sexuality*. Vol. 2, *The Use of Pleasure*. Harmondsworth: Penguin.

Freitag, Sandria B. 1989. *Collective Action and Community: Public Arenas and the Emergence of Communalism in North India*. Berkeley: University of California Press.

———. 1996. "Contesting in Public: Colonial Legacies and Contemporary Communalism." In David Ludden, ed., *Contesting the Nation: Religion, Community and the Politics of Democracy in India*. Philadelphia: University of Pennsylvania Press.

———. 2001. "Vision and the Nation: Theorizing the Nexus between Creation, Consumption, and Participation in the Public Sphere." In Rachel Dwyer and Christopher Pinney, eds., *Pleasure and the Nation: The History, Politics and Consumption of Public Culture in India*. New Delhi: Oxford University Press.

Gates, Henry Louis. 1997. *Speaking of Race, Speaking of Sex: Hate Speech, Civil Rights and Civil Liberties*. New York: New York University Press.

Greenough, Paul. 1995. "Nation, Economy and Tradition Displayed: The Indian Crafts Museum, New Delhi." In Carol Breckenridge, ed., *Consuming Modernity: Public Culture in a South Asian World*. Minneapolis: University of Minnesota Press.

Guha-Thakurta, Tapati. 1992. *The Making of a New "Indian" Art: Artists, Aesthetics, and Nationalism in Bengal, c. 1850–1920*. Cambridge: Cambridge University Press.

———. 1995. "Recovering the Nation's Art." In Partha Chatterjee, ed., *Texts of Power: Emerging Disciplines in Colonial Bengal*. Minneapolis: University of Minnesota Press.

Gupta, Akhil. 1998. *Postcolonial Developments: Agriculture in the Making of Modern India*. Durham, N.C.: Duke University Press.

Gupta, Charu. 2002. *Sexuality, Obscenity, Community: Women, Muslims, and the Hindu Public in Colonial India*. London: Palgrave.

Gupta, Dipankar. 1982. *Nativism in a Metropolis: The Shiv Sena in Bombay*. New Delhi: Manohar.

Hansen, Kathryn. 2001. "The *Indar Sabha* Phenomenon: Theatre and Consumption in Greater India (1853–1956)." In Rachel Dwyer and Christopher Pinney, eds., *Pleasure and the Nation: The History, Politics and Consumption of Public Culture in India*. New Delhi: Oxford University Press.

Hansen, Thomas Blom. 2001. *Wages of Violence: Naming and Identity in Postcolonial Bombay*. Princeton, N.J.: Princeton University Press.

———. 2004. "Politics as Permanent Performance: The Production of Political Authority in the Locality." In John Zavos, Andrew Wyatt, and Vernon Marston Hewitt, eds., *The Politics of Cultural Mobilization in India*. New Delhi: Oxford University Press.

Hawley, John Stratton. 1995. "The Saints Subdued: Domestic Virtue and National Integration in *Amar Chitra Katha*." In Lawrence Babb and Susan Wadley, eds., *Media and the Transformation of Religion in South Asia*. Philadelphia: University of Pennsylvania Press.

Haynes, Douglas E. 1992. *Rhetoric and Ritual in Colonial India: The Shaping of a Public Culture in Surat City, 1852–1928*. New Delhi: Oxford University Press.

Heumann, Milton, Thomas W. Church, and David P. Redlawsk. 1997. *Hate Speech on Campus: Cases, Case Studies and Commentary*. Boston: Northeastern University Press.

Inglis, Stephen. 1995. "Suitable for Framing: The Work of a Modern Master." In Lawrence Babb and Susan Wadley, eds., *Media and the Transformation of Religion in South Asia*. Philadelphia: University of Pennsylvania Press.

Israel, Milton. 1994. *Communications and Power: Propaganda and the Press in the Indian Nationalist Struggle, 1920–1947*. Cambridge: Cambridge University Press.

Jaikumar, Priya. 2003. "More Than Morality: The Indian Cinematograph Committee Interviews (1927)." *Moving Image* 3(1): 83–109.

———. 2006. *Cinema at the End of Empire: A Politics of Transition in Britain and India*. Durham, N.C.: Duke University Press.

Jain, Kajri. 2007. *Gods in the Bazaar: The Economies of Indian Calendar Art*. Durham, N.C.: Duke University Press.

Jansen, Sue Curry. 1988. *Censorship: The Knot That Binds Power and Knowledge*. New York: Oxford University Press.

John, Mary, and Janaki Nair, eds. 2000. *A Question of Silence: The Sexual Economies of Modern India*. London: Zed Books.

Jones, Derek. 2001. "India." In Derek Jones, ed., *Censorship: A World Encyclopedia*. Chicago: Fitzroy Dearborn.

Kapur, Geeta. 2000. *When Was Modernism? Essays on Contemporary Cultural Practice in India*. New Delhi: Tulika.

Kasbekar, Asha. 2001. "Hidden Pleasures: Negotiating the Myth of the Female Ideal in Popular Hindi Cinema." In Rachel Dwyer and Christopher Pinney, eds., *Pleasure* and the Nation: *The History, Politics and Consumption of Public Culture in India*. New Delhi: Oxford University Press.

Katzenstein, Mary Fainsod. 1979. *Ethnicity and Equality: The Shiv Sena Party and Preferential Policies in Bombay*. Ithaca, N.Y.: Cornell University Press.

Kaul, Chandrika. 2003. *Reporting the Raj: The British Press and India, c. 1880–1922*. Manchester: Manchester University Press.

Kaur, Raminder. 2003. *Performative Politics and the Cultures of Hinduism: Public Uses of Religion in Western India*. New Delhi: Permanent Black.

Kaviraj, Sudipta. 1997. "Filth and the Public Sphere: Concepts and Practices about Space in Calcutta." *Public Culture* 10(1): 83–113.

Khilnani, Sunil. 1998. *The Idea of India*. Harmondsworth: Penguin.

Kishwar, Madhu. 2001. *Off the Beaten Track: Rethinking Gender Issues for Indian Women*. New Delhi: Oxford University Press.

Kumar, Girja. 1990. *Censorship in India, with Special Reference to* The Satanic Verses *and* Lady Chatterley's Lover. New Delhi: Har-Anand.

Kumar, Shanti. 2005. *Gandhi Meets Primetime: Globalization and Nationalism in Indian Television*. Champaign: University of Illinois Press.

Lelyveld, David. 1995. "Upon the Subdominant: Administering Music on All-India Radio." In Carol Breckenridge, ed., *Consuming Modernity: Public Culture in a South Asian World*. Minneapolis: University of Minnesota Press.

Levinson, Sanford. 1998. "The Tutelary State: 'Censorship,' 'Silencing,' and the 'Practices of Cultural Regulation.'" In Robert C. Post, ed., *Censorship and Silencing: Practices of Cultural Regulation*. Los Angeles: The Getty Research Institute.

Little, John. 1995. "Video *Vacana: Swadhyaya* and Sacred Tapes." In Lawrence Babb and Susan Wadley, eds., *Media and the Transformation of Religion in South Asia*. Philadelphia: University of Pennsylvania Press.

Lutgendorf, Philip. 1995. "All in the (Raghu) Family: A Video Epic in Cultural Context." In Lawrence Babb and Susan Wadley, eds., *Media and the Transformation of Religion in South Asia*. Philadelphia: University of Pennsylvania Press.

Lyotard, Jean-Francois. 2004. *Libidinal Economy*. New York: Continuum.

Mankekar, Purnima. 1999. *Screening Culture, Viewing Politics: An Ethnography of Television, Womanhood and Nation in Postcolonial India*. Durham, N.C.: Duke University Press.

Manuel, Peter. 1993. *Cassette Culture: Popular Music and Technology in North India*. Chicago: University of Chicago Press.

Mazzarella, William. 2003. *Shoveling Smoke: Advertising and Globalization in Contemporary India*. Durham, N.C.: Duke University Press.

———. Forthcoming. "The Obscenity of Censorship: Rethinking a Middle-Class Technology." In Amita Baviskar and Raka Ray, eds., *"We're Middle Class": The Cultural Politics of Dominance in India*. New Delhi: Routledge.

———. n.d. "'Cannibals Enjoy Comedies': Apprehending the Cinema in Late Colonial India." Unpublished manuscript.

Mehta, Monika. 2001a. "Selections: Cutting, Classifying and Certifying in Bombay Cinema." Ph.D. diss., University of Minnesota.

———. 2001b. "What Is Behind Film Censorship? The *Khalnayak* Debates." *Jouvert* 5(3): 1–12.

Nandy, Ashis. 1995. *The Savage Freud and Other Essays on Possible and Retrievable Selves*. Princeton, N.J.: Princeton University Press.

———. 2002. "An Anti-secularist Manifesto." In *The Romance of the State and the Fate of Dissent in the Tropics*. New Delhi: Oxford University Press.

Ohm, Britta. 1999. "Doordarshan: Representing the Nation's State." In Christiane Brosius and Melissa Butcher, eds., *Image Journeys: Audio-Visual Media and Cultural Change in India*. New Delhi: Sage.

Orsini, Francesca. 2002. *The Hindi Public Sphere, 1920–1940: Language and Literature in the Age of Nationalism*. New Delhi: Oxford University Press.

Pinney, Christopher. 1997a. *Camera Indica: The Social Life of Indian Photographs*. Chicago: University of Chicago Press.

———. 1997b. "The Nation (Un)pictured? Chromolithography and 'Popular' Politics in India, 1878–1995." *Critical Inquiry* 23(4) (Summer): 834–67.

———. 2004. *"Photos of the Gods": The Printed Image and Political Struggle in India*. London: Reaktion.

Post, Robert, ed. 1998. *Censorship and Silencing: Practices of Cultural Regulation*. Los Angeles: The Getty Research Institute.

Prasad, M. Madhava. 1998. *Ideology of the Hindi Film: A Historical Construction*. New Delhi: Oxford University Press.

Rabinow, Paul. 1989. *French Modern: Norms and Forms of the Social Environment*. Cambridge, Mass.: MIT Press.

Rajagopal, Arvind. 2001. *Politics after Television: Hindu Nationalism and the Reshaping of the Public in India*. Cambridge: Cambridge University Press.

Roy, Srirupa. 2007. *Beyond Belief: India and the Politics of Postcolonial Nationalism*. Durham, N.C.: Duke University Press.

Roy, Tapti. 1995. "Disciplining the Printed Text: Colonial and Nationalist Surveillance of Bengali Literature." In Partha Chatterjee, ed., *Texts of Power: Emerging Disciplines in Colonial Bengal*. Minneapolis: University of Minnesota Press.

Sangari, Kumkum, and Sudesh Vaid, eds. 1990. *Recasting Women: Essays in Indian Colonial History*. Piscataway, N.J.: Rutgers University Press.

Sarkar, Kobita. 1982. *You Can't Please Everyone! Film Censorship: The Inside Story*. Bombay: IBH.

Sharma, K. M. 1968. "Obscenity and the Law." In A. B. Shah, ed., *The Roots of Obscenity: Obscenity, Literature and the Law*. Bombay: Lalvani.

Singh, B. P. 1998. *India's Culture. The State, the Arts and Beyond*. New Delhi: Oxford University Press.

Smith, H. Daniel. 1995. "Impact of 'God Posters' on Hindus and Their Devotional Tradition." In Lawrence Babb and Susan Wadley, eds., *Media and the Transformation of Religion in South Asia*. Philadelphia: University of Pennsylvania Press.

Sorabjee, Soli J. 1977. *The Emergency, Censorship and the Press in India, 1975–77*. London: Writers and Scholars Educational Trust.

Strum, Philippa. 1999. *When the Nazis Came to Skokie: Freedom for Speech We Hate*. Lawrence: University of Kansas Press.

Taussig, Michael T. 1999. *Defacement: Public Secrecy and the Labor of the Negative*. Stanford: Stanford University Press.

Tharoor, Shashi. 2003. *Nehru: A Biography*. New Delhi: Oxford University Press.

Thomas, Rosie. 1989. "Sanctity and Scandal: The Mythologisation of *Mother India*." In "Indian Popular Cinema," ed. M. Binford, special issue of *Quarterly Review of Film and Video* 11(3): 11–30.

Thompson, Kenneth, ed. 1997. *Media and Cultural Regulation*. Thousand Oaks, Calif.: Sage.

Uberoi, Patricia. 1990. "Feminine Identity and National Ethos in Indian Calendar Art." *Economic and Political Weekly*, April 28: 41–48.

Vaidyanathan, T. G. 1996. *Hours in the Dark*. New Delhi: Oxford University Press.

Varma, Pavan K. 1998. *The Great Indian Middle Class*. New Delhi: Penguin.

Vasudev, Aruna. 1978. *Liberty and License in the Indian Cinema*. New Delhi: Vikas.

Visvanathan, Shiv. 1998. "Revisiting the Shah Commission." In Shiv Visvanathan and Harsh Sethi, eds., *Foul Play: Chronicles of Corruption*. New Delhi: Banyan Books.

Visvanathan, Shiv, and Harsh Sethi, eds. 1998. *Foul Play: Chronicles of Corruption*. New Delhi: Banyan Books.

Walker, Samuel. 1994. *Hate Speech: The History of an American Controversy*. Lincoln: University of Nebraska Press.

Iatrogenic Religion and Politics

Christopher Pinney

Iatrogenics

Firstly, iatrogenics. This is a concept and process which will help explicate how it is that reflexive interventions in culture themselves produce culture. In this chapter I will investigate the impact of the colonial censorship of images on the contemporary political constitution of India. I hope to explore the ways in which the proscription of certain forms of "political" activity led to a reconfiguration of activities that were categorized as "religious." My broader claim is that the particular intersection of religion and politics that characterizes much of the public life of contemporary India reflects—in part—a history and practice of censorship, both colonial and postcolonial.

As Ivan Illich explains, "iatrogenesis" is derived from the Greek words for "physician" (*iatros*) and "origins" (*genesis*) and denotes "illness that comes about as a direct result of the physician's intervention" (cited in Hooper 2000, 676). Thus, for instance, Edward Hooper has argued that the 1976 Ebola epidemic in Yambuku, in the northern Congo—like most other Ebola outbreaks—was facilitated by the presence of a mission hospital. He hypothesizes that in its unmedicalized condition Ebola emerges periodically but does not progress, because the loose settlements in which it occurs disperse, leaving behind a few individuals or families affected by the disease. Under conditions of medical intervention, however, sufferers are brought into close contact with other potential infectees: the closeness of beds in cramped mission hospitals and cross-infection through medical instruments and blood quickly allow the disease to prosper (Hooper 2000, 96). Ebola in its epidemic form is, apparently, the consequence of the physicians' interventions.

Secondly, some Indian background. My initial assumptions include the following: in precolonial India the ideal polity fused religion and politics in a unified lifeworld. During the colonial period they were conceptually titrated into separate domains, politics being strictly surveilled and religion conceptualized as (within these colonially instituted parameters) autonomous. As Sandria Freitag puts it, the colonial state "labelled issues related to religion, kinship, and other forms of community identity as apolitical—as private, special interest, and domestic and therefore not requiring the attention of the state and its institutions" (Freitag 1996, 212). Then, in large part because of the practice of colonial censorship and proscription, an authorized "religion" increasingly became the vehicle for a fugitive politics.[1] Indians were able to do things under the guise of "religion" that they were not able to do in the name of "politics." But these two domains were now (to recall Adorno's phrase), "torn halves of an integral freedom, to which however they do not add up" (Adorno 1980, 123).[2] Incapable of being recombined, they were realigned in a new deadly cosmo-politics. Visual culture was perhaps the major vehicle for this reconfiguration.

In thinking about this issue I have contemplated finding a more appropriate neologism—perhaps "anthropogenesis"—to understand the feedback loops in what Nicholas Dirks (2001) has termed the Ethnographic State. But "iatrogenesis" retains its saliency, because of the forensic and symptomological discourses that lay at the heart of the late colonial Indian state.

The 1910 Press Act

Colonial state interventions into what were perceived to be pathological Indian conditions were tortuous. The repressive 1823 Adams Regulations (Shaw and Lloyd 1985, vii) were overturned by Metcalfe's Act of 1835 (see Barrier 1974, 4). Various surveillance and censorship protocols introduced after the convulsions of 1857 were consolidated in 1867 by the Press and Registration of Books Act, which required that three copies of all publications be deposited with local governments (see Barrier 1974, 5, and Ahmed's chapter in this volume), and popular theater (especially the worrying activities of itinerant *jatra* groups) was brought under surveillance through the 1876 Dramatic Performances Act.

Notwithstanding the broadening of the definition of "seditious" material in the 1898 Code of Criminal Procedure to encompass that which "brings or attempts to bring into hatred or contempt, or excites or attempts to excite disaffection towards Her Majesty, or the Government established by law in British India" (Shaw 1985, vii), the first decade of the twentieth century focused further anxieties which the 1910 Indian Press Act attempted to address. Various violent incidents gave additional impetus: a bomb was thrown at Lord and Lady Minto's carriage in Ahmedabad in November 1908 (it failed to explode), and one month later A. M. T. Jackson, a magistrate in Nasik, was shot and killed by members of the Abhinav Bharat (Barrier 1974, 45).

Whereas the 1898 Code of Criminal Procedure vaguely gestured to disaffection created by "words, either spoken or written, or by sign, or by visible representation" (Barrier 1974, 6), the 1910 Act extended the proscriptional net and explicitly targeted the circulation of images. Section 2(a) noted that the term "book" included every "volume, part or division of a volume, and pamphlet in any language, and every sheet of music, map, chart or plan, separately printed or lithographed." Section 2(b) defined "document" as including "any painting, drawing, or photograph or other visible representation."

What were the anxieties that provoked such an encompassing attempt at suppression? In his speech introducing the Act, Herbert Hope Risley, a new Home Member, made a detailed inventory of the political aspirations that print culture was increasingly purveying:

> Everyday the Press proclaims, openly or by suggestion or allusion, that the only cure for the ills of India is independence from foreign rule, independence to be won by heroic deeds, self-sacrifice, martyrdom on the part of the young, in any case by some form of violence. Hindu mythology, ancient and modern history, and more especially the European literature of revolution, are ransacked to furnish examples that justify revolt and proclaim its inevitable success. The methods of guerilla warfare as practiced in Circassia, Spain and South Africa; Mazzini's gospel of political assassination; Kossuth's most violent doctrines; the doings of Russian Nihilists; the murder of the Marquis Ito; the dialogue between Arjuna and Krishna in the *Gita*, a book that is to Hindus what the *Imitation of Christ* is to emotional Christians—all these are pressed into the service of inflaming impressionable minds. The last instance is perhaps the worst. I can imagine no more wicked desecration than that the sacrilegious hand of the anarchist should be laid upon the Indian Song of Songs and that a masterpiece of transcendental philosophy and religious ecstasy should be perverted to the base uses of preaching political murder.[3]

Something of the intensity of the conflicted anxiety about the new forms of cosmological politics is apparent in Risley's lament "Is the Sakuntala of the future to grow up in an atmosphere of treason, plotting murder and designing bombs?" Risley's anxiety is but a late manifestation of a concern about the rise of a cosmological politics which has its origins as early as the 1870s, the decade during which several important lithographic presses were established (see Pinney 2004 for a more detailed account). Risley hoped to counter the recourse which Indian politics made to religion.

A key force in developing this imbrication of the political in the cosmic was Vishnu Krishna Chiplunkar, the founder of the Chitrashala Press in Poona in 1878. It was on the Chitrashala Press's premises that (as the press itself bragged) the first bomb in the Deccan was constructed. Chiplunkar's journalism and his publication of pictures were intended to be no less explosive, and many of the early chromolithographs invoked a past Maratha glory and disseminated a pantheon in a milieu of incipient violence.

Chiplunkar's (and, later, B. G. Tilak's) conjuring of a past as a kind of master political code was famously, and perceptively, analyzed by Richard Temple, Governor of Bombay:

> Throughout the whole of the Deccan, the mind of the people is . . . affected by the past associations of Maratha rule, which, so far from being forgotten,

are better remembered than would ordinarily be expected. . . . This memory constantly suggests the analogy between the position of the British and that of the Moguls in the Deccan. (quoted in Johnson 1973, 54)

One key effect of this historical imagination was a creeping allegorization. The past became part of a present, and correspondences between past and present became significant. Coincidence and accident were replaced in this new historiography by resonance and significance. History and present-day events became parallel systems with a converging significance.

This sense of the world as a system of signs to be read by those in possession of the code—rather than as an aleatory flux to be simply experienced—was especially apparent in the visual field, where signs could more easily evade colonial surveillance. Political intent was easy to identify in certain kinds of propositional and imperative language (e.g., a slogan such as "Murder the Colonisers!"). However, similar intentions could be more subtly embedded in visual representations, especially if the imagery appeared at first sight to be simply the visual reiteration of a deity, or an episode in a religious epic. Take Chitrashala's *Narsimha*, for example. Published around 1880, this striking chromolithograph depicts a seated Narsimha, the man-lion incarnation of Vishnu, killing Hiranyakashipu, the king of the Daityas.[4] Narsimha sits in the center of the image, on a threshold in front of an astonishing vista, a position which establishes his liminality. Likewise, Hiranyakashipu is suspended between air and earth as Narsimha plunges his liminal claws into the flesh of his victim. On either side, human devotees look on in admiration as this avatar does his work.

In an account first published in 1930, the liberal missionary-turned-historian Edward Thompson describes one of the ways in which such images circulated. He notes that in 1920 in a Bengal town where he was based, "in the very centre of the Bazaar, the vegetable market, appeared a thirty-foot-high image of Vishnu in his Man-Lion incarnation, tearing out the bowels of a figure flung face upwards across his knees. The figure was pale-complexioned, and dressed like an Englishman" (Thompson 1930, 90). The description matches the Chitrashala print very closely and suggests that it may well have served as referent for the Bengali installation.[5] Thompson also describes differences: "In front of the figure, and gazing reverently towards it, were Mr. Gandhi and the Ali Brothers (to signify the Hindu-Mohammedan rapprochement), a woman ('Mother India') and a cow. I have often seen the tableau, and am glad I saw it" (Thompson 1930, 90–91). These images were able to occupy such prominent public spaces because of their double coding: when accused of politicality they could seek refuge in the mythic. "This is Hiranyakashipu, slain by our god."

This double coding was mobilized even more potently by Chiplunkar's strategy of establishing, though his journalism, the discursive infrastructure for images which might otherwise appear wholly innocuous. Take, for instance, the Chitrashala Press's interest in parrots. It produced large chromolithographs of a young Ram held in his mother's arms while she releases a parrot from a cage,

Figure 2.1

Artist unknown. Narsimha. Chromolithograph published by
Chitrashala Press, Poona, c. 1880s. Author's collection.

and in the early twentieth century it printed postcards showing parrots sitting
in the branches of trees. Colonial surveillance might have seen in the former
a simple reference to mythic lore, and in the latter an echo of Indian folkloric
preoccupations with the bird. An audience familiar with Chiplunkar's Marathi

journalism, however, is likely to have freighted these images with other significance, framing them with Chiplunkar's celebrated observation that

> there is a great difference between the bird who roams at will through sky
> and forest and the parrot who is put into a large cage of gold or even jewels!
> It is a great disaster when a bird whose God given power is to move wherever
> he pleases unrestrained on the strength of his beautiful wings must remain
> always chirping in a confined place! The same applies to a nation. (quoted in
> Wolpert 1961, 10–11)

Chiplunkar's journalism provided Chitrashala prints with captions whose syn-
tactic and semantic specificity closed down the volatile possibilities of images.

We can see a similar double coding in the use of the trope of chastity in
several Ravi Varma images. In 1870 Ravi Varma was commissioned to paint *Sita
Bhoopravesam* (Sita's Ordeal), a work which was to play a key role in his career.
This image was subsequently bought by the young Gaekwad of Baroda, one of
a small group of key princely modernizers. Venniyoor has noted the "sensation"
that *Sita Bhoopravesam* caused when it was first exhibited in Baroda (Venniyoor
1981, 21). The painting depicts an Ayodhya-returned Sita disappearing—in the
arms of Bhoomi Devi—into the earth, unable to bear the questioning of her
chastity after her abduction by Ravan. This narrative, with which most Hindus
would have been intimately familiar, placed a set of key tropes within a matrix
whose relevance to a colonized India would have been lost on few: the exile
of Ram from Ayodhya as a deferment of just rule ("Ram Rajya"), Sita as the
Motherland, and the rape of the Motherland by a foreign ruler.

The dynamics of these metaphors, and strategies that might be enacted to
overturn past wrongs, were further elaborated in another popular Ravi Varma
image, *Keechak-Sairandhri*, which also become the subject of a popular—and
subsequently proscribed—play (Pinney 2004, 68–71). Colonial anxieties about
the capacity of print media to disseminate sedition had been intensified by the
upsurge of picture production during the Cow Protection agitation from the
1890s onward. The idea that the growth of nationalist sentiment was intimately
linked to the development of print capitalism (Anderson 1991) was prefigured
in the conclusions of some British officials as they thought through the consequences of new media during the early 1890s. Landsdowne, the Secretary for
India, and others expounded such a thesis in a memo in 1893. This was in part
a response to the Earl of Kimberley's earlier question as to "why . . . disturbances
are becoming more frequent than in past years," and Lansdowne argued that

> one of the causes [is] the greater frequency of communication and the
> interchange of news by post and telegraph between different parts of the
> country. . . .
>   This rapid dissemination of news and increasing activity of controversy,
> carried on through the Press, by public meetings, and by the addresses of
> itinerant preachers, is in some respects a new feature in Indian life, and is one

Figure 2.2
Ravi Varma. *Sita Bhoopravesam.* Painting, reproduced here from an early
photographic copy reproduced in S. N. Joshi, *Half-Tone Reprints of the
Renowned Pictures of the Late Raja Ravi Varma* (1911). Author's collection.

which is likely to grow and add considerably to the difficulties of administration. . . . pamphlets, leaflets . . . and placards of an inflammatory tendency
have been disseminated throughout the country.[6]

In the later phases of the Cow Protection agitation, locally produced images
were mobilized through collective action in a manner that prefigured the use of
the ubiquitous Hindu chauvinist images of the 1980s and 1990s. The cow, an
enormously potent and sacred sign, was to emerge as a symbol of the nation,
and this and other visual symbols were to play a vital role in the organization
as well as the ideology of the Cow Protection Movement. Cow protection
involved a struggle not only over a "sacred symbol" but also, locally, over "sacred
spaces," and the specificity of local struggles also forged new senses of community: "the common experience of being incorporated in a 'process of sanc-
tification' defined group solidarity" (Yang 1980, 582). At a regional level, this
spatialization took the form of a network of messengers and traveling preach-
ers who could rapidly disseminate the cause over wide areas. Geographic reach
was combined with the insertion of Cow Protection into the spaces of the
everyday: "no space, no occasion, it seemed, was inappropriate to organize and
direct attention towards the issue of the cow" (Yang 1980, 587). This colonization of quotidian space replicated the infestation of the body of the cow itself

with the divine; in numerous lithographs the cow becomes a proto-nation, a space which embodies a Hindu cosmology. Among the earliest images is that published by P. C. Biswas of Calcutta and, after the turn of the century, designs which circulated in the 1890s were widely commercially produced and would even appear on commercial packaging such as textile labels. These lithographs can be seen as mythic charters whose metaphors were instantaneously transformed into everyday spatial practice, an iconic mythopraxis that convulsed much of northern India.

The historical record is unusually rich in the detail it provides of the consumption of these kinds of visual images. Lansdowne's memo provides a clear sense of the gamut of visual and performative signs which were made to do the work of cow protection during this period.

> In addition to the inflammatory harangues delivered to meetings of Hindus, [wandering ascetics] have distributed throughout the country pictures of the cow, of a kind calculated to appeal strongly to the religious sentiment of the people. One of them, for instance, depicts a cow . . . being slaughtered by three Muhammadan butchers, and is headed "the present state." Another exhibits a cow, in every part of whose body groups of Hindu deities and holy persons are shown, being assailed by a monster with a drawn sword entitled the "Kali Yug" but which has been largely understood as typifying the Muhammadan community.

A memo from Forbes, Commissioner of the Patna Division, to the Chief Secretary of the Government of Bengal in the same year describes a similar image which had been seized in Champeran: "the picture of a cow stamped with images of Gods, also contained a representation of a Musalman advancing to slay the cow and a Hindu beseeching him to refrain."[7]

Sandria Freitag has also drawn attention to an account of a meeting in Azamgarh District in 1894 which provides invaluable data on how meanings were constructed in the process of consuming these images. A wealthy landholder named Ram Saran Singh organized the meeting in the town of Lar on March 18, 1893. A lithographed copy of rules adopted by other Cow Protection societies was circulated and amended after discussion. Attention then turned to the visual propaganda which the organizers had brought with them:

> A cow picture was placed on a stool before the platform and copies of it were circulated. This picture represents a cow in whose body all the Hindu gods are depicted as residing. A calf is at her udder and a woman sits before the calf holding a bowl waiting for her turn. This woman is labelled "the Hindu." Behind the cow, above her tail, is a representation as of Krishna labelled "Dharmraj," and in front of the cow, above her head, is a man with a drawn sword labelled "Kaliyug." The Hindu who produced this picture expatiated on its meaning. The Hindu must only take the cow's milk after the calf has been satisfied. In the "Dharmraj" of the Satyug no Hindu would kill a cow, but the Kaliyug is bent upon killing the cow and exterminating kine.

Figure 2.3

Artist unknown. *Chaurasi Devata Auvali Gay* (The Cow with Eighty-four Deities). Chromolithograph published by Ravi Varma Press c. 1915.

As every man drinks cow's milk just as he as an infant has drawn milk from his mother, the cow must be regarded as the universal mother, and so is called "Gao Mata." It is matricide to kill a cow. Nay more, as all the gods dwell in the cow, to kill a cow is to insult every Hindu. The Magistrate [at Deoria] found Muhammadans excited because they heard a picture was in circulation representing a Muhammadan with a drawn sword sacrificing a cow, and this they considered an insult.[8]

Images from the 1890s do not survive, but later versions (figure 2.3 is from around 1915) which bear a close resemblance to those described above do. In the later Ravi Varma image the figure with drawn sword is clearly labeled in the image as a representative of the *kaliyug*, presumably the demon *kali*. The caption about his head reads, "he manusyaho! kaliyugi mansahari jivom ko dekho" (mankind, look at the meat-eating souls of the kaliyug), and the figure in yellow (labeled *dharmaraj*) beseeches him with the words "mat maro gay sarv ka jivan hai" (don't kill the cow, everyone is dependent on it).

The deluge of imagery associated with the Cow Protection Movement forms part of the frame within which we can understand the anxieties driving the intensification of colonial surveillance and censorship from the end of the nineteenth century. "We are overwhelmed with a mass of heterogeneous material, some of it misguided, some of it frankly seditious," declared Herbert Hope

Risley in 1907, and these concerns would lead him to draft the major substance of the 1910 Press Act. One ambivalent colonial anxiety centered on the possibility of a "deformed" political theology—a fusing of Hinduism with a politics of revolution and apotheosis—in the analysis of which ordinary political theory would be useless. The prospect of this paradigmatic shift, which might transform rational political action into a cosmological strategy, was at once thrilling and terrifying. Only a few months before that 1907 speech, Risley had sent his assistant to trawl the streets of Calcutta for seditious imagery, and he had turned up a Calcutta Art Studio lithograph in which Kali seemed to be garlanded with European heads and the fall of the British empire was predicted.

The assistant, B. A. Gupte, wrote to Risley, "Of those I could collect last evening, I feel that the one printed for a cigarette manufacturer is the most effective and significant."[9] This lithograph had been in circulation in various forms since the early 1880s. Gupte was alarmed by it, though quite why is sometimes hard to discern. He remarked on "the artistically cunning 'modulation' of the caste marks" on Kali's garland of heads, noting that some lacked these marks and apparently concluding that they must be the heads of Europeans. In a similar vein, Gupte noted "the symbolical British lion couchant in the . . . N. W. corner, his fall in the N. E. corner and a decapitated *red coated* soldier in the S. E. corner." "The falling head near the toes of the prostrate 'husband'" [Siva], he continued, "leaves no doubt as to the intention of the designer."[10] Gupte concluded with the observation that he was "promised more 'editions'" and would forward them to Risley.[11]

Operation of the Act

The main instruments of control imposed by the Press Act were financial securities which were vulnerable to confiscation in the event of any breach of the exceptionally wide provisions of the legislation. All presses that had made declarations under the 1867 Act were required to deposit security (up to Rs 5,000) unless expressly exempted by local magistrates. Securities were to be forfeited if a local government declared in writing to the press concerned that the act had been breached. A press subject to such a ruling and wishing to publish further material was required to make a further application and deposit a further security with a magistrate, "not being less than one thousand or more than ten thousand rupees, as the Magistrate decides" (1910 Act, section 5). In the event of further breaches, more securities could be required or the entire assets of the press could be forfeited. As Barrier notes, "The press bill therefore provided for new deterrents (securities) and executive action to remove publications from circulation" (1974, 47).[12] Between 1910 and 1914 at least ten vernacular newspapers ceased publication following demands for the deposit of securities. The Gujarati *Kathiawar and Mahi Kantha Gazette* of Ahmedabad was required to deposit Rs 2,000 and it "continued publication[,] for which the editor was convicted under Section 23(2) of the Press Act,

Figure 2.4

Artist unknown. The goddess Kali. Chromolithograph, first published
by Calcutta Art Studio in the early 1880s, this copy collected in 1908.
Royal Anthropological Institute, London.

1910, and fined Rs. 300. After this the paper ceased publication" (Natarajan
1955, 267).[13]

The remit of the Act was extraordinarily wide, placing within its sights the
"printing or publishing [of] any newspaper book or other document contain-
ing any words, signs or visible representations which are likely or may have a

tendency, directly, or indirectly, whether by inference, suggestion, allusion, metaphor, implication or otherwise," to incite murder, hatred of the administration, or a variety of other responses (section 4[i]). Within a longer frame one might see this as part of a post-Newtonian war against metaphor. The seventeenth-century scientific revolution staged science against metaphor so powerfully that even Bishop Parker wanted Parliament to proscribe the use of metaphors in sermons (Shapin 1996). One can see an anxious colonialist-rationalist disparagement in this exasperated list of "suggestion, allusion, metaphor, implication." In a profound sense, these subtleties are all affronts to a rational politics.

Predictably, the overwhelming impact of the Act was on Indian-run presses. In 1910 the number of proceedings under the Press Act was 48, in 1911 it was 51, in 1912 it dropped to 36, and in 1913 rose again to 80. Of this total of 215 proceedings, only one was taken against a European-owned press, all the rest being aimed at Indian-owned concerns.

Some sense of the real human cost of these proceedings is apparent from the following examples: Shridhar Waman Nagarkar of Nasik was sentenced by the Bombay government on August 11, 1910, to three years' rigorous imprisonment for "publishing and distributing seditious pictures." Likewise, Devising Mohansingh was sentenced on August 18, 1910, to three years' rigorous imprisonment for the same misdemeanor.[14]

However, the act was fraught with problems. As Barrier notes, "Manoeuvring a controversial measure through legislative shoals was relatively simple compared with putting it into operation" (1974, 48). The pathological politicality of some artifacts was easy to establish. For instance, a *dhoti* sold in Calcutta in 1910 on which was printed a song in praise of Khudiram Bose (who had been executed in 1908) was clearly seditious. The dhoti was five yards long, presumed to be of Midnapore manufacture, and sold for Rs 4. The government translator S. K. Mahaptra noted that "some boys and women are going about with these *dhotis* and selling them. This is a new method of disseminating sedition." He provided the following translation of the Bengali text which covered the border of the *dhoti*:

> Mother, farewell,
> I shall go to the gallows with a smile.
> The people of India will see this.
> One bomb can kill a man.
> There are a lakh of bombs in our homes.
> Mother, what can the English do? If I come back,
> Do not forget, Mother,
> Your foolish child Khudiram.
> See that I get your sacred feet at the end.
> When shall I call you again "Mother" with the ease of my mind?
> Mother, do not keep this sinner in another country.
> It is written that you have 36 crores of sons and daughters.

Mother, Khudiram's name vanishes now.
He is now turned to dust.
If I have to rise again,
See that, Mother, I sit in your lap again.
In this kingdom of Bhisma who else is there like you?
You are unparalleled Mother.
When shall I depart from this world with a shout of Bande Mataram?
This is the saying of Bhabataran.
Farewell Mother,
I shall go to the gallows with a smile.
The people of India will see this.
One bomb can kill a man.
There are lakhs of bombs in our homes.
Mother what can the English do?[15]

The *dhoti*'s seditious nature was clear. What was problematic was whether it could be considered a "document" under section 2(6) of the act: it was finally deemed to be so and notification no. 1350-P was published in the *Calcutta Gazette Extraordinary* declaring that all such *dhotis* should be "forfeited to His Majesty."

Beyond these relatively straightforward dilemmas concerning the remit of the Act lay the much more complex issue of where the "seditious" began, and the merely "religious" or "mythic" ended. The phrase "signs or visible representations which are likely or may have a tendency, directly, or indirectly, whether by inference, suggestion, allusion, metaphor, implication or otherwise," while reassuringly encompassing in theory, proved in practice to involve very difficult encounters with vernacular cultural production. "Inference" and "metaphor" quickly revealed themselves to be difficult areas for the colonial state to police.

A case from 1912 demonstrates the extraordinary complexity of the operation.[16] In January of that year, the Local Government of the Central Provinces issued a notification under the 1910 Act to prevent the dissemination of the "Ashtabhuja Devi" image published by the Ravi Varma Press. All copies of the picture found in the Central Provinces were to be forfeited to His Majesty. The justification for this was that the picture, in which

> the Hindu Goddess called Ashtabhuja Devi is depicted riding a lion and furiously attacking two butchers who have apparently just decapitated a cow, printed at the Ravi Varma Press Karla and elsewhere[,] contains visible representation likely to incite to acts of violence and to bring into hatred and contempt certain classes of His Majesty's subjects in British India.

An attached memo from C. A. Kincaid, Secretary to the Government of Bombay, was intended to make clear that "the picture was interpreted by the Government of the Punjab and by the Bombay Government as an anti-cow-killing document."

In a petition to the Bombay High Court, Schleicher, the then proprietor of the Ravi Varma Press, claimed that the description of the picture given in the notification of proscription was "gravely erroneous and absolutely misconceived." He made a claim for its pure "religiosity," arguing that the image was no more than a mimetic visualization of an episode in the Mahabharata. Ashtabhuja Devi, otherwise known as Mahishasuramardini, rode on a lion to battle with the demon Mahishasur, whom Vishnu had requested she slay. Schleicher's petition continued:

> When she saw the extensive army of demons which occupied the ten directions, she was annoyed and assumed such a big form that her eight arms reached the eight directions and the crown on her head reached the sky above. The battle commenced and the result was that hundreds of thousand[s] [of] demons fell down and the bloodshed was so great, that even the elephant, chariots and foot soldiers in the demon's army were swept away in a flood of blood. Then Mahishasur with the assistance of his general Bidalaksha pushed forward to fight a duel with the great Goddess. The lion gave a blow to Bidalaksha with his paw and lay him flat on the ground. The Goddess pierced Mahishasur with her Trishul (trident). As soon as the demon was shot in his chest with the Trishul he assumed the form of a buffalo. The Goddess mounted on him and separated his head from his body.

The picture shows the lion springing on Bidalaksha and the goddess is shown simultaneously severing Mahishasur's head, piercing the demon buffalo with her trishul, and treading on the decapitated buffalo.

Schleicher claimed in his petition that "it is erroneous to interpret the two demons shown in the picture as butchers and that it is also erroneous to interpret that they are apparently decapitating a cow." But a closer look complicates the matter greatly, for the buffalo is very definitely cow-like in coloring and physiology. Similarly, there is a subtle displacement of agency marked by the presence of blood on Bidalaksha's sword and its absence on the goddess's. The implication is clearly that it is the foregrounded figure with the sword who has just slain the buffalo/cow and upon whom the lion wreaks vengeance. In the absence of clear textual knowledge among the popular consumers of this image, a reading that constructs it as the goddess's retribution upon two Muslim or untouchable butchers who have just slaughtered a cow seems highly plausible.

The precise nature of the agreement reached between Schleicher and the government indicates that those who sought to proscribe it had a clear sense of the deliberate misrecognition that the image was seeking to provoke. When government officials were advised that they were likely to be unsuccessful, they proposed that if Schleicher agreed to "make certain alterations in the pictures" and withdraw his suit, they would pay compensation for the pictures seized earlier by the police. Consequently, Schleicher agreed that in future copies of the picture "the blood stains on the sword of one of the two men will be removed and the animal will be coloured black." Schleicher did this and the print was quickly reissued with these marginal changes.

Figure 2.5

Artist unknown. *Ashtabhuja Devi*. Chromolithograph published
by Ravi Varma Press c. 1911. Ashmolean Museum, Oxford.

Figure 2.6

Artist unknown. Revised version of *Ashtabhuja Devi*.
Chromolithograph published by Ravi Varma Press
c. 1912. Ashmolean Museum, Oxford.

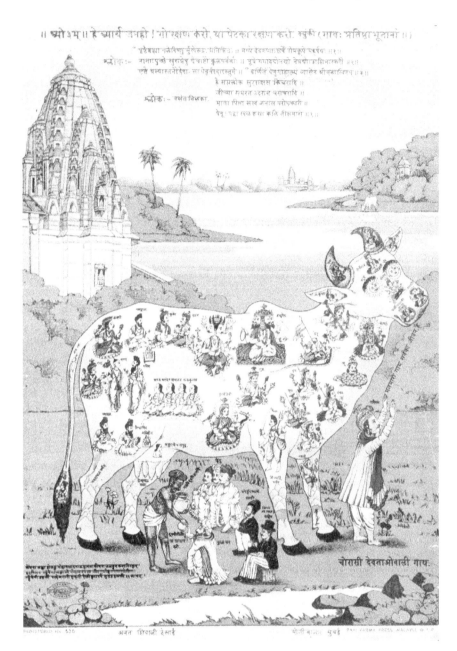

Figure 2.7

Artist unknown. Amended version of *Chaurasi Devata Auvali Gay*.
Published by Ravi Varma Press c. 1915. Author's collection.

A similar compromise was reached regarding another Ravi Varma Press image which I have already discussed (figure 2.3) and which was but the latest in a line of similar images stretching back two decades. Under the terms of the compromise Schleicher agreed that in future copies "the figure of the demon in front of the cow shall be removed." Shortly thereafter a similar print was issued, this time in vertical portrait format, in which Dharmaraj beseeches the empty void where once the sword-wielding demon stood.

Risley no doubt would have been pleased by these manifestations of surveillance and regulation. From the point of view of the state seeking to titrate the increasingly compound relationship between the "religious" and "political," these cases may have seemed exemplary instances of diagnosis and correction. Recall Risley's lament: was "the Sakuntala of the future to grow up in an atmosphere of treason, plotting murder and designing bombs?" Well, in this case, apparently not. The atmosphere of treason had been separated out from the mythic and Ashtabhuja Devi restored to her Sakuntala-like purity, or so it seemed.

The crackdown on picture publishers and newspapers continued for a decade after the introduction of the Act. A 1919 memorandum from the Press Association of India noted that 991 printing presses and newspapers which had existed prior to the Act had had some form of action taken against them. Of these, 286 received warnings, and 705 received demands for heavy securities with the subsequent "forfeitures thereof by executive orders whenever the Government thought any publication objectionable." A further 70 presses founded after the implementation of the Act were subject to forfeitures, and the Association estimated that more than 173 new presses and 129 new newspapers "were stifled at their birth owing to the demand of a security which they could not furnish." The total amount of sureties forfeited to the government by sundry presses had reached five lakhs (Rs. 500,000) by 1915 (Natarajan 1955, 158).

This suppression intensified during the later years of the First War, and official returns for 1918 indicated that more than five hundred publications had been proscribed under the Act (Natarajan 1955, 159). Further appeals were made for the repeal of the Act, and while these were considered by the Secretary of State, the official response was that nothing could be considered until after the introduction of the Montagu-Chelmsford Reforms.

Following the introduction of the Rowlatt Bill in February 1919, Gandhi launched a satyagraha in Bombay, in the course of which he urged further protest against the Press Act. In the first issue of his unregistered publication *Satyagraha*, Gandhi urged every satyagraha center to publish "a written newspaper without registering it." This handwritten paper was to be disseminated scribally: "it will be the duty of those who receive the first copies to re-copy till at last the process of multiplication is made to cover if necessary, the whole of the masses of India."[17] The Press Act was to be systematically flouted, all unregistered scribes offering themselves for arrest: "Satyagrahis should so far as possible, write their names and addresses as sellers so that they may traced easily when wanted by the Government for prosecution" (Natarajan 1955, 160).

The Jallianwala Bagh massacre in Amritsar spurred numerous further breaches of the terms of the act. The *Amrita Bazar Patrika* lost a security of Rs 5,000 and was ordered to supply a security of Rs 10,000 if it wished to continue publishing. The *Punjabee* suspended publication altogether. The editor of the *Tribune* was sentenced to imprisonment, and the editor of the *Bombay Chronicle*, Benjamin Guy Horniman, was deported, an action, the 1955 Press Commission subsequently observed, "reminiscent of the days of the East India Company" (Natarajan 1955, 161).

The overzealous implementation of this catch-all piece of legislation led to a number of critical legal judgments which were to culminate in its repeal in 1922. Muzaffar Husain Khan's *The Indian Press Act, Act 1 of 1910* is a manual specifically aimed at "lawyers, as well as . . . journalists and proprietors of Printing establishments" (Khan 1919, 1) and draws attention to a series of judgments concerning the Act's undisciplined rubric which were to undermine its efficacy. A judgment in *Mahomed Ali v. the Emperor* ruled that

> the provisions of Section 4 are very comprehensive and its language is as wide as human ingenuity could make it. Indeed it appears to me to embrace the whole range of varying degrees of reassurance from certainty on the one side to the very limits of impossibility on the other. It is difficult to see to what lengths the operation of this section might not plausibly be extended by an ingenious mind . . . much that is regarded as standard literature might undoubtedly be caught. (Ibid.)

In March 1921, Sir Tej Bahadur Sapru (a Law Member in the viceroy's executive council) formed a committee, with himself as chairman, for the repeal or amendment of the Press Act. Both the 1910 Act and the Indian Press (Incitements to Offences) Act of 1908 were repealed shortly thereafter. The Press Law Repeal Act of 1922 led to a retroactive reliance on section 99A of the 1898 Code of Criminal Procedure and a reduction in the number of prosecutions for the production of seditious pictures until 1930, when the combined effect of Bhagat Singh's Hindustan Socialist Republican Army and Gandhi's "salt march" to Dandi precipitated the introduction of a Press Ordinance which reintroduced many of the features of the hated 1910 Press Act. As Natarajan noted, "the peace between the Press and the Government which had been maintained for nine years, snapped as the peace of the country was disturbed" (1955, 166).

The Slipperiness of Metaphor

In July 1930, the Bombay Provincial Congress Committee issued stamps bearing the words "Boycott British Goods," with the intention that its supporters would affix these to envelopes and postcards. The colonial state's response to these "boycott stamps" was to throw into stark relief the difficulties it faced in regulating the visual "everyday." Initially it appeared that there would be no objection to the use of such stamps. The Bombay Presidency's Postmaster told the *Indian Daily Mail* on July 4, 1930, "You can write anything you like on your cover. If you like you may even affix your photograph to it. So long as it bears our usual stamp there can be no objection." Such indifference caused concern among others in the government, who sought legal clarification as to whether the slogan "Boycott British Goods" might be considered "seditious," "scurrilous," or "grossly offensive" under the relevant section of the Post Office Act. The advice they received indicated that the government could act if it wished, but it would then also have to proscribe slogans such as "Shop with Selfridge's." Extensive correspondence between the Home Political Department and the Bombay postmaster general ensued, and further legislation was suggested before the Legal Department again pointed out the difficulties of isolating these specific stamps in any new proscription. "I have found great difficulty," opined D. G. Mitchell, "in devising a formula which is free from obvious objection":

> I have tried several variants of the term "political significance," but could not find one which did not cover harmless activities. . . . The difficulties may be seen from a consideration of the following actual cases—or probable cases— (1) Photographs of Mr. Gandhi with no accompanying text; (2) reproductions of the "national flag"; (3) the device of the Overseas League, from whom I have just received a communication; (4) an open post-card soliciting a vote at an election; (5) post-cards bearing the slogan "Vote for Swaraj" (or any other political cause); (6) the device on the envelopes of the P. & O. [Company].

The boycott stamps revealed an undecidable public space where contestatory images could operate in the gaps of preexisting practice. In general, allegorical and propositional anticolonialism was vulnerable to surveillance. Its referents could be easily ascertained in a process of translation and adequation. Between 1920 and 1940 many anticolonial images appeared which invoked the logic of the simile in which both terms of comparison are present. The simile here also has the quality of discourse as Lyotard defines it. An example—taken from many—is the 1930 image *Non-co-operation Tree and Mahatma Gandhi*, published by N. D. Sahgal and Sons and printed by the National Art Press, both of Lahore. The proscription order issued for this image makes surprisingly clear reading. The image is described in these orders as "showing" (which, given the argument I shall develop shortly, is a revealing term)

> (1) Mahatma Gandhi sitting at the foot of a non-co-operation tree, with the "goddess of union" holding its two branches on which are seated leaders of the No-Change Party and the *Swarajya* Party, respectively, while a European is trying to pull down the branch carrying the leaders of the No-Change Party;

Figure 2.8

Svatantra Bharat: Boycott British Goods, Non-Violence.
Postage stamp–sized sticker issued by Bombay Provincial
Congress Committee, 1930. Author's collection.

(2) Bharat Mata and Shri Krishna with the inscription—
"The virtuous people to protect
And to destroy the sinful ones,
To set up firmly righteousness,
From age to age I enter birth."
(3) a jail with a sentry on duty in front of it;
(4) the Lawrence Statue with policemen standing in front of it;
(5) a *Swarajya Ashram*;
(6) a Congressman intervening to stop a quarrel between the Hindus and
Mohammadans, and a gulf of differences crossed by a bridge constructed
as a result of the constructive programme, the sacrifice of leaders and the
voice of the masses, leading to the Council Chamber, showing the influence of Mahatma Gandhi, etc;

> The proscription order declares the forfeiture of the image under
section 124-A of the Indian Penal Code "on the ground that it contains matter [tending] to promote hatred and disaffection towards the
Government established by law in British India."[18]

This image is strikingly transparent. Its visual logic is akin to a diagram: all
the parts are labeled, and their identity made doubly clear. Noncooperation was
like a tree, as Gandhi said, and a bridge over a river is like a bridge over a gulf

of differences. The terms of this image—rooted in simile—are so amenable to linguistic translation that one almost does not need to see the image to visualize it precisely.

The surveillance and suppression of these easily identifiable modes of visual propaganda encouraged a movement away from simile to the more metaphorical, and from the discursive to the figural, from a sphere of language-like knowability to zones "where intensities are felt." Just as in the composer Shostakovich's oeuvre we can trace the emergence of a secret zone of intensity in which his deep feelings were expressed in a manner that was not susceptible to the increasingly close scrutiny of the Stalinist regime, so we can see in the work of certain key artists a move away from publicly identifiable political assertions and toward increasingly figural fields of affect.

We have already seen in B. A. Gupte's cryptological paranoia concerning the 1907 Kali image the difficulties that the colonial state faced in surveilling images that it deemed problematic. Gupte attempted to map a propositional or discursive translation onto the image; looking for similes, he wanted the slain head to be "like" that of a British soldier, he wanted the lion to be "like" the British imperial lion couchant. In attempting this unconvincing translational interpretation he was able to avoid engaging with the most obvious—but least easily analyzable—fact about the picture, namely that it conjured *figurally* an atmosphere of apocalyptic foreboding.

The India Office and the National Archives of India preserve more proscribed images created by Rup Kishor Kapur (1893–1978) than by any other known artist. Active in Kanpur from the 1920s, when the city was known as "lal Kanpur," Rup Kishor first came to prominence following the execution of Bhagat Singh in 1931. As his grandson Kamal Kapoor phrased it,

> The day Bhagat Singh was hanged, he painted in a day [a picture] of Bhagat Singh beheaded, giving his head on a plate to Bharat Mata. Bharat Mata is weeping. He painted it and [displayed it in Sambal] and shouted Bande Mataram and he was taken by the police and was imprisoned for one or two years. (Interview)

The images he produced in his Kanpur period include many of the martyrs of the Lahore Conspiracy trial. *Sardar Bhagat Singh's Wonderful Presentation* depicts Bhagat Singh (behind whom stand Raj Guru and Sukhdev) giving his head on a plate to an enthroned Mother India; *Three Heroes in the Prison* depicts the three prisoners chained and behind bars; another image depicts B. K. Dutt in prison; and *Azad Mandir*, one of Rup Kishor's most complex images, arranges vignettes of Bhagat, B. K. Dutt, Raj Guru, Sukhdev, and four other martyrs around a portrait of Chandrashekhar Azad and the scene of his killing in Allahabad.[19]

Azad Mandir is a fascinating ensemble of images whose dissemination was originally authorized, in many cases, by the colonial state through the press. The individual portraits (with the possible exception of that of the corpse of

Figure 2.9

Rup Kishor Kapur. *Azad Mandir*. Black-and-white print published by
Laksmibilas Press, Cawnpore, 1931. Courtesy British Library Board.

Roshan Singh) were all police portraits, in the public domain only because they
had officially been made available.[20] The Home Department contemplated court
action against the *Pioneer*, the *Hindustan Times*, and *Bande Mataram* (Lahore) for
printing pictures of Bhagat Singh and B. K. Dutt, but only on the grounds that
they did so before Singh and Dutt had been identified in a second lineup, and the

defense might have tried to use the pictures' publication to invalidate the lineup. This did not happen, and the Home Department's interest waned.[21]

It is unclear whether the photograph of Azad's corpse under a tree that is included in *Azad Mandir* was released by the police (as seems possible) or was taken by a newspaper photographer and disseminated directly by the press. Whatever its origins, it quickly become a piece of potent propaganda once it had been linguistically framed. The Home Political files (KW to 159/1931, pp. 1–10) in the National Archives record, in exceptional detail, a public meeting held in memory of Chandrashekhar Azad under the auspices of the Naujawan Bharat Sabha on March 13, 1931. Songs and poems were sung and recited, and printed copies of the photograph of Azad's body under the tree were sold "for one anna a copy." These foolscap sheets reproduced the photograph with two lines of Urdu text above and below, reading,

> On the place of sacrifice for freedom
> We shall have our name included in the
> List of these living whilst dying
> We shall save the honor of India.[22]

Rup Kishor Kapur undertakes a similar captioning in *Azad Mandir*, but instead of words, he frames the central image with other images, other celebrations of martyrdom, which create what Eco calls "chains of syntagmatic concatenation imbued with argumentative effect" (1982, 38). The argumentative effect is such that the image would surely have been immediately identified as seditious, even in the absence of the didactic title "Azad Mandir" ("temple of freedom").

My conversations with picture publishers and with Rup Kishor's grandson, and the evidence of those images housed in the Proscribed section of the India Office Library, indicate that nearly all Kishor's early politically motivated images were proscribed and that he was imprisoned.

In 1937–38 he met Kalicharan, the son of a blacksmith, with whom he would paint (under the pseudonym "Chitrashala Kanpur" and then "Chitrashala Dehradun"). In these later images, there is a striking transformation of the explicitly political and topical into the divine. But the powerful evocations of divine potency that Rup Kishor and Kalicharan jointly conjured seem to pursue politics by other means, a means that evaded the proscriptional net of the state. I do not wish to negate other factors that may have been at play. The Meerut painter Yogendra Rastogi recently told me that he no longer paints contemporary political subjects because they "lack weight": he has rejected the "timely" in favor of the enduring. In part this shift reflects Rastogi's increasing years and his desire to address the permanent, and it is reasonable to presume a similar preoccupation on the part of Rup Kishor. However, by the late 1930s, the anticolonial allegorical and metaphorical infrastructure was sufficiently substantial for politics to be articulated through "religious" images. Thus Rup Kishor and Kalicharan's *Sudarshan Chakra*, depicting Krishna on the battleground, operated in a field conditioned by Tilak's discussions of political action and the

Figure 2.10

Rup Kishor Kapur and Kalicharan. *Mahamaya Shakti.*
Chromolithograph published by Hem Chander Bhargava
c. 1940s. Author's collection.

Mahabharata, and their *Mahamaya Shakti* is one of a long line of political manipulations of the Mahishasuramardini trope.[23] However, these articulations would have operated by equating motifs and elements of narrative (e.g., Krishna on the battlefield = political action by Hindus). In *Mahamaya Shakti* and other images figural effects work much more subtly and build upon an apocalyptic expressivity. One of the earliest mass-produced forms of this expressivity is the

Calcutta Art School lithograph of Kali whose analysis by Gupte played a significant role in Risley's interest in the 1910 Press Act. I am suggesting that part of *Mahamaya Shakti*'s power lay in its ability to evoke a—by now easily recognizable—apocalyptic scene of destruction and cleansing through, for instance, the shadowy sword-wielding armies in the background and the ominous clouds of smoke illumined by a red (blood-red?) sun. And all this, of course, in a securely "religious" image whose apparent lack of politicality placed it beyond the reaches of the various press laws and their definitions of sedition.

A similar figurality can be seen at work in "national" landscape in popular images from the late 1920s. Associated with the work of artists from Nathdvara published by the company S. S. Brijbasi, this terrain would constitute an inestimable resource to the imagination of Indian religious nationalists. First crystallized by Bankim Chandra Chatterjee, it was continually invoked by nationalists in the form of the poem or song "Vande Matram." But the landscape was also figured as an actual, fecund, moonlit terrain in countless millions of chromolithograph depictions. Nathdvara pastoralism gave embodiment to that richly watered, richly fruited, utopic space of a free India and fused it with the erotics of *bhakti*.[24] Images produced in the mid-1930s by Narrottam Narayan Sharma (particularly *Murli Manohar* and *Shankar Kailash*) are among the most widely reproduced in the world, and are immediately recognizable to those with a knowledge of India. Nathdvara's aesthetic produced a national figure whose effects were similar to that of the music of Beethoven and Verdi on certain European nationalisms. The Nathdvara landscape, which has now become the normative visual space of contemporary India, was born out a relationship with colonial censorship. It is the iatrogenic result of the anxiety displayed by the British colonial state.

"Techno-materialism"

There is also an important techno-material dimension to surveillance: certain forms of cultural production are obviously much easier to police because of the material basis of that production. The efficacy of the 1910 Press Act rested fundamentally on the material basis of letterpress production. Presses required considerable capital investment and were dependent on a relatively immobile infrastructure of printing technology. The levying of securities against the production of certain kinds of materials was predicated on this immobility and the ease with which premises could be closed and equipment confiscated. Confronted with this surveillance of apparatus, some artists and publishers, as we have seen, sought refuge in the slipperiness of metaphor, escaping surveillance in the density of figure.

Immobility and mobility were aspects of the techno-material dimensions of cultural production. Production rested within different techno-material regimes: lithography required fewer resources than movable type, and the passing of songs from mouth to mouth occurred within a wholly different techno-material space than the printing of music and lyrics or the manufacture of gramophone records. Theodore Bhaskaran has traced the growth of political song in late colonial India. The Swadeshi movement in Bengal took its cue from Rabindranath Tagore's July 1904 Swadeshi Samaj address, in which he suggested that "festivals, open-air folk entertainments like the *jatra,* and song should be used to reach out to the masses." Not only Tagore, but Kamin Kumar Bhattacharya, Rajni Kantha Sen, and Jogindranath Sarkar were prolific producers of Bengali songs. At the same time the Tamil poet Subramanya Bharathi started to produce "nationalistic lyrical poetry in a simple and lucid style suitable for singing" (Bhaskaran 1981, 47).

The colonial state's anxieties about techno-material transformations can be seen as one of the motivations driving the trial of B. G. Tilak for sedition in 1908. The pretext for this trial was an article in *Kesari*—the Marathi paper which Tilak himself edited—titled "The Country's Misfortune," published on May 12, 1908, and a subsequent piece published on June 9, 1908, which was titled "These Remedies Are Not Lasting." Following the trial in Bombay, Tilak would be imprisoned for six years.[25]

"These Remedies Are Not Lasting" forecasts the end of an iniquitous British rule in India. Earlier oppressive and unjust colonizers such as the Mughals, Tilak suggests, prompted discontent and extreme acts of self-sacrifice, but no report of this ever reached "the ears of the Government." In the twentieth century all this has changed: "turn-headed men" now have access to bombs and can make everyone sit up and listen. Tilak articulates this historical transformation in terms of the oppressed's new access not simply to weaponry but also to the dissemination of a very particular chimerical technology of vernacular bomb-making. "The bomb," he told *Kesari* readers, "is not a thing like muskets or guns," "it is a simple sport of science":

> Muskets and guns may be taken away from the subjects by means of the Arms Act; and the manufacture, too, of guns and muskets without the permission of Government, may be stopped; but is it possible to stop or do away with the bomb by means of laws or the supervision of officials or the busy swarming of the detective police? The bomb has more the form of knowledge, it is a (kind of) witchcraft, it is a charm, an amulet. (Kelkar 1908, exhibit D)

Vernacular bombs, Tilak went on to argue, can be produced from materials stored in a few bottles. What is more, the knowledge needed to produce vernacular bombs is simple: "the formula of the bomb does not at all appear to be a lengthy one and [its] process also is very short indeed." If the bomb, for Tilak, was significant because of its portability and its nonindustrial and essentially indigenous—or *swadeshi*—identity, it was also a technology which revealed itself to be an intellectual strategy. Its "witchcraft" lay in its knowledge-based nature and its transformation of an infrastructural practice into an epistemological one. The parallels with the small printing press are striking, for, as Landsdowne and the colonial state had already nervously discovered as early as 1893, new informational flows ("the interchange of news"), floating free of their earlier infrastructural constraints, were potentially highly destabilizing.

In his summation, the judge had sections of the disputed translations of Tilak's piece written out for him in what he termed a "readable calligraphy." The original of the passage which was translated as "The bomb has more the form of knowledge, it is a (kind of) witchcraft, it is a charm, an amulet" was *hi ek jadu ahe / ha ek mantra todga ahe* (Kelkar 1908, 12). As in Hindi, in Marathi *jadu* connotes "magic, sorcery, witchcraft." Likewise, *mantra*, as in other North Indian languages, connotes "a charm, an incantation." The word *todga* means "Any wild, magical or superstitious device for the removal of demon[ic] influence or disease; a charm, an amulet, a spell" (Vaze 1928, s.vv. *jadu, mantra, todga*). The opening address for the prosecution asked, "How does a bomb become a witchcraft, or amulet or charm, unless it is intended to be used?" and the judge suggested that "in the similes you have the effects of the bombs explained [in] various ways." Here we see a whole set of anxieties about the cosmologization of politics, the fluidity of new forms of knowledge, and the changing techno-materialist basis of resistance elided into a single preoccupation with the mystical yield of *todga*. The colonial state's experimentation with censorship might be seen as a parallel quest for its own "device for the removal of demonic influence."

The nationalist trope of a psychic, internalized mobility was perhaps most perfectly expressed in a Bengali *jatra* song, for the possession of which one Mukunda Lal Das was prosecuted in the Court of the Additional District Magistrate, in Bakarganj, in 1908 under section 124-A of the Indian Penal Code. The song was translated for the purposes of the trial as follows:

> O foreigner, what do we care for the threats you hold out? The body is under control, but the mind (thought) is free. You may bind us hand and foot, at most you may commit us to prison. But are you powerful enough to change our minds? The things of your . . . country are beautiful to look at, but they are really worthless, like the dead sea apple with a fair exterior but black interior. The charming mirrors, combs, toys and bracelets of your country are easily reduced to powder.[26]

If Indian nationalism, energized by the vitality of its own ideology, adopted an increasingly mobile attitude toward media apparatus, the colonial state— indexing its own uncertainty about the rationale of continuing dominion— increasingly reified the apparatus as a thing in itself. While nationalists abandoned the gramophone for the memorized song, and the printed newspaper for the hand-copied news-sheet, colonial police officers interrogated captives for proof of their contamination by media. Thus in September 1931 the Intelligence Bureau reported on a number of "terrorists who admitted they had been led astray by the reading of newspapers." Among those interrogated was one Hansraj Vohra, an "approver" in the Lahore Conspiracy case who confessed, "I commenced reading newspapers and their study converted my ideas to political ones." Madan Gopal, an approver in the Punjab Conspiracy case, was reported as saying, "I started daily perusal of papers. Later on I occasionally read in the papers the proceedings of the Lahore Conspiracy case. These accounts converted my ideas to those of sympathy for the revolutionaries." Bhag Ram, an accused in the Punjab Conspiracy case, reported that in his early days, "I spent a greater part of my time in the perusal of newspapers" and that subsequently a "perusal [of *Chand* magazine] inflamed my ideas more than before."

Beneath the absurdity of these confessions lies a profound refusal to acknowledge the political and affective content of nationalist ideologies. Transforming them into pure media effects was the colonial state's final, unwitting, acknowledgment of its own inability to imaginatively engage Indian aspirations.

Coda: Iatrogenics and Film

Early film was subject to a surveillance similar to that described in the main body of this chapter. The 1918 Cinematograph Act required that "the licensee will not exhibit, or permit to be exhibited ... any film other than a film which has been certified as suitable for public exhibition." In surveilling film the regional censor boards rigorously prevented the dissemination of the kinds of political expressions that the 1910 Press Act and subsequent surveillance practice also policed (see Mazzarella, this volume, and Ganti, this volume).

The records of the Bombay Censor Board from 1920 to 1928 reveal in remarkable detail the manner in which explicitly political comment was controlled and the attempt to control the efforts of politics to take refuge in the mythic. Although newsreels by Congress Topical News were generally passed uncut, Madan Theatre's *Mahatma Gandhi at Calcutta and Delhi* (February 1922) was refused a certificate. Newsreels were frequently heavily cut and intertitles removed or altered. In February 1923 the Bombay Universal Film Manufacturing Company was required to cut 74 feet out of its *International News*, from the portion titled "India mobs foreign made cloth: Mahatma Gandhi's disciples destroy the white man's products in campaign for 'Home Rule.'" In June of that year the same company was ordered to delete four intertitles: "Native leaders demand independence of India at the National Congress," "C. R. Das the new leader of India's 'rebels,' successor to Gandhi—and his wife," "Mrs Gandhi, wife of the jailed leader, keeps up her husband's fight," and "The apostles of non-violence give an imitation of a peaceful riot."

Foreign newsreels were also surveilled for anything that might resonate in ways deemed inappropriate. In February 1923 the Pathe Gazette was passed with endorsement on condition that the title "Out of a Land of Bondage etc" and scenes showing the Greek exodus from Turkey be omitted. Foreign feature films also had to be monitored for any reference to oppression and injustice— in any context—which might suggest parallels with an Indian audience's own predicament. In July 1924 Warner Brothers' *The Jungle Princess* was required to

delete the word "white" from the intertitle "We must get rid [of] our white enemies. We must capture the girl and dispose of the men." Later that same month
another Warner Brothers film, *Peaceful Alley*, was required to omit the intertitle
"Today—as in days gone by—the struggle between wealth and poverty goes on
to prove that the rich get richer while the poor get children." In August 1920
the Maharashtra Film Company's *Sairandhri* was passed subject to excision of a
scene in which "the head of Keechak is pulled off, till after Bheema throws it on
the ground"; in August 1921 Kohinoor Film's *Bhakta Vidur* was passed subject
to excision of the scene in which "some troublesome and disobedient subjects
are flogged and yoked to a grinding mill" and the scene "in which Bhima is
shown tearing out the entrail and swallowing the blood of his dead enemy."

I have argued that the increasing surveillance of print culture culminating
in the 1910 Press Act led—paradoxically—to the further articulation of political aspirations through religious idioms. The prospect of Sakuntala designing
bombs—the very possibility that Risley had hoped to avert—was made much
more likely as a result of the particular ways in which the Act was applied.
What I hope to have shown here is that the increase of surveillance of all forms
of dissent, for which Risley was in part responsible, led to an intensification of
the condition that he hoped to cure. A reified domain of "customary" religious
practice and belief became the last resort of a politics whose open public display
was almost completely prohibited. As the defense for the journal *Pallichitra*
argued in 1910, during its trial for the publication of a poem titled "Come
Mother, Queen of the Night," "if a man is to be punished for referring to Hindu
Mythology as in this poem it will be necessary to forbid all reference to Hindu
Mythological history."[27] That very Hindu mythology which Risley had hoped
to decontaminate increasingly became the last redoubt of a politics that was
not allowed to surface in other forms.

A parallel trajectory is clearly evident in film production. What is unsay-
able in the conventional discourses of civil society finds refuge in the *todga* of
mythological film. Once expressed mythopoetically, these political aspirations
fuel an even more anxious state response. It is in the late colonial period that this
cyclical iatrogenics is most evident. This late colonial iatrogenics put in place
a tenacious paradigm whose effects are still apparent in the fusing of political and religious aspirations, especially in the visual field. Here I have tried to
document some elementary aspects of colonial surveillance, whose legacy still
informs key aspects of the religio-political landscape of modern India.

Notes

1. See Mazzarella, n.d., for an illuminating discussion of this.
2. Adorno is referring here to "high" and "low" art (Adorno 1980, 123, letter of
March 18, 1936).

3. "Press Bill," *Proceedings of the Council of the Governor General of India,* February 4, 1910, p. 7.

4. Hiranyakashipu was angered by his eldest son Prahlad's devotion to Vishnu. He asked Prahlad whether Vishnu could appear from a pillar. When Prahlad said that he could, Hiranyakashipu smashed the pillar, whereupon Vishnu appeared as Narsimha and killed Hiranyakashipu with his claws. Brahma had promised Hiranyakashipu that he would not be killed on earth or in space, in fire or water, by either humans or gods, by the animate or the inanimate. Vishnu as man-lion, using his claws and holding his victim on his knees, managed (like Asdiwal) to elude all these determinacies (Krishna 2002).

5. Satyajit Ray gives a fascinating account, in his childhood memoirs, of nationalist automata in Calcutta c. 1930: "The most striking displays . . . were wax figures of famous Indian leaders. . . . In one, Mahatma Gandhi sat writing on the floor in a prison cell, with an armed guard at the door. Gandhiji had a writing pad on his lap, and a pen in his hand. His hand moved across the pad from one side to the other, and his head followed the movement of his hand. In another cubicle there was an enormous statue of Bharat Mata, with the body of Deshbandhu Chittaranjan Das in her arms. She looked at Deshbandhu, then closed her eyes and turned her head away mournfully . . . These figures created a huge stir in Calcutta" (Ray 1998, 31).

6. Memo dated December 27, 1893, India Office Records L/P & J/6/363, file 84, p. 4.

7. File 84 for 1894 dated October 27, 1893, India Office Records.

8. "Note on the Cow-Protection Agitation in Gorakhpur District," 1894, India Office Records, file 84, pp. 1–2; see also Freitag 1980, 130–31.

9. Letter dated December 11, 1908, from Gupte to Risley in the Royal Anthropological Institute Photographic Collection, London.

10. Strangely, Gupte did not mention what Partha Mitter (1994, caption to color plate 12) describes as "the hidden message in its colour symbolism of the black goddess dominating a supine white-skinned Siva."

11. See Gupte 1916, xliii, for a letter from Risley written in February 1910 in which he notes his exhaustion as a result of his work on the Press Bill, and his concession that "Whatever credit I have gained in Europe in the departments of Ethnology and Archaeology is, I feel, due in large measure to your indefatigable industry and careful judgment in furnishing me with materials and in drawing attention to the points of importance."

12. Barrier also discusses (47–48) Gokhale's, Mudholkar's, and Malaviya's minute of dissent requesting judicial oversight of the act's operation, and Minto's informal reassurance that existing presses would be dealt with leniently.

13. Appendix 2 in Natarajan 1955 provides details of the different sureties demanded. Not surprisingly, Tilak and Kelkar's *Kesari* was required to deposit the full Rs 5,000.

14. National Archives of India, Home Political, January 1911, nos. 1-14.

15. National Archives of India, Home Political, April 1910, 36–39A, p. 3.

16. National Archives of India, Home Political B, February 1912, file no. 86-104.

17. This call needs to be situated within Gandhi's wider communication strategy, which—despite his enthusiastic involvement in industrialized mass media such as

the radio, the gramophone and photography—also urged an artisanal approach. As an alternative to electric amplification he urged that "at meetings volunteers should be dispersed among the crowd. They should learn flag and *whistle signalling* in order to pass instructions from one to another when it is impossible for the voice to carry" (quoted in Amin 1995, 56n).

18. National Archives of India, Home General, February 17, 1931, no. 11661-1-S-B.

19. All four images described here were published by Shyam Sunder Lal, Cawn-pure [Kanpur].

20. For instance, Bhagat Singh's portrait was reproduced in the center of the front page of the *Tribune* (Lahore) on Wednesday, March 25, 1931, under the headline "Bhagat Singh, Rajguru and Sukhdev Executed."

21. National Archives of India, Home Political, 1930, 28A, pp. 284–84A and photographic annexures.

22. I am indebted to Vinay K. Srivastava for translating this.

23. See Pinney 1999 for some earlier examples.

24. See Jain 2007. The erotic density of Nathdvara *bhakti* is much more marked and systematic than that of Tamil-language devotion (Ramaswamy 1997, 114ff.).

25. For a general account of the trial and its wider context see Chicherov 1966.

26. National Archives of India, Home Political A, March 1909, nos. 112–31, pp. 29–30.

27. National Archives of India, Home Department, October 1910.

References

Interviews (all by author)

Kapoor, Kamal. 1996. Mathura.
Rastogi, Yogendra. 1999. Meerut.

Published Works

Adorno, Theodor W. 1980. "Letters to Walter Benjamin." In Ronald Taylor, ed., *Aesthetics and Politics*. London: Verso.

Amin, Shahid. 1995. *Event, Metaphor, Memory: Chauri Chaura, 1922–1992*. Berkeley: University of California Press.

Anderson, Benedict. 1991. *Imagined Communities: Reflections on the Origins and Spread of Nationalism*. 2nd ed. London: Verso.

Barrier, N. Gerald. 1974. *Banned: Controversial Literature and Political Control in British India, 1907–1947*. Columbia: University of Missouri Press.

Bhaskaran, S. Theodore. 1981. *Message Bearers: Nationalist Politics and Entertainment Media in South India, 1880–1945*. Madras: Cre-A.

Chicherov, A. I. 1966. "Tilak's Trial and the Bombay Political Strike of 1908." In I. M. Reisner and N. M. Goldberg, eds., *Tilak and the Struggle for Indian Freedom*. New Delhi: People's Publishing House.

Dirks, Nicholas B. 2001. *Castes of Mind: Colonialism and the Making of Modern India*. Princeton, N.J.: Princeton University Press.

Eco, Umberto. 1982. "Critique of the Image." In Victor Burgin, ed., *Thinking Photography*. London: Macmillan.

Freitag, Sandria. 1980. "Religious Rites and Riots: From Community Identity to Communalism in North India, 1870–1940." Ph.D. diss., University of California, Berkeley.

———. 1996. "Contesting in Public: Colonial Legacies and Contemporary Communalism." In David Ludden, ed., *Making India Hindu: Religion, Community, and the Politics of Democracy in India*. New Delhi: Oxford University Press.

Gupte, B. A. 1916. *Hindu Holidays and Ceremonials*. Calcutta: Thacker, Spink and Co.

Hooper, Edward. 2000. *The River: A Journey Back to the Source of HIV and AIDS*. Harmondsworth, UK: Penguin.

Jain, Kajri. 2007. *Gods in the Bazaar: The Economies of Indian Calendar Art*. Durham, N.C.: Duke University Press.

Johnson, Gordon. 1973. *Provincial Politics and Indian Nationalism: Bombay and the Indian National Congress*. Cambridge: Cambridge University Press.

Kelkar, N. C. 1908. *Full and Authentic Report of the Tilak Trial (1908)*. Poona: N. C. Kelkar.

Khan, Muzaffar Husain. 1919. *The Indian Press Act, Act 1 of 1910*. Calcutta: R. Cambray and Co.

Kittler, Friedrich A. 1999. *Gramophone, Film, Typewriter*. Trans. Geoffrey Winthrop-Young and Michael Mutz. Stanford, Calif.: Stanford University Press.

Krishna, Prasad. 2002. "Hiranyakashipu." *Encyclopedia Mythica*. http://www.pantheon.org/articles/h/hiranyakashipu.html, accessed August 26, 2008.

Mazzarella, William. n.d. "'Cannibals Enjoy Comedies': Making Sense of the Cinema in Late Colonial India." Unpublished manuscript.

Mitter, Partha. 1994. *Art and Nationalism in Colonial India, 1850–1922: Occidental Orientations*. Cambridge: Cambridge University Press.

Natarajan, J. 1955. *History of Indian Journalism: Part II of the Report of the Press Commission*. New Delhi: Government of India.

Pinney, Christopher. 1999. "Indian Magical Realism: Notes on Popular Visual Culture." In *Subaltern Studies: Writings on South Asian History and Society*, vol. 10, ed. Gautam Bhadra, Gyan Prakash, and Suzie Tharu. New Delhi: Oxford University Press, 201–33.

———. 2004. *"Photos of the Gods": The Printed Image and Political Struggle in India*. London: Reaktion.

Ramaswamy, Sumathi. 1997. *Passions of the Tongue: Language Devotion in Tamil India, 1891–1970*. Berkeley: University of California Press.

Ray, Satyajit. 1998. *Childhood Days: A Memoir*. New Delhi: Penguin.

Shapin, Steven. 1996. *The Scientific Revolution*. Chicago: University of Chicago Press.

Shaw, Graham, and Mary Lloyd, eds. 1985. *Publications Proscribed by the Government of India: A Catalogue of the Collections in the India Office Library and Records and the Department of Oriental Manuscripts and Printed Books*. London: British Library.

Thompson, Edward. 1930. *The Reconstruction of India*. London: Faber.

Vaze, Shridhar Ganesh. 1928. *The Arya-Bhushan School Dictionary, Marathi-English*. Poona: Arya-Bhushan Press.

Venniyoor, E. M. J. 1981. *Raja Ravi Varma.* Trivandrum: Director of Museums and Zoos and Art Gallery, Government of Kerala.

Wolpert, Stanley A. 1961. *Tilak and Gokhale: Revolution and Reform in the Making of Modern India.* Berkeley: University of California Press.

Yang, Anand A. 1980. "Sacred Symbol and Sacred Space in Rural India: Community Mobilization in the 'Anti–Cow Killing' Riot of 1893." *Comparative Studies in Society and History* 22(4): 576–96.

THREE

Making Sense of the Cinema in Late Colonial India

William Mazzarella

"Cannibals Enjoy Comedies"

n late 1927 or early 1928, the American Trade Commissioner in India, Charles B. Spofford, Jr., submitted an extraordinary memo to the Indian Cinematograph Committee (ICC), a commission of inquiry into the cinema appointed by the colonial government of India in the autumn of 1927.[1] Hefty to the point of absurdity, Spofford's memo comprised something like thirty-five closely typed, single-spaced pages. Its purpose was to defend the cinema in general, and the American cinema in particular, against a rising tide of moralizing condemnation.

Spofford was writing at a time when Hollywood films constituted approximately 80 percent of the movies being shown on Indian screens.[2] Consequently, he was particularly keen to defuse any apprehensions about untoward ideological effects, to insist that the desire for entertainment was a basic aspect of human nature, and to explain that the cinema could provide such entertainment in a form that was far more universal than anything the world had hitherto seen.

Responding to the mounting British suspicion that American films, with their eroticized egalitarianism, were undermining the civilizing mission, Spofford declared,

> There is no intention on the part of American film producers to fill their pictures with propaganda of a nature to subvert certain institutions in other countries. American films do not constitute a 4th International. Who really imagines that the images of humanity produced in Hollywood are likely to replace or blow everything native out of the soul of India or Europe?[3] American films are only meant to entertain, whether in India or any other part of the world. (Indian Cinematograph Committee [ICC] 1928a, 4:298)

The cinema, in its global diffusion, was bringing light—if not yet enlightenment—to the world's hinterlands and, as we shall see, laughter to cannibals.

In the best evangelical style, Spofford reported the heartening testimony of an Arctic explorer "who told us how the Eskimos enjoyed their movies in the perpetual night which descended upon them in the Frozen North." Under the subheading "Cannibals Enjoy Comedies," Spofford then relayed the experience of a Presbyterian missionary to the Belgian Congo who had screened films in the rural interior to

> hundreds and even thousands of savages—some of them indeed still cannibals. . . . He told us how he puts up a canvas sheet in a clearing in the wilderness and how the natives sit by hundreds in front of this and in back of it. Of course, for those sitting in back, the lettering of the titles is reversed, but that makes no difference, since they are unable to read anyhow. They laugh as delightedly at the slap-stick antics of our screen comedians as do any of our American audiences, which shows, of course, that human nature is alike the world over. (4:305)

This was not simply a matter of pacification through pleasure. Rather, the principle of universal entertainment was, in the final analysis, the true bedrock of social contentment. Building to a climax after a detailed description of the workings and capabilities of Hollywood (and not forgetting to mention its host of "canine histrionic talent" [4:330]), Spofford proclaimed, "The world must be amused. Men must have recreation and relaxation. . . . Just as you serve the leisure hours of the masses, so do you rivet the girders of society" (4:326). Indeed,

> It has always been so. Back in the days of Rome's supremacy the cynical poet and satirist, Juvenal, said sneeringly of the Roman populace: "All they care for is their bread and their games." He needn't have sneered. The populace did care for their bread and their games—for life and relaxation from life. It was as it should be. Man, whatever his environment, has always felt the same. Therein again lies your explanation of Hollywood. (4:327)

One of the recurrent themes in the literature on cinema in the colonial world is that Hollywood films of the silent period often occasioned a kind of moral panic. Some of this panic was simply an importation to India of anxieties and controversies that had already been circulating in Europe and the United States for several decades. The cinema was going to corrupt the young, the unlettered, women, or whatever other subaltern population seemed most likely to succumb to its curiously visceral charms. The cinema was tasteless, it was low, it was base and unseemly. Cinema halls were a breeding ground not only for lax moral hygiene but also for physical disease.

Indeed, the archive overflows with impassioned alarmism. The following passage, dispatched in 1925 by one Rattan Barorji Cooper to the editor of the *Bombay Chronicle*, is distinctive only by virtue of its singular degree of purpleness:

Sir, with all fairness and frankness I strongly protest against our modern cinema shows. I do not for a moment claim the abolition of this innocent and favourite public resort [although he would, as was common, go on to call for more stringent censorship]. But it is only when this innocent plea-sure house is turned into a veritable infernal dungeon where vilest trickeries and rogueries are taught to its frequenters that any one has every reason to protest, and protest vehemently and emphatically. For so many years I have been visiting cinema shows, but with the lapse of every day my abhorrence for them gets greater and greater. I go everytime [*sic*] with a hope to see something new or original but I am eternally disappointed, and by this time I am practically disgusted. All that I see, and so many others see, is women, wine, gambling, staking, racing, plotting, scheming, murder, roguery, rascal-ity, robbery, trickery, prudery, sycophancy, pomp, magnificence and a host of other vices.[4]

Cooper's letter manifests a telling tension. His tone strives, on the one hand, for a pitch that might match the sensory intensity of cinemagoing itself. On the other hand, he also tries to enumerate the determinate forms of the cinema's crimes, as if an adequately capacious taxonomy might contain, and thus somehow con-trol, the troubling mediations of the movies. In India, among both British offi-cials and indigenous elites of the kind to which the vehement and emphatic Mr. Cooper belonged, these fears were inevitably diffracted through anxieties of empire and racial hierarchy. The European discourse on the roiling energy of crowds during this period rested quite routinely upon a metaphorical equation of the modern urban crowd and an impressionable state of childlike savagery. In the colonies, this metaphor ran right up against its own reality, where emerging mass publics—including cinema audiences—were substantially composed of individuals that British colonial thought did in fact classify as childlike savages.

This sense that the cinema possessed an intensity that was something to be not simply contained or limited but also carefully harnessed and deployed was typical of the discourse of the period. The American Trade Commissioner Charles Spofford appended to his memo the words of several contemporary authorities on the cinema. Among these none was more infamous than Will Hays, the man who within just a few years would give his name to the obscenity-busting Hollywood production code that ruled the American film business well into the 1960s. True to his position as a representative of industry interests, Spofford insisted on a sol-idly market-liberal approach to evaluating the films of his country: "There is noth-ing much wrong with them, for if there was, it is scarcely likely that every week 50,000,000 people would patronize the picture houses and would come out of them smiling and satisfied, saying to each other 'When shall we go again?'" (ICC 1928a, 4:300). But Hays, embroiled as he was in debates on cinema censorship, refuses to equate films with commodities in general: "Motion pictures are not dead things, to be regulated like commodities such as freight and good. They are not wares, to be monopolized and traded in by tickets and statues, or marked like iron and soap. They contain a potency of life in them to be as active as the soul whose progeny they are" (4:309).

Now this attribution of vital energy to films is worth some attention, because Hays's comment was not an isolated or eccentric figure of speech. Indeed, it was very much at the root of contemporary concerns over the risks and the possibilities of the cinema. And in colonial India, the problem took on a special urgency: was the cinema, visceral as it was, beyond the pale of an imperial pedagogy? Were the spectacular, performative forms of the British colonial project—such as they were—at odds with the short-cut mimesis of the cinema? Or was the cinema precisely the elixir that the Raj required, an intimate, sensuous engagement on a mass scale that might finally enable a *felt* connection between colonial subjects and their alien government?

At the root of this British ambivalence lay the intimation that Hollywood had solved the global communicational puzzle by deploying a hypermodern technology to resonate with a savage sensorium. Colonial officers were not alone in their suspicions. Rachel Moore (2000) has shown how early European film theorists—Epstein, Benjamin, Balazs, Eisenstein, Lindsay, and others—posited a kind of radical and often romantic connection between the cinema image and "savage thought." The ICC's final report, published in the summer of 1928, argued that cinema worked by an appeal to the more basic "human emotions," an appeal that presumably worked for audiences everywhere. And yet, at the same time, it also noted that Indians seemed preternaturally adapted to its mode of address: "Despite some evidence to the contrary we are fully satisfied that Indians gain the cinema sense very quickly—the uneducated sometimes more quickly than the educated" (ICC 1928b, 112).

So could an apparently savage medium be adapted to a civilizing mission? On the one hand, the cinema presented the British in India with an unprecedentedly efficacious means for conveying the blandishments of civilization. On the other, it was the conditions of the cinema's efficacy—its startlingly visceral appeal to the senses—that seemed to implicate it in precisely that infantile, even savage sensorium that marked the uncivilized. As Rachel Moore puts it, "Technology, as manifested in cinema at least, created a different mode of perception more equipped to work in the new dimensions and at the new speeds that characterize[d] the advent of modernity. At the same time, the cinema forced a re-encounter with that which progress was meant to have left behind" (Moore 2000, 53–54).

From the 1820s onward, and particularly after the great rebellion of 1857, the British had striven to distinguish their forms of life in India from those of their subjects. The stiffly Victorian-bourgeois comportment of the imperial *sahib* displaced the more porous engagement of the Company nabob (Collingham 2001), while the British sequestered themselves away from the native towns in their civil lines, military cantonments, and hill stations. The apparent humanitarianism of the white man's burden increasingly depended upon a radical discourse of racial difference. During the preimperial, East India Company phase of British presence in India, the foreign interlopers had sought legitimacy by observing ritual forms of tribute and obeisance to Mughal rulers and local kings, even as their advance across India steadily "hollowed out" the political power of these polities. After 1857, with the Mughals gone and the empire installed, the British found themselves increasingly conscious of their self-imposed alienation from what C. A. Bayly (1996) calls Indian "affective knowledge."

Bernard Cohn (1983) has given us a wonderfully wry description of British experiments with harnessing indigenous rituals of royal incorporation and spectacular display to the legitimation of empire. Lord Lytton, who served as viceroy between 1876 and 1880, famously insisted that "the further East you go, the greater becomes the importance of a bit of bunting." Conventionally, the remark gets read as an expression of the Raj's more or less reluctant concession to the natives' love of *tamasha* or spectacle. But as Thomas Metcalf points out, Lytton himself was a "romantic medievalist" (1995, 76), enthusiastically developing a whole heraldic system of insignia for the Imperial Assemblage of 1877, at which India's princes were to perform their loyalty to the Queen-Empress Victoria (Wheeler 1877).

The spectacularization of imperial power during these years was neither confined to the colonies nor necessarily dependent upon an archaic symbolic repertoire. In England, emergent forms of commodity spectacle were energetically being adapted to the public reinvention of royal authority (Richards 1990), even as new branded consumer goods both popularized images of empire to Europe (MacKenzie 1984) and represented empire around the world (Burke 1996; McClintock 1995). Perhaps more than any other medium, the cinema—which emerged almost simultaneously in Europe and in India in the middle of the 1890s—represented at once the raucous culmination of this new mass culture and the promise of an unprecedented instrument of propaganda. And in India, the cinema appeared on the scene precisely at the time when the more creatively populist wings of anticolonial mobilization were capitalizing on the affective deficit that haunted the Raj by forging a direct connection between the intimate aesthetics of popular cultural forms and nationalist struggle (Freitag 1989; Kaur 2003).

Writings on Hollywood in the colonial world often imply a dialectical interpretation: these films, saturated as they were with a new globalizing consumerist ontology, nevertheless also, through a kind of ruse of history, served a genuinely liberatory and democratizing purpose by helping to displace the repressively racist social hierarchies of European colonialism. For starters, this kind of argument would have to be confronted with the fact that, as Prem Chowdhry (2000) points out, during the 1930s and 1940s Hollywood was churning out so-called empire films that were so jingoistically pro-imperial and so clumsily racist that the Raj itself had to request restraint from American producers.

More interestingly, it seems to me, the cinema appeared to the British both as a frightening extension of the culture-mobilizing vernacular protests that they were increasingly trying to contain *and* as a potential weapon with which they might be able to tackle their opponents on their own terrain.

A New World Space of Publicity

By the 1920s, Hollywood was well on its way to global dominance. In the United States, the regulatory initiatives that would culminate in the Hays Code (developed in 1930, made binding in 1934) were coming into view (French 1997; Jowett 1999). The irresistible rise of Hollywood was causing significant anxiety in the non-American world; in many European countries, the imposition of import quotas on film was linked to efforts to forge national cinematic autonomy (Levin 1999; Vasey 1999). In this emergent space of world publicity, the promise of instant enlightenment was always shadowed by the fear of global contagion. In particular, the experience of the Great War brought home to governments, with some urgency, the potentials of the new technologies and channels of mass mediation (Mattelart 1994). From this standpoint, the growing obsessions with the possibilities of propaganda and with the need for censorship were two sides of the same coin.

As I have suggested, there was anxiety as well as excitement about the sensuous force of the new medium, whose effectiveness—and therefore also its danger—was understood first of all to reside in its appeal to the senses rather than to the intellect. The cinema would therefore be of especial utility—and of especial concern—when it came to communicating with the uneducated and the unlettered. Whether it was the communists or the Western imperialists, the world stage of cinematic publicity was understood to be a volatile one in which, as a 1926 article in the London *Times* famously put it, the "simple native,"" very deficient in the sense of proportion," was being subjected to wholly unprecedented provocations.

In India, the 1920s also saw a mass nationalist public come into being, especially around that galvanizingly charismatic publicist, Mahatma Gandhi. But the nationalist movement's relation to the cinema was notably ambivalent. This should not have been surprising in the case of the Oxbridge-educated nationalists, schooled in paternalist condescension for the popular. But Gandhi himself, despite—or perhaps because of—his exquisitely tuned understanding of the public efficacy of mass corporeal spectacle, mustered only a terse response to the ICC's questionnaire. The following three sentences were, famously, all he sent from his Sabarmati ashram: "Even if I was so minded, I should be unfit to answer your questionnaire, as I have never been to a cinema. But even to an outsider, the evil that it has done and is doing is patent. The good, if it has done any at all, remains to be proved" (ICC 1928a, 4:56).

Gandhi's personal dismissal of the cinema didn't stop the Indian movie business from constantly affixing his name and likeness to its products during the 1920s and 1930s (Chowdhry 2000). Nor did it prevent the British from sensing an affinity between them. Constance Bromley, former manager of the Opera House cinema in Calcutta, warned in the pages of the London *Times* around the time of Gandhi's noncooperation movement that "scores of unsuitable serial films still find their way on to the screens in hundreds of native cinemas, a first-class handbook to the teachings of Mr. Gandhi" (Bromley 1922).[5] The British may not have been entirely mistaken. Although the majority of the films of the period were certainly beyond the pale of a Gandhian body politics, they shared with the latter an insistence upon calling into question imperially approved demarcations between public life and intimate concerns.

Print was already a mass medium in India by the turn of the twentieth century, but one whose impact was constrained by limited literacy. Newly politicized popular practices—such as Bal Gangadhar Tilak's nationalist refashioning of the Ganesh festival in western India (Kaur 2003)—were thought to be more affectively powerful than print, but their impact was more or less limited to their performative setting. Crucially, the cinema bridged this gap, because it united in an explosive way the mass reach of print with the corporeal appeal of theatrical and ritual performance.

Such communicative force needed equally forceful containment—and one sees this impulse toward containment at work in the taxonomical frenzy of the early film censor boards. For example, the British Board of Film Censors report of 1920 contains no less than sixty-seven separate categories of unacceptable representations and themes. Almost without exception, the political potentials and risks of the cinema were closely associated with the erotics of the screen image. And these erotics were, within the moralizing calculus of an imperial pedagogy, usually and reductively literalized as sexual. The same 1926 London *Times* article that speaks of the "simple native" complains that the diffusion of the cinema in "the tropical world" is diminishing the prestige of Europeans and, to add insult to injury, probably preparing the ground for communist agitation as well. But the moments of actual cinematic reception that are invoked are directly sexual, typically involving "prolonged and often erotic exhibitions of osculation."

At the same time, the colonial administration found itself repeatedly attracted to the propagandistic claims made by a motley crew of entrepreneurs about what the cinema might do for the teetering Raj. In the words of one such, the cinema was "admittedly the greatest educational agency of our time—an agency which has the unique advantage of instructing the uneducated with a completeness rivaling that of the ordinary methods which penetrate the consciousness of the educated classes only."[6] The colonial government had always insisted that its true and unshakable constituency was, precisely, the uneducated masses, the simple folk whose "natural" interests were in fact undermined by the hotheaded verbiage of the nationalist agitators who claimed to speak for them. Any medium that might make the government's case in the language of this silent majority was not to be ignored.

The Savage Screen

Many existing critical studies of Hollywood in the colonies have suggested that the subversive force of the movies resided in the viewpoints and identifications that they—often unwittingly—offered colonized audiences. Particularly troubling was the relatively intimate view of white women that the screen offered for the viewing pleasure of brown men. Indeed, this was precisely the concern that the alarmists of the 1920s harped on and bequeathed to the ICC. The records of the committee's proceedings, however, show its members constantly struggling with the limitations of this anxiety. Typically, the committee would ask their informants for examples of particular kinds of objectionable content or scenes, and receive answers that were so vague, so obviously chauvinistic, or so illogical as to drive the committee's formidable chairman, Mr. Rangachariar, to the point of exasperation.

Pushed harder, many informants would point beyond specific representations or subject matter to a *generally* unsettling quality in film, a tendency to stir up or agitate audiences. Mr. Dwarkadas, Secretary of the Bombay Vigilance Association, spoke of "scenes which violently shake and upset the emotions. . . . They stimulate the quickly-excitable emotions of children and adolescents in a wrong way" (ICC 1928a, 1:262). "Sensuous films" were particularly likely to produce "high excitement" in the impressionable (1:644), to "stimulate uncontrolled passions" (2:1085), again, particularly among the young or the uneducated sections of the population.

If no conclusive causal links could be established between behavior shown in films and subsequent behavior in spectators' lives, a more generalized vulnerability of the nervous system could nevertheless be posited. H. C. Mukharjee of Amalgamated Newspapers in Calcutta worried that constant exposure to "these thrilling scenes" would have "a bad effect on the nerves" of youth. "Constant thrills have an injurious effect upon the human mind, speaking psychologically. You see a harassing thing and it tells upon your brain and makes undue demands on the mind" (2:1019). U. B. Romesh Rao of the Radha Picture Palace in Calicut similarly felt that "the Western serials are unnecessarily and injuriously working on the nerves of the audiences by depicting hair-raising stunts" (3:446).

Other respondents pursued something like a comparative ontology of media, suggesting that the cinema image was "much more striking" than the printed word, and more liable to make "a lasting impression" than either print or oral discourse (2:556, 339). The moving picture's quality of being so incomparably "full of life" (2:509) appeared both beneficial and treacherous. On the one hand, as a Trivandrum chemistry professor argued, the inherent fascination of moving pictures promised to make both the producer's and the consumer's tasks easier: "The demonstrative value of pictures saves a person from a heavy strain on his imagination and his faith" (3:461). The value of the cinema lay not just in its communicative facility but also in its immersive appeal. Bhagwat Prasad, a Lucknowi judge, enthused,

> The Picture House possesses all the attractions of real life. We find ourselves in the midst of people in the screen and become interested in them. Our tears for their sorrows and our delight at the successes are immediately called forth. The effect which is produced in our minds is instantaneous and it is not soon effaced. We hear an orator and are impressed. Modern novels move us by their reality, but the greater reality of this vivid presentation of everyday life before our eyes moves us more readily and almost more deeply (4:108).

And yet precisely this "vivid presentation" was understood by others to be the mark of cinema's lack vis-à-vis, say, the novel. In its apparent bypassing of reasoned judgment, the cinema was, par excellence, the medium of the crowd, of the masses. Some worried that its facility constituted its greatest danger. Reflected a judge of Peshawar, Mufti Abdul Latiff, "In my view there is much difference between novel reading and seeing a thing in the cinema. In the one case one's own brain is reasoning things out, while in the other the actual thing is shown on the screen, which is quite different" (2:276).

Indeed, the spatial arrangement of the audience in the cinema halls was itself imagined on a sliding scale from rabidity to reason. The cheaper seats were downstairs and in front. The people who sat there were, literally, both inferior and more intimately absorbed in the image on the screen and, as such, assumed to be incapable of critical distance. The fancier folk sat in the balconies further back, at a safer distance from the distracting force of the image as well as physically elevated above and behind the rabble, whom they could survey without being so easily examined in return.

To those who had access to a more elevated vantage point, nothing was so immediately indicative of the dangerously infantile fusion of screen and mass than the raucous noises emitted by the great unwashed in the cheap seats. Then as now, the theme was obsessive. Many elite ICC respondents, frustrated by their inability to present coherent evidence of objectionable image-content, would often end up pointing to the palpable excitation triggered in audiences by the films as a corporeally concrete index.

At times, the effect would be described as a pregnant, barely contained agitation in the cinema hall, a kind of audible thickening of the air. Lieutenant-Colonel Gidney, an all-India representative of Anglo-Indians and "domiciled Europeans," reported that "when there is anything suggestive [on the screen] there is often a sort of hushed silence and suppressed extasy [sic] over the suggestion" (ICC 1928a, 2:1082).[7] But containment did not appear to be the rule. One Karamchand Bulchand, involved in the production of educational and propaganda films, remarked, "You have only to visit a downtown cinema to see how the lower classes of people gloat over scenes when there is kissing or embracing. . . . I wish you could come and hear the screeches and howls of the audience when the kissing is going on" (1:679, 684). *En masse*, these responses conjure all the acoustic density and variety of a veritable bestiary in the stalls: "hissing and jeering" (1:51), "catcalls and exclamations" (1:248), "hooting" (2:275), "shouting and Ah-Ahing" (2:225). Indeed, on occasion the atmosphere apparently became so charged that the cinema management felt obliged to stop the film and turn on the lights until the audience could be subdued (2:380). If the perceived threat of the cinema was moral as well as physical, then it was moral *because* it was so physical. "All you have to do," averred H. W. Hogg, Secretary of the Punjab Boy Scouts' Association, "is sit in the cinema and listen to the remarks made by some of these young men, just to realize how this thing is getting really under their skin" (2:69).

In India, as Brian Larkin (n.d.) and Poonam Arora (1995) have both pointed out, the cinema hall provided a novel and uneasy space of physical proximity in which—for the first time in many decades—Europeans attended the same entertainments as Indians, and social elites shared an auditorium, although not a seating area, with the less privileged. The obsessive focus on audience noise may certainly be interpreted as a mark of the anxiety aroused by the possibility of the Indian spectator's gaze lustfully traversing the distance between the white women on the screen and those in the theater. (The situation was somewhat different in many parts of British Africa during this same period, where a much more rigorous separation of whites and nonwhites was enforced at the movies.)

But I would also like to take into account the possibility that some of this anxiety was a response to the novelty of the cinema *as* a mass medium. Benedict Anderson (2006) has, of course, given us a theory of nationalism in which the impersonal simultaneity of what he calls print capitalism made it possible to imagine a national public or collective which consisted of individuals who not only would never physically interact but could also be imagined as formally equivalent under the abstract sign of citizenship. The cinema in colonial India shared something of this property, what one might call "the open edge of mass publicity." But the colonial context also brought to the fore the obverse of this open edge, namely its unknowability. The cinema was troubling to colonial governmentality not only because it brought together populations that were supposed to keep at least at arm's length from each other. More than this, it served as a constant reminder of the coming-into-being of an abstract, general public, unknowable in its contours—not necessarily nationalist, not necessarily activist, but certainly straining the categories of what Nicholas Dirks (2001) has called "the ethnographic state." The bestial noises emerging from the pit were thus an index of both an uncomfortable proximity and an unsettling anonymity. The complacent certitude with which the administrative files speak of "the masses," of "coolies," and of "the uneducated" as if these are known quantities is constantly haunted by its corollary question: "Who *are* these people?"

The Filmic Image

The question of the identity of cinema audiences—whether generic or specific—was never entirely separable from that of the nature of cinema images. Indeed, one could say that the discourse on cinema regulation, then as now, relies on two intersecting constructs. The first is that of the unacceptable image, the second is that of the susceptible audience. In this and the following section, I would like to examine each of these constructs a little more closely, before moving toward a series of concluding reflections.

Some, as we have seen, have argued that the cinema was threatening to colonial authorities because the camera eye seemed to reverse the surveying gaze of the administration, granting the brown masses apparently intimate access into the private spaces of European life. A spectacular scopophilia in which the intrusive close-up combined with the life-like moving picture breached the distance that was the precondition of the charismatic authority of the whites. As ICC Chairman Rangachariar put it in conversation with a local notable in Trichinopoly, "Is not that a difficulty about the cinema, that it really removes the wall of one's private house and exhibits your private life[?] I mean to say what happens in a room is shown on a screen" (ICC 1928a, 3:997).

And yet alongside these themes—the reversal of the gaze, the refiguring of the relation between the public and the private—or, perhaps better, *embedded within* these themes was a persistent attempt to describe something that was seen as still more fundamental. With mounting frustration, the members of the ICC—and especially Rangachariar—demanded of its informants how one might presume to effectively regulate something as apparently evanescent as the cinema. In a characteristic exchange, L. K. Mitter, an Assistant Public Prosecutor in Mandalay, when pushed to identify exactly what details he found troubling in the cinema image, pointed beyond its specific content to something more along the lines of attitude, the potentialities implied, the habitus that seemed implicitly to organize the elements of the image: "[It is] not exactly the scanty clothing. It is the gestures and the postures which are suggestive of something more gross, to which I object" (ICC 1928a, 3:675). After a similar round of attempted specification Owen Roberts, a Member of the Legislative Council in Punjab, proceeded by way of an analogy to the then recently published sensational exposé on Indian civilization by the American author Katherine Mayo: "I have been thinking how I could put it to you. You know the publication *Mother India*. Well, the facts in it may be correct but one puts it down to the feeling that the whole thing is wrong, that the perspective of the book is wrong and that it does not do justice to the country. It is the same thing with these films" (2:196).

Perhaps the single most frequently mentioned formal source of discomfort was the close-up. Now it hardly requires repeating that the close-up involves a spatial transformation of the audience's relation to that which the image represents, in that it both provides a new, intimate access to that object and allows audiences to identify with the spectatorial position implied by the camera eye. And of course, in a colonial setting, this transformation had potentially subversive implications. What, as one Indian journalist mockingly put it, were these poor natives going to make of such proximate "sidelights on the Sahib at play"?[8] But there is also evidence in the ICC transcripts to suggest that the close-up generated anxieties that were less about viewpoint and more about the camera's qualitative transformation of its objects.

During the course of the ICC's peregrinations, both the committee and its respondents regularly struggled to specify the relationship between the close-up and the sense of indecent intensity that it so frequently seemed to evoke. At the most general level, one might say that the close-up was, in several ways, associated with anxieties over intemperate disproportion. For example: the art of making silent films, many insisted, necessarily led to overacting and, more generally, to the kind of corporeal exaggeration of sentiment and gesture to which uncivilized peoples were thought to be prone. As the British Board of Film Censors put it in its 1920 report, "The besetting danger of the cinema in the expression of emotion is almost inevitably over-emphasis in action" (O'Connor 1920).

Predictably, an important fulcrum of this debate—as indeed it was in Britain around the turn of the century (French 1997)—was the screen kiss. In today's discussions of Hindi film, the unwritten prohibition on kissing (which appears to have stretched from the 1940s to its partial breaching in the 1990s) has become both the bête noire of cosmopolitan critics and, in a more allegorical mode, a figure for the apparent impossibility of domestic intimacy in the mainstream Hindi cinema (Prasad 1998). It has become customary nowadays to figure the post-Independence era as puzzlingly prudish in this regard, by recalling that there appears to have been a healthy quota of kissing in early Indian films.

To be sure, the ICC certainly encountered the odd kiss-booster on its travels. One particularly lively written submission from S. Nanjundier, a cinema buff in Rangoon, affirmed that "some sentimental and over-modest people may not like *kissing* to take place in the public gaze and more especially *long* and *lingering kisses*. Without such kisses at the appropriate time the play [film] will be insipid and dry. . . . People who revolt against kisses perhaps like warm and half naked dances; so far it is creditable and I thank them for the [*sic*] small mercies" (ICC 1928a, 4:263, emphasis in original).

But in general, the ICC transcripts are full of adjectivized attempts to express the crossing of an affective boundary in which the kiss marks the crucial spot. What is objectionable, again, is not so much the literal substance of the act depicted, but rather the mode of its dramatization: the "*pregnant sex film*"[9] (ICC 1928a, 1:6), the "*frantic*" or "*gushing* love scenes" (1:367, 373), the "*strenuous* kissing and this *violent* hugging" (2:993, all emphases added). Visual précis of intimacy that it was, the kiss became the fount of a startling profusion of varieties. Something of this dramatic versatility was captured by Pherozeshah Marzban, the editor of the stalwart Parsi periodical *Jam-e-Jamshed:* "Kissing may be here and there, but not indiscriminate kissing. You have got the long kiss, the prolonged kiss, the hot kiss and the soft kiss, all sorts of kisses" (1:497).

While for some the besetting sin of the close-up was exaggeration, others identified an effect more akin to temporal—and perhaps, for the audience, cognitive—retardation. Punjabi scoutmaster Mr. Hogg explained, "What I object to is the 'close up,' where you get a man and woman standing for a considerable time, the slow movement of either the man or the woman putting his or her hands over the shoulders of the other. I mean, the whole thing is deliberately and slowly done, and that, to my mind, is certainly undesirable" (2:73). Some actually went so far as to suggest quantitative limits: "You can even define that the kissing should be only for one second or some such thing. But kissing for 30 seconds or even one minute is not proper, I think. It affects every man who sees the film" (3:981).

Of course, there was a great deal of talk about the fact that Indians, unlike Europeans, did not kiss in public and that on-screen kissing in Indian cinemas—whether by Europeans or Indians—was for this reason problematic. Ostensibly, then, it was a matter of simple cultural difference. But many of the ICC's informants kept returning to the uncomfortable way that the camera transformed the kiss. Again, there was a sense that the close-up created discomfort by forcibly disrupting the normalized proportions and rhythms of everyday life. J. Henderson, a Lahore College Principal and member of the Punjab Censor Board, remarked to the ICC that the screen kiss, unlike "real life" public kissing between Europeans, was never "a passing kiss" (2:5).

The cinema image was perceived as too slow, too fast, too close and too distant. In its lingering fixity and probing intimacy, the camera eye—particularly in close-up—seemed complicit with the languid, sluggish sensuality routinely attributed to tropical populations. At the same time, the cinema also seemed to enjoy an uncanny affinity with the natives' savagely accelerated but necessarily superficial mimetic capacities. The Headmaster of Mylapore High School, Krishnaswami Ayyar, described the effect of the cinema on his students thus: "It is artificial mimicry but carried to excess. . . . The point is every odd moment they can snatch they indulge in imitations and they are very sincere but lamentable imitations" (3:71).

Underlying all this one senses an anxiety triggered by the cinema's capacity to denaturalize the naturalized mediations of colonial life, to open up—in a sensuous rather than primarily a discursively critical register—the routinized relationships between bodily experience and ideological truth that a nineteenth-century colonial pedagogy had bequeathed. The perceived threat was sense untempered by sensibility—a condition already diagnosed as chronic by many contemporary critics of the dawning mass society in Europe and the United States.[10] In some ways, then, the cinema was scandalous because its spatiotemporal gimmickry sat awkwardly with the stately unfolding of an approved imperial *Bildung.* But from the point of view of publicity, its striking affective intimacy seemed at once perilous and promising.

The Cinema Sense and Imperial Pragmatics

Doubtless, audiences—when not simply bored or restless—were enjoying themselves. But did they understand what they were seeing? The colonial mimic man sitting in the cinema hall was, in the debates of the time, figured as a kind of spectatorial idiot savant—a cynical innocent who understood both nothing and everything about these flickering images. On one level, the working administrative theory posited that colonial audiences needed to be protected from the cinema because they lacked the cultural and aesthetic prophylaxis—generally glossed as a European-style education—that would enable them to exercise proper judgment vis-à-vis what they were seeing. On another level, the British suspected the cinema itself of being a strangely savage medium because of the way that it addressed its audiences so affectively, so corporeally, because it addressed them in a language they understood all too well.

For the British, the fact that Hollywood seemed capable of producing the most popular films confirmed their long-held suspicion that American civilization was in some sense fundamentally childish.[11] And yet it also set off a jealous anxiety (exacerbated by self-consciousness about the affective deficits of colonial governmentality) around whether the British Empire was ever going to be able to harness this kind of communicative magic for its own ends. On the one hand, the alleged Indian predisposition to a "cinema sense" was understood as a primitive tendency to become unproductively— perhaps dangerously—absorbed in the hypnotically diverting play of light and shadow. On the other, many colonial officers were keen to exploit the propagandistic potentials of the then-current belief that the "oriental" had "a firm belief in the veracity of the camera" (quoted in Woods 1995, 543). The compelling link between the gestural emphasis of the (silent) cinema, Indians' purported corporeality, and the needs of colonial publicity was encapsulated in the reflection offered to the ICC by E. Villiers of the European Association in Calcutta:

> You have got a peculiarly constituted people, they are intensely dramatic in thought and action. When you see a cooly [*sic*] and talk to him you realize how intensely dramatic he is. Their language is a very graphic language, much more than the Western, and that is a material which could be made very much better use of. (ICC 1928a, 2:957)

Many felt, of course, that the sensuous short-cut of the cinema was the devil's work precisely because it combined engagement with incomprehension. L. K. Mitter, a Public Prosecutor in Mandalay, remarked, "Western films are too rarely intelligible to the uneducated class. The result is that they form a low opinion of the people" (ICC 1928a, 3:677). And Dorothy Jinarajadasa of the Indian Women's Association in Madras shuddered at the sense of an elevation which was more priapic than proper:

> Also you can tell from the way the audience behave that when they see a thing which excites them emotionally, scenes between men and women and drinking and racing and that kind of thing, you can tell from the kind of way they applaud or cheer that it is not having at all an elevating effect on them. It does not help them to self-control or purity of mind. It debases them, this kind of thing, even if they don't understand exactly. (3:113)

But others speculated that the civilizing project might actually finally take wing by means of the cinema image. In a country where poverty and illiteracy meant that few could afford to "see the world," the cinema offered an opportunity to bring the world to the remotest village. In the words of Dr. K. L. Moudgill, the Trivandrum chemistry professor I quoted earlier,

> I would deprecate and I believe a very large majority of educated Indians would deprecate any attempt that is made to prevent the Indian public from availing themselves of this instrument of enlightenment. Correct understanding of a people has a humanizing effect and I would be in favour of Indians being freely educated in this respect. (3:463)

The ICC interviewed the legendary Punjabi nationalist leader Lala Lajpat Rai not long before his death at the hands of the colonial police in 1928. Although his attitude toward the cinema was, like that of much of the nationalist leadership, generally rather dismissive, he nevertheless found in it a principle of education-by-inoculation: "I don't want the youth of this country to be brought up in a nursery. They should know all these things, because then they will be better able to resist those things when they go out. They should see all those things here and they will be able to understand better all the points of modern life" (2:201).

In some respects, then, the discourse on the cinema resembled a debate on a particularly volatile *pharmakon*, a drug that, depending on the constitution of the patient, might either heal or kill.[12] The magic formula would be a specific conjuncture of culture, education, and spectatorial attitude—a conjuncture that would allow the cinema's indubitable powers to be not exactly resisted, but rather most effectively harnessed for the production of social value. In relation to the cinema, then, a Western-style education was conceived at once as a kind of shell that would protect its beneficiary from the raw force of sensory stimulus and as a kind of prism through which this onslaught could be refracted and perhaps sublimated into something resembling a more sober aesthetic judgment. This distinction between, as it were, the raw and the cooked spectator also carried an implied contrast between affect-intensive provinciality and detached universalizing judgment.

On the one hand, Indian audiences—particularly the uneducated—were thought to respond to themes and content that were substantively familiar to them. Conversely, concerns or settings far divorced from their experience were liable to be dismissed as irrelevant. On the other hand, a Western-style education would liberate filmgoers from a dependence on such correspondences and allow them to ascend to a more properly "aesthetic" engagement with films. Education, in other words, represented the passage from the particular to the universal. The distinction upon which this ideal was based was evident even in the relatively casual comments of the likes of Mr. Ardeshir Bilimoria, the Director of the Bombay Circle of the then nearly all-powerful Madan Theatres Company. Bilimoria stated that educated Indian audiences appreciated Western films because of their superior production values. But uneducated audiences liked the (technically inferior) Indian films because they could relate to them better. In Rangachariar's summation of the position, "they want to see their own class of society. That is what it comes to" (ICC 1928a, 1:328).

Then as now, we confront the irony that precisely the greatest colonial mimic men—the Westernized professional classes—were the ones who professed themselves entirely immune to the mimetic seductions of the cinema. The ICC's more elite Indian informants often tended to voice sentiments like those of a graduate of Lucknow University who insisted that he and his friends could attend the cinema without fear of corruption or contagion because "we can control. We are educated. We can control ourselves more than ignorant people" (2:478). And in terms that might have caused Wilhelm Reich to raise an ironic eyebrow, Mr. Villiers of the European Association noted that uneducated audiences were more excitable since they lacked the benefit of "the armour which knowledge and true perspective gives" (2:953).[13]

Of course, Indian nationalists of a more culturalist-populist bent tended to make the opposite claim: namely, that it was precisely the deracinated middle-class *babus* who had lost their souls to modern distractions like the cinema. The unlettered salt of the earth, on the other hand, firmly grounded in their lifeworlds, might have limited uses for such urban fripperies. But insofar as the medium might be dangerous, precisely their "healthy" grounding in local life would protect them from it. As Lala Lajpat Rai put it, "I am very strongly of opinion [*sic*] that the rural people are much more moral to resist any demoralizing influences than the townspeople and I think the Punjab peasantry is such a sturdy peasantry that a few films would not have any demoralizing influence on it at all" (2:205). (Indeed, there were those who claimed that the so-called "martial races" of the northwest in fact *required* sturdier cinematic fare than their more effeminate compatriots to the south and east. Being "full of vigour," Punjabi men, for instance, were said to appreciate "strong scenes" [2:68]).

The colonial debate on the social effects of the cinema, then, involved a constitutive oscillation between two claims. On the one hand, spectators educated in the ways of the West would be well equipped to withstand the sensory barrage of the films, indeed, perhaps so well-equipped that the cinema's unique efficacy as a communicative medium might be lost on them. On the other hand, non-Westernized Indians were thought to be at once more vulnerable—which could also be interpreted as more open—to the cinema *and* more effectively insulated from its predations by the bulwark of tradition. A (probably unsolicited) written statement from a Calcutta organization calling itself the Publicity Campaign waxed indignant along these lines: "It is an insult to the intelligence and an affront to moral instincts to be continually alleging that Indians could see nothing but evil in a pair of dainty, tripping ankles and nothing but devil himself [*sic*] in arms that may be undraped. The average Indian is neither prurient in mind nor putrid in thought. The Savitris and Sitas of old still inspire his thoughts and ideas" (4:149).

Note how the debate on the cinema swings, in a matter of seconds, from a concern with the enlightening or demoralizing *force* of its images to a question of audience *comprehension*. In other words, the issue of what the cinema might *do* to its audiences bore an ambiguous relation to the issue of whether or not they *understood* it. One variant of this problem was the recurrent complaint that the cinema misled naïve Indian audiences by scandalously misrepresenting European and American life. Here, the issue of verisimilitude sat awkwardly bundled with that of comprehension. During the ICC hearings, as the committee traveled around India, Rangachariar frequently grew exasperated at the complacency with which the educated would attribute gullibility to illiterate audiences. At one point he exploded at the British supervisor of the Bombay Entertainment Duties Act: "Do you think that the Indian is so extraordinarily simple . . . ? I think you rather exaggerate the importance of the uneducated classes. They are shrewd people, are they not?" (1:40). The issue of "education" was of course even more complicated, once the debate moved away from a simplistic opposition between the cosmopolitan educated and the provincial uneducated. As N. C. Ghose, a Calcutta lawyer, demanded rhetorically, "The first thing I would like to know is, what do you mean by 'uneducated' people[?] Take the lascars or people who are employed aboard a ship and who have been to England and other places. They certainly know much more than some of us who have been to England and lived in the country. What are you going to teach them? They know more of some phases of Western life than I do" (2:916). Of course, the unstated implication was that whatever Indian ship-hands might know of Western life was unlikely to find favor with any officially sanctioned view of Europe.

In fact, as the ICC traveled around India, its conversations manifested a mounting suspicion that the entire alarmist colonial discourse on the cinema suffered from a basic logical contradiction. It was this: the types of audiences who were supposed to be particularly vulnerable to the cinema (in shorthand, the "uneducated") were apparently not capable of understanding the kinds of films that were thought to be most potentially demoralizing (typically, social dramas with intimate or eroticized content). ICC and Bombay Censor Board member A. M. Green neatly summarized the objection: "If the illiterate do not understand it and the literate do not mind it or are not affected by it, there does not seem to be very much reason to object to it?" (2:273).

The members of the ICC were soon confronting their more alarmist informants with the argument that a so-called "sex film" whose content was not understood—even if, against all odds, the "man in the street" decided to patronize a cinema showing such a film—could not possibly have damaging effects. To this, Mr. Healy, the Commissioner of Police in Bombay, retorted that while the uneducated might have trouble following the plots, "at the same time they see what is going on" (1:77).[14]

But there was still another variation on the theme, namely the claim that it was precisely ignorance or a lack of comprehension that was going to be socially productive. Particularly beloved of educationalists and propagandists, this perspective shared something with the Brechtian notion of an estrangement effect, whereby insight arrives through a sudden and shocking reorientation of familiar assumptions. Sometimes the estrangement might be unintentional but nevertheless productive. One J. D. Khandhadia (whose occupation is, unusually, not listed in the transcripts) asserted that the majority of Indian audiences were, indeed, unlikely to understand Western films but that this was, in world-historical terms, a good thing: "Strife is the essence of evolution. Without wars there can be no world and without misunderstandings, misrepresentations, there can be no wars. It can never be helped" (1:554).

✳   ✳   ✳

In the longer work of which this paper is a part I develop many of the connections and questions that I have only been able to touch upon here: the historical and institutional foundations of film censorship in India, and the troubled relation between its precepts and its practice; the relation of the cinema to other forms of entertainment and publicity of the period; the question of the "verisimilitude" of the cinema and its vexed relation to the problem of dramatic misrepresentation, as well as the complex connections that were argued between misrepresentation and demoralizing effects. I deal with the shifting constellations of class, caste, religion, and age that were empirically documented among cinema audiences but also mobilized as explanatory counters in the attempt to account for this peculiar media apparatus.

What I have attempted to present here is, in a sense, what I take to be the core of the matter, that part of the debate in 1920s India which gets to what one might call the tension between an ontology and an epistemology of the cinema. When the debate dealt with cinema images, the ontological question had to do with the force or potentialities of these images, and the epistemological problem was one of these images' verisimilitude, in other words their relation to something called "real life." When the debate focused on audiences, its ontological side obsessed over the sensory agitation that the cinema might provoke in audiences and its epistemological side had to do with audiences' capacity to comprehend what they were seeing. These concerns about image and audience were, of course, inseparable from the larger question of how to regulate the cinema in India. In this way, the entire debate is really an attempt to fix, to pin down the novel processes of social mediation that the cinema enabled. In part, of course, this pinning down was improvised as a response to unforeseen public cultural challenges. But it also quite obviously drew on models and metaphors, some of which were well-established clichés of the imperial project, and some of which—particularly those quasi-electrical figurings of the shock of the image—were current in contemporary European concerns about the relationship between industrial modernity, crowds, and the mass society.

It seems to me that the experience of Hollywood near-hegemony in British India during these years involved both a kind of melancholy fulfillment and an uneasy augury. A melancholy fulfillment in that the encounter with these movies laid bare in several ways the contradictions and tensions upon which colonial cultural politics were based. An uneasy augury in that this challenge to the colonial imaginary pointed forward to the norms and forms of the American Century. Not least among these norms was the equation of both progress and happiness with a highly eroticized sensory engagement with commercial mass-mediated images.

This is not a one-way street, and my interest in the contradictions and tensions of the 1920s is not merely—or even primarily—antiquarian. Rather, it seems to me that these contradictions and tensions, repressed by the formulas of the American Century which—in good Hegelian fashion—appeared to supersede and transcend them, return strengthened today the more this arrogant American successor to the European imperial project drives itself toward caricature.

Notes

The research for this project was made possible by the National Science Foundation. For comments and critical reflections I am particularly indebted to friends and colleagues at Princeton University, Columbia University, and the Franke Institute for the Humanities at the University of Chicago, as well as to Filipe Calvao, Dianna Frid, Raminder Kaur, and Marcos Mendoza.

1. The proceedings and report of the ICC are themselves an extraordinary resource, upon which I have drawn heavily in the composition of this essay: thousands of pages of interview transcripts, questionnaires, and miscellany. The ICC was publicly announced in October 1927, and conducted its inquiry during several months in late 1927 and early 1928. It was chaired by a former Madras High Court judge, T. Rangacha-

riar, and further comprised Sir Ebrahim Haroon Jaffer (Kt.), Colonel J. D. Crawford (DSO, MC, MLA), K. C. Neogy (MLA and *vakil* of the Calcutta High Court), A. M. Green (Collector of Customs and Member of the Bombay Board of Film Censors), J. Coatman (MLA and Director of Public Information) and, as Secretary, G. G. Hooper (MC, ICS). In its scope, the committee was in many ways quite remarkable: in order to examine 353 witnesses across the length and breadth of British India, it traveled some 9,400 miles. It sent out 4,325 copies of its question-naire and received 320 replies. Its members visited 45 cinemas, saw 57 features, and inspected 13 producing studios. In 1927 terms, the ICC cost the colonial administra-tion around Rs 200,000.

2. The remaining 20 percent was made up of the declining European and the surging Indian cinemas. By the middle of the 1930s, the ratio of domestic to foreign films screened in India had already approached 50/50. Today, of course, India is one of the few film markets outside the United States in which domestic product remains dominant.

3. Interestingly, to buttress this claim, Spofford appealed to the supposed cul-tural affinity between the United States and Britain:

> We must not forget that a very large percentage of Americans are Anglo-Saxons comparatively recently transplanted. It is difficult to cut them off and make a separate race of crude people out of them. Even 300 years is not enough to clear racial traditions and folkways out of a man's unconsciousness and consciously there is not an American fam-ily of educated or semi-educated classes which does not bear in mind knowledge of its particular European descent, near or distant. America is Anglo-Saxon by tradition, custom, speech and law. American chil-dren are brought up on English classics, English fairy tales, English myths. It was America that discovered such British writers as Mer-edith, Conrad, Wells, Galsworthy and to a great extent Bernard Shaw. (ICC 1928a, 4:298)

4. Letter to the editor, *Bombay Chronicle*, January 31, 1925, contained in India Office Library [IOL], L/P&J/6/1747 (2601/21).

5. This particular intervention by Constance Bromley appeared, as Larkin notes, in a special *Times* supplement devoted to the cinema. Bromley's hand in raising the stakes of the moral panic of the 1920s is invariably noted by students of the period—hers is the one voice guaranteed to appear in any article on the topic. More interestingly, her screeds were also among the principal exhibits for the prosecution during the ICC's deliberations.

6. IOL, L/P&J/6/1882/2695.

7. In the silent era, and particularly in the theaters catering to a more "vernacu-lar" public, it was common for literate audience members to read out intertitles to their illiterate neighbors, thus creating a constant "confused murmur" (ICC 1928b, 41) in the halls. On other occasions, the cinemas would employ announcers to read out the titles, sometimes simultaneously in several languages, and sometimes, apparently, pro-viding a dialogue "track" of their own devising to accompany the images.

8. The article appeared in the April 21, 1926, issue of the *Times of India*. Maharash-tra State Archive, Home Dept. (Poll), 1925, 194.

9. The term "sex film" did not, of course, refer to what even by the standards of the 1920s would have been recognized as pornographic films. When asked by the ICC what the term might mean, Bombay exhibitor R. N. Bharucha responds, "I do not know whether I shall be able to evolve a definition offhand but I will put it this way—any film which has for its main theme the relations of the sexes" (ICC 1928a, 1:115). S. A. Alley, a cinema manager in Calcutta, is rather more specific, suggesting that "sex films" are films "where there are passionate love-making scenes, kissing—not the ordinary kissing, but kissing passionately, all over the body" (2:822).

The ICC proceedings do contain a handful of scattered references to pornographic movies. Mr. Watkins of the Bombay Board of Film Censors notes that "of course we have from time to time obtained obscene films, usually toy size, bits of films, and I can remember now a little toy cinema which worked quite well" (ICC 1928a, 1:104). The oral evidence given by K. Dwarkadas in camera suggests that European as well as Indian pornographic films circulated clandestinely. The Bombay suburb of Santa Cruz is specified as a production location, and Dwarkadas suggests that European films may have reached India through a form of diplomatic immunity: "They found their way, I was told, through some Maharajah or Rajah" (5:7). Rangachariar admits to some direct experience, but only of a fragmentary nature: "I did see a bit of a film like that on the Bombay side which was destroyed for fear of the police and they showed me a small portion" (3:117).

10. One place where a lament over the crudeness of mass man in the West comes together with an explicit appeal to prevent the cinema from achieving the same thing in the colonies is in the travel writings of Aldous Huxley, quoted and discussed in Larkin, n.d.

11. Moore, again, notes that Vachel Lindsay in one of the very earliest serious works on the cinema, *The Art of the Moving Picture* (1915), expressed precisely this apprehension: that "America, like cinema itself, was . . . both primitive and advanced" (quoted in Moore 2000, 54).

12. Christopher Pinney has developed a related argument around photography in colonial India. I am grateful to him for illuminating conversation on this topic.

13. Moral vulnerability to the cinema was, typically, someone else's problem. I did find one instance, however, in the ICC transcripts of a respondent who directly acknowledged the cinema's demoralizing effect on himself. This was B. Das, a Member of the Legislative Assembly from Delhi who couched his comment in a theory of cultural difference:

> These Western sex films and emotional films in India have that [pernicious] effect. They do not suit our national characteristics. . . . You know the Indian social life is quite different from the Western social life. Naturally when I saw these emotional films, there was a mental and moral fall in me, even in my own estimation. I felt a bit impulsive and emotional. What is natural to the West is not natural to the East. (ICC 1928a, 3:978, 981)

14. The question of audience comprehension was also debated among representatives of the cinema business, where obviously it was thought to have a direct bearing on financial prospects. So, for instance, R. N. Bharucha, a Bombay exhibitor-entrepreneur, argued that Western films involving "sex topics" were the preserve

of the educated. Note the direct connection that Bharucha draws between popular entertainment, uneducated audiences, and the affective density of religious practice.

> My experience is if you pay a millhand a ten rupee note and give him a complimentary ticket into the bargain to go to the [upscale] Excelsior, the chances are he will run away because he would prefer any day to go to one of his own shows at Parel which are run by Mr. Engineer and wholly devoted to the labouring classes. They will flock around there and they will go with the same enthusiasm as if they were going to their temple. (ICC 1928a, 1:115)

On the other side of the transnational coin was the testimony of Alexander Hague, at that time the "sole proprietor" of Pathe films in India. Invested—both materially and ideologically—in the idea that there was a vast Indian market for Western films, he suggested that the local masses' engagement with foreign product was marked by measured but enthusiastic judgment rather than either unseemly frenzy or bored incomprehension.

> It is *not* a fact that films of Western life are unintelligible to an uneducated Indian, or are largely misunderstood by him. I would recommend the Committee go to any Picture Theatre and sit with these *uneducated* audiences in the gallery and watch them, how they appreciate the finer points of highly social Western dramas. I think the cinema-going Indians are quite intelligent people and I have seen them even 20 years ago follow a picture and applaud all good points in it. And to-day the same audience, both educated and uneducated, is even more intelligent as they show their disapproval of a bad picture in no unmistakable manner. (1:509)

References

Anderson, Benedict. 2006. *Imagined Communities: Reflections on the Origins and Spread of Nationalism*. Revised edition. London: Verso.

Arora, Poonam. 1995. "Imperiling the Prestige of the White Woman: Colonial Anxiety and Film Censorship in British India." *Visual Anthropology Review* 11(2): 36–50.

Bayly, C. A. 1996. *Empire and Information: Intelligence Gathering and Social Communication in India, 1780–1870*. Cambridge: Cambridge University Press.

Bromley, Constance. 1922. "India. Censorship and Propaganda. Influence of Foreign Films." *Times Cinema Supplement*, February 21.

Burke, Timothy. 1996. *Lifebuoy Men, Lux Women: Commodification, Consumption and Cleanliness in Modern Zimbabwe*. Durham, N.C.: Duke University Press.

Chatterjee, Partha. 1993. *The Nation and Its Fragments: Colonial and Postcolonial Histories*. Princeton, N.J.: Princeton University Press.

Chowdhry, Prem. 2000. *Colonial India and the Making of Empire Cinema: Image, Ideology and Identity*. Manchester: Manchester University Press.

Cohn, Bernard. 1983. "Representing Authority in Victorian India." In Eric Hobsbawm and Terence Ranger, eds., *The Invention of Tradition*. Cambridge: Cambridge University Press.

Collingham, E. M. 2001. *Imperial Bodies: The Physical Experience of the Raj, c. 1800–1947.* Cambridge: Polity.

Dirks, Nicholas B. 2001. *Castes of Mind: Colonialism and the Making of Modern India.* Princeton, N.J.: Princeton University Press.

Freitag, Sandria B. 1989. *Collective Action and Community: Public Action and the Emergence of Communalism in North India.* Berkeley: University of California Press.

French, Philip. 1997. "No End in Sight." In Ruth Petrie, ed., *Film and Censorship: The Index Reader.* London: Cassell.

Guha-Thakurta, Tapati. 1992. *The Making of a New "Indian" Art: Artists, Aesthetics and Nationalism in Bengal, c. 1850–1920.* Cambridge: Cambridge University Press.

Gupta, Charu. 2002. *Sexuality, Obscenity, Community: Women, Muslims and the Hindu Public in Colonial India.* London: Palgrave.

Hussain, Nasser. 2003. *The Jurisprudence of Emergency: Colonialism and the Rule of Law.* Ann Arbor: University of Michigan Press.

Indian Cinematograph Committee. 1928a. *Indian Cinematograph Committee, 1927–28: Evidence.* 5 volumes. Calcutta: Government of India Central Publication Branch.

———. 1928b. *Report of the Indian Cinematograph Committee, 1927–28.* Calcutta: Government of India Central Publication Branch.

Jowett, Garth. 1999. "'A Capacity for Evil': The 1915 Supreme Court *Mutual* Decision." In Matthew Bernstein, ed., *Controlling Hollywood: Censorship and Regulation in the Studio Era.* New Brunswick, N.J.: Rutgers University Press.

Kaur, Raminder. 2003. *Performative Politics and the Cultures of Hinduism: Public Uses of Religion in Western India.* New Delhi: Permanent Black.

Larkin, Brian. n.d. "Film, Empire and Anxious Colonialists." Unpublished manuscript.

Levin, David. 1999. *Richard Wagner, Fritz Lang and the Nibelungen: The Dramaturgy of Disavowal.* Princeton, N.J.: Princeton University Press.

MacKenzie, John. 1984. *Propaganda and Empire: The Manipulation of British Public Opinion, 1880–1960.* Manchester: Manchester University Press.

Mattelart, Armand. 1994. *Mapping World Communication: War, Progress, Culture.* Minneapolis: University of Minnesota Press.

McClintock, Anne. 1995. *Imperial Leather: Race, Gender and Sexuality in the Colonial Contest.* London: Routledge.

Metcalf, Thomas. 1995. *Ideologies of the Raj.* Cambridge: Cambridge University Press.

Moore, Rachel. 2000. *Savage Theory: Cinema as Modern Magic.* Durham, N.C.: Duke University Press.

O'Connor, T. P. 1920. *Report of the British Board of Film Censors for the Year Ending December 31st, 1919.* London: British Board of Film Censors.

Orsini, Francesca. 2002. *The Hindi Public Sphere, 1920–1940: Language and Literature in the Age of Nationalism.* New Delhi: Oxford University Press.

Pinney, Christopher. 2004. *"Photos of the Gods": The Printed Image and Political Struggle in India.* London: Reaktion.

Prasad, M. Madhava. 1998. *Ideology of the Hindi Film: A Historical Construction.* New Delhi: Oxford University Press.

Richards, Thomas. 1990. *The Commodity Culture of Victorian England: Advertising and Spectacle, 1851–1914.* Stanford, Calif.: Stanford University Press.

Sinha, Babli. 2005. "Fearing the Close-Up: The Threat of Spatial Intimacy in Cinema in Colonial India." *Biblio: A Review of Books* 10(9–10): 20–21.

Smyth, Rosaleen. 1979. "The Development of British Colonial Film Policy, 1927–1939." *Journal of African History* 20(3): 437–50.

Times (London). 1926. "The Cinema in the East." September 18.

Vasey, Ruth. 1999. "Beyond Sex and Violence: 'Industry Policy' and the Regulation of Hollywood Movies, 1922–1939." In Matthew Bernstein, ed., *Controlling Hollywood: Censorship and Regulation in the Studio Era*. New Brunswick, N.J.: Rutgers University Press.

Wheeler, James Tallboys. 1877. *History of the Imperial Assemblage at Delhi*. London: Longmans, Green, Reader and Dyer.

Woods, Philip. 1995. "Film Propaganda in India, 1914–23." *Historical Journal of Film, Radio and Television* 15(4): 543–54.

FOUR

The Limits of Decency and the Decency of Limits
Censorship and the Bombay Film Industry

Tejaswini Ganti

n July 2002, veteran Hindi filmmaker Vijay Anand abruptly resigned as chairman of the Central Board of Film Certification—more commonly known as the Censor Board—even before completing his first year of a three-year term. His resignation provided the basis for a cover story about film censorship in the national English-language newsmagazine *India Today* titled "Is Sex Ok?" with the subtitle "Indian Cinema Tries to Break Free from the Clutches of Prudish and Archaic Censorship but the Government Dithers." Though filmmaking in India is a private enterprise, in order to have a theatrical release, films have to be cleared and rated by the state's Central Board of Film Certification—a practice initiated by the British in 1918 to protect the image of the colonizer. Perceived threats to the reputation of white women as well as any allusion to self-governance, the Indian nationalist movement, or Indian independence were heavily censored by the colonial authorities.

Anand had made news earlier because he was considering a recommendation from the regional censor board in Kerala that "sexually explicit films" be legally exhibited in specially designated theaters with a rating of X-A or M/A (for "matured adults"). Kerala is regarded as the center of the adult film industry in India, and while such films are either prohibited or censored heavily, they continue to be exhibited clandestinely throughout the country with the censored portions added back in.

In an interview with the English-language newspaper *The Indian Express*, Anand explained, "The committee thought it wasn't possible to stamp out the sex film trade. The better option is to regulate it, like they do in other countries: set up special halls, levy 2–3 times the regular entertainment duty" (Nair 2002). Anand presented his position as a pragmatic one, making arguments similar to those for decriminalizing other socially taboo or morally suspect activities like drug use or prostitution: such films exist because there is a market for them, and the state may as well earn revenues from them rather than expend resources trying to police and prohibit them. Individual states in India earn a significant amount of revenue from the entertainment tax imposed upon cinemagoing. This issue was merely one aspect of a general overhaul of the censorship process that Anand was attempting during his tenure as chair.[1]

During his review of the censorship process, Anand received sixty recommendations that were to be placed in a report to a core committee of the Ministry of Information and Broadcasting, under whose purview the Censor Board operates.[2] However, to officials in the Ministry the suggestion of screening X-rated adult films in specially designated theaters overshadowed all of the other recommendations and Anand was ordered to not even raise the issue at an upcoming committee meeting. Anand's response was to resign immediately. In an interview with *India Today*, he stated, "I wasn't being allowed to do my job." He characterized the order from Delhi as "taking away my freedom of speech" (Bamzai and Unnithan 2002, 46). In other words, the censor was himself censored.

Though Anand's resignation and the adult film proposal received a good deal of coverage in the Indian press, little outrage or even concern was reported on the part of the Bombay film industry. As someone who has been researching the Hindi film industry for over a decade, I was not surprised. While the popular press in India represents film censorship as a state-imposed regulation that is anathema to filmmakers—as evident in the subtitle of the above-mentioned *India Today* article—I discovered during the course of my initial fieldwork among Hindi filmmakers (in 1996) a great deal of ambivalence toward the Indian state's policies and practices of film censorship. In my interviews with filmmakers, discussions about censorship were rarely articulated in a language of rights or artistic or creative freedom, but rather in a language of cinematic power, social responsibility, and self-control. While most filmmakers had problems with the implementation of censorship policies, many actually agreed with the idea of censorship and expressed anxiety about a culture free of state censorship. These anxieties were articulated primarily through the tropes of the audience, the market, and opportunistic peers.

In this chapter, I examine these concerns as a way of broadening the discussion of film censorship beyond issues of content, policy, and regulation to incorporate issues of citizenship, subjectivity, and social relations. I detail the varied perspectives held by Hindi filmmakers on the practice, rationale, and efficacy of film censorship. While some filmmakers clearly endorsed the idea of state censorship, many were ambivalent about the whole issue. Even those who disagreed with the practice of state censorship did so on the basis of its redundancy rather than its iniquity.

Rather than a textual (specific films) or regulatory (state legislation) perspective on film censorship, I approach the issue ethnographically, focusing on Hindi filmmakers' ambivalent attitudes toward censorship. I argue that this ambivalence arises from two distinct but related features of the historical context and social world of the contemporary Bombay film industry. First is the

ideology of developmentalism that both informs state policy and shapes subjectivities in postcolonial India. India's particular relationship to modernity
has been defined primarily by the apparatus and discourse of development
which positions "Third World" nation-states like India as "behind" the West,
and therefore "inhabiting a period that lay in the dim recesses of the history
of the 'developed' world" (Gupta 1998, 10). Though the Indian state since the
mid-1980s has replaced a Nehruvian-style development agenda with a neo-
liberal one, it has not abandoned its obsession with "catching up" with the West.
While the methods may have changed, a teleological ideology of modernization still undergirds state economic and social policy. Development discourse
is not just about the economic position of a nation-state relative to others, but
more significantly "has created the 'underdeveloped' as a subject and 'under
development' as a form of identity in the postcolonial world" (Gupta 1998, 11).
I have discussed elsewhere how this identity of underdevelopment is manifest
in the film industry both in its self-representation and in its representation of
its audiences (Ganti 2000). Here, I examine how the sense of "backwardness"
and incomplete subject formation implicit in the label "developing country" is
internalized and articulated by Hindi filmmakers in their discussions of audiences and the need for censorship.

The second factor necessary to contextualize filmmakers' ambivalence about
censorship is the Bombay film industry's desire for respectability and acceptance
within Indian middle-class and elite social spheres. The film industry has long
been viewed by elites and represented by the media as an unsavory and illicit site
because of its historical connections to courtesan culture, the "black" or undocu-
mented economy, money laundering, organized crime, and stereotypes about the
"casting couch." Since the 1930s it has been possible to discern Bombay filmmakers' concerns about such characterizations and efforts to counter them,[3] and from
the mid-1990s the self-representations of the film industry have been marked by
a narrative of increasing respectability accruing to the profession (Ganti 2000).
In this narrative, filmmakers assert that the Bombay film industry is becoming
respectable because of the middle- to upper-class backgrounds of new entrants;
filmmakers also make distinctions between legitimate, committed filmmakers
who make films for the sake of storytelling and entertainment and those who
make films for reasons that are morally suspect. Here, I reveal how such concerns
about respectability and legitimacy manifest themselves in discussions of censorship through the figure of the errant filmmaker who is unable or unwilling to
control the desire to cater to audiences' prurient instincts for commercial gain.
The inability of the industry to regulate and discipline itself is offered as another
rationale for censorship; therefore the discussion about censorship also serves as
a commentary on the identity of the Bombay film industry and the subjectivities
of its members.

Film censorship in India exemplifies the distinction and tension between
citizen and population that is a characteristic feature of contemporary democracy

(Chatterjee 2004). Though the discourse of democracy is predicated on the figure of the citizen and its corollaries of autonomy, equal rights, and self-representation, the modernizing agendas of postcolonial nation-states like India presume "populations," which are the objects of government policy, rather than citizens (Chatterjee 1998). Debates over censorship in India are commonly framed in terms of the tension between democracy and modernization. While the argument against censorship is based on the idea of the discerning spectator whose subjectivity is autonomous from the act of film-viewing, i.e., the belief that citizens are formed prior to cinema, the argument for censorship is predicated upon the social significance of film and its potential to shape subjectivities in ways that could advance or limit the state's efforts at modernization. These tensions are manifest in filmmakers' attitudes toward censorship, since the practice interpellates them both as citizens with rights and as a population that requires regulation. Sometimes in the course of their career, members of the Bombay film industry are asked to become a part of the censorship apparatus, either as the chair of the Censor Board, as in the case of Anand, or as a part of the body of viewers who make up the board; they therefore occupy what would appear to be conflicting positions, those of the censor and the censored. Examining Hindi filmmakers' discourses about censorship complicates our understanding of the institution of state censorship and reveals how its concerns move beyond the restriction of expression or the regulation of content and become centrally involved with the production of citizenship, class identity, and subjectivity in a postcolonial setting.

Before launching into an examination of the Bombay film industry's discourse about censorship, I provide a brief history of film censorship legislation in India and then outline the process by which a film gets certified. After establishing the context, I turn to a discussion of filmmakers' explanations of and attitudes toward censorship. Two broad sets of themes emerge from their statements. The first set I discuss, which includes the power of cinema, filmmakers' social responsibility, and the immaturity of audiences, is consistent with the discourse and ideology of developmentalism. The second set of themes, which includes the redundancy of state censorship, the presence of self-censorship, and the (in)ability of the film industry to regulate itself, corresponds to the Foucauldian notion of governmentality (1991), in terms of "the conduct of conduct" and self-regulation.

Film Censorship Regulation

Anxiety about the filmic image and distrust of filmmakers' intentions result in a continuous effort on the part of the Indian state to discipline and regulate films, filmmaking, and filmmakers. Film censorship in India dates back to the colonial period; the Cinematograph Act of 1918 dealt with the licensing of movie theaters and the certification of films. The Act enabled provincial governments to set up authorities to examine and certify films for release.

However, no guidelines were established in the Act to assist those authorities in determining what type of films should be certified. By 1920, boards of film censors had been set up in Bombay, Calcutta, Madras, and Rangoon. A certificate granted by any of these boards was valid throughout British India, but could be revoked in any province by the provincial government (Rangoonwalla 1983, 153).

The first Indian film to become embroiled in a censorship controversy was *Bhakta Vidur*, released in 1921. Ostensibly a mythological film based on the Mahabharata, the film, which was produced, certified, and successful in Bombay, was banned first in Karachi and then in Madras. According to the Indian Cinematograph Committee's 1928 report, the film was perceived by the authorities as "a thinly veiled resume of political events in India, Vidur appearing as Mr. Gandhi clad in Gandhi-cap and khaddar shirt" (quoted in Rajadhyaksha and Willemen 1999, 244; see also Pinney's chapter in this volume).

The 1918 Act was not amended until after Independence. The Cinematograph Act of 1949 created two categories of censorship certificates: A for films restricted to adults (18 and older) and U for unrestricted exhibition. This Act also established the Central Board of Film Censors in place of the provincial boards, although regional subcommittees were retained to review non-Hindi-language films. Rather than becoming more relaxed, censorship became much stricter after Independence. The censors indulged their reformist tendencies in the process of certifying films. They expressed their disapproval of most films, increasingly exercised aesthetic judgment, and ordered indiscriminate cuts. Censors began to reject both Indian and foreign films in a manner that seemed arbitrary and unfounded to filmmakers (Barnouw and Krishnaswamy 1980).[4]

The Cinematograph Act of 1952 invalidated all existing censor boards and granted the central government the authority to form a Board of Film Censors consisting of a chairperson and nine members. The central government reserved the power to invalidate the certification of any film in the whole or any part of India, change a film's certification from U to A, suspend the exhibition of any film for a stated period of time, and exempt certain films from the operation of censorship (Rangoonwalla 1983, 153). The 1952 Act was amended in 1981 and 1984 and two new categories for certifying films were added in 1983: UA for unrestricted public exhibition but with parental guidance suggested for children below age 12 and S for public exhibition restricted to specialized audiences, such as doctors.

Throughout these changes, what remained constant was the guiding principle, instituted in 1918, that a film could not be certified (and therefore released) if it was "against the interests of the security of the State, friendly relations with other foreign states, public order, decency or morality" (Rajadhyaksha and Willemen 1999, 23). In subsequent amendments to the 1952 Act, the phrase "security of the State" was changed to "sovereignty and integrity of India." The Act also authorized the central government to issue principles to guide censors in their task of viewing and certifying films. The principles currently guiding the Censor Board were drafted in December 1991.

While film censorship was instituted by the British to uphold the legitimacy of colonial rule, the independent Indian state characterized the continuance of the practice in paternalist terms, befitting its role as the main agent of development and modernization. According to the 1991 guidelines, the objectives of film certification are to ensure that

a. the medium of film remains responsible and sensitive to the values and standards of society;
b. artistic expression and creative freedom are not unduly curbed;
c. certification is responsible to social changes;
d. the medium of film provides clean and healthy entertainment; and
e. as far as possible, the film is of aesthetic value and cinematically of a good standard. (Central Board of Film Certification, n.d., "Guidelines")

The Act then goes on to list twenty-two principles that members of the Board of Film Certification should bear in mind while evaluating films.[5]

Despite the plethora of guidelines, many filmmakers, journalists, and social commentators have criticized them for being too vague and confusing. In September 2005, the Ministry of Information and Broadcasting began an attempt to overhaul and make more explicit the Cinematograph Act to take into account changes in technology and content in the Indian media landscape since the onset of satellite broadcasting in 1991. The proposed changes included adding the category MA—for "mature" adults 25 and older—to the existing certification categories of U, UA, A, and S, as well as allowing the depiction of sexual foreplay (though prohibiting explicit sex) in films rated MA (Raman 2005).[6]

The Process of Film Censorship

While a film can be submitted to any of the nine regional censor boards in the country for certification, the majority of Hindi films are certified through the Central Board of Film Certification, located in Bombay. The board and its chair are not involved in the routine work of viewing and certifying films, but rather are called upon only in special circumstances. The routine work is carried out by advisory panels located in the regional centers.

The CBFC office in Bombay has nearly a hundred members, drawn from the public, who view and certify films. In an attempt to have a wide spectrum of backgrounds and viewpoints represented, these members are drawn from a variety of professions, including the film industry, as well as homemakers. One of the members whom I knew while I was in Bombay was the mother of one of my friends; she was designated a representative "house-wife." My conversation with Mrs. Kapoor made clear that training for this position was minimal, with footage that had been previously censored serving as the primary tool of orientation.[7] She described the training process:

When you're selected by the Censor Board, there's a workshop where all the new members are given a basic training—what is a mid-shot, what is a long shot, and what they have been deleting in the past. They show them the visuals which have been deleted from the past movies. They show them what should be deleted from the film when you're watching it. (Interview)

Films are first viewed by an examining committee comprising four or five members and the board's regional officer, who is frequently a member of the Indian Administrative Service. The committee recommends cuts and issues a U, UA, or A certificate, which establishes the limits on a film's circulation. A filmmaker who disagrees with the committee's decision can appeal to the revising committee, which is made up of eight members. However, there is no guarantee that this committee will not ask for further cuts. If dissatisfied with the revising committee's decision, a filmmaker can appeal further, to the appellate tribunal, headed by a retired high court judge whose decision is usually final. A determined filmmaker, however, can still appeal to the courts.

While the process of submitting a film for certification and appealing the board's decision is bureaucratized and systematic, the guidelines are an entirely different matter. When viewing a film, members are instructed to pay attention to whether it conforms to the twenty-two guidelines stipulated by the Ministry of Information and Broadcasting. Twelve of these guidelines are reprinted on the forms that committee members fill out in the course of filing their report about a film, reminding them to ensure that "pointless or avoidable scenes of violence, cruelty, and horror are not shown" and "human sensibilities are not offended by vulgarity, obscenity, and depravity." The application of the guidelines is therefore a highly interpretive, subjective, and idiosyncratic exercise. In fact, if the guidelines were followed strictly, many films would be denied a certificate. Kapoor, when describing the process of viewing a film within the framework of the guidelines, presented a very subjective and fluid scenario:

There are about nineteen or twenty codes—it's not any strict procedure as such. You see, broadly, you have to apply, you have to use your own discretion. After the film is over, we call the applicant and we tell him our views, and he can argue. If he convinces us, we can change, but if he doesn't convince us, it remains as it is. Sometimes we have given an A certificate and he wants UA, so we tell him, we can give you further cuts and make it UA. There are also some times when we've given U and he wants A—clear A [laughs]. If he argues his point well, we consider it. And still if he's not happy, then he can go to the chairman and ask for a second committee. (Interview)

Kapoor's statements and the fact that most films are released demonstrate the somewhat arbitrary nature of the process and the tremendous emphasis placed upon cuts, or removal of the troublesome portions of a film. Filmmakers have figured out strategies to deal with the guidelines—either shooting extra footage in anticipation of cuts ordered by the censors, or trying to influence members of the board through favors or gifts. Many of my informants stated quite bluntly that with the right contacts, favors, or outright bribery, anything could get passed by the censors. Top box-office star Aamir Khan characterized such a scenario as symptomatic of the larger corruption of society:

> *Suppose I make a film that is extremely crude and has excessive violence . . . so if I am exploiting sex and violence unduly, then what I do is, to get it passed by the censors, because the society is corrupt I manage to pay my way through, or I manage to get favors, and I somehow manage to get the film passed. That is the fault of the corruption in society today, you can't blame cinema for that, you can't blame films for that. You've got to blame the human beings for that. We are misusing it, we should correct ourselves.* (Interview)

The vagueness of the guidelines and the arbitrariness with which they are applied frustrates most Hindi filmmakers. Every time they submit a film for certification, something which seemed innocuous or was allowed in the past may be singled out for prohibition. For example, the censors ordered the word "sexy" removed from a popular song in the 1994 film *Khuddar*, so the original refrain "sexy, sexy, sexy, *mujhe log bole*" (people call me sexy) was changed to "baby, baby, baby, *mujhe log bole*." However, another film song of the '90s, "*Mera pant bhi* sexy, *mera* shirt *bhi* sexy" (my pants are also sexy, my shirt is also sexy) was left alone.

Screenwriter Sutanu Gupta commented upon what he described as the incoherence and absurdity of film censorship in India. The Censor Board had refused to grant his film *Anjaam* (Consequence) a certificate for exhibition.

> *They found it very violent and they found it very this, that, and the other. What eventually happened was that they just asked for ten feet, two feet, seven feet cut out of some violent scenes, and they were being fooled, because anyway we had kept twenty feet. We knew they will be asking for seven feet to be cut off. So happily the director did it and that's it. And I was sitting there and watching and I said, "My God! these guys are fools, yaar! They don't understand. They're not getting the point." Either you argue on a valid reasoning, on a proper ground. This kind of a film is this, either we don't lagao [show] the film or put an A certificate. Don't ask for ten feet to be cut off and five feet to be cut off and all that, that kind of a thing. I personally feel that our censor system is not working. What happens is, either we all go by precedents: "How come you allowed Zeenat Aman to wear a two-piece [bathing suit] in Raj Kapoor's film? Why can't Karisma wear two-piece?" Our arguments are always on that level. The Censor Board arguments are always about five feet and ten feet and two feet. Cut this off and cut that off.* (Interview)

Gupta believed the problem was due to the composition of the Censor Board—that it included people who basically did not like cinema or had an axe to grind about the "poisonous" impact of cinema on the nation's youth—and the vagueness of the guidelines. What is interesting is that he never explicitly argued that censorship should be done away with—his main complaint was about its implementation.

While many people I spoke to voiced the same criticism and argued that the censorship guidelines needed to be applied with consistency, they also acknowledged the difficulty of creating more precise guidelines because of the subjective nature of the enterprise. In response to my question about whether censorship was necessary, Madhuri Dixit, one of the leading stars of the industry in the 1990s, said,

> Yeah, I think some code is necessary. And they should follow the code, they should lay down specific rules and just follow them. Right now that's not happening; it's very vague. You know, what is vulgar and what is not is a very vague and abstract idea. So I don't think it's an issue that can ever be resolved. What is vulgar to me might be very aesthetic to you, so it's a very vague issue. (Interview)

While Dixit acknowledged the near impossibility of defining a category such as vulgarity, she was still definite about the need for guidelines and the consistent application of them. Though filmmakers complained about censorship and the composition of the advisory committees and I heard many an anecdote about filmmakers' experiences with the Censor Board, many were uncomfortable with the idea of getting rid of censorship completely.

In the following section, I describe filmmakers' perceptions of the undue power of cinema and present the perspectives of those who are either explicitly or implicitly in favor of state censorship. I demonstrate how these perspectives are located in a developmentalist framework, which leads them to fall in with state discourses about censorship.

The Power of Cinema—Censorship and Developmentalism

Films are too important to be left to filmmakers alone.

—H. Y. Sharada Prasad, Director, Indian Institute of Mass Communication, in a welcome speech at the 1979 Symposium on Cinema in Developing Countries

One of my standard questions to Hindi filmmakers during my fieldwork concerned the significance of cinema in everyday life in India. Without fail, filmmakers would launch into a description of the power and social significance of popular film in India. Viveck Vaswani, an actor and producer, responded to my question in a manner that indicated he found it trite:

> I'll give you the same clichéd answer. It has infiltrated every town, every village, every city. Therefore it has a tremendous impact on the masses. And if you show the wrong things, they'll do wrong things. And if you show the right things, they'll do right things. But you can't underestimate its importance. It's there in front of you. You know? Sridevi has a fancy hairstyle, the whole country's wearing it. Madhuri wears a purple sari in Hum Aapke Hain Koun, they're

all doing it. Naturally, it is powerful, but that answer you can get in any history book on cinema. (Interview)

Cinema's influence on the "masses" was a common refrain during my field-work, and remains so now.[8] In state- and media-generated discourses about cinema, the vast majority of film audiences are categorized as the "masses," mostly illiterate or poorly educated spectators easily influenced or incited by onscreen images.

When I asked if he accepted such a "clichéd" description of the power of cinema, Vaswani answered,

I accept it. I accept it. It is too powerful a medium to really ignore the social implications of making the kind of films that you should. I have no doubts, not just here, in the world, that a film like Natural Born Killers will have the kind of impact that it shouldn't, but it will, because it is such a powerful medium. That doesn't mean that all of us should make Raju Ban Gaya Gentlemans [Raju Has Become a Gentleman][9] all our lives, but, because we're infiltrating to even the small towns, therefore we have to have a social conscience, certain responsibility, not of what we are showing, but we should have a social respon-sibility in terms of what we're not showing. . . . The power of not showing is in your hand. So you have to realize what you don't have to show. (Interview)

His statements about the mimetic power of cinema, the need for self-restraint on the part of filmmakers, and the social responsibility they have to audiences were echoed by many others in the industry. Though members of the film industry emphasized that their main task is to entertain, they claimed that that task car-ries with it the responsibility to maintain standards of decency and decorum, because of the impact of the medium. I heard frequent statements about the need for limits and boundaries on visual expression. For example, popular box-office star and producer Aamir Khan asserted during our interview,

I do feel that filmmakers and people involved in films should have a certain amount of sense of responsibility, because what they are making is certainly having a certain impact on the viewer and especially on the younger minds. So to say that we can do what we want and it doesn't matter is wrong, and to say that we have to only do things which are educational, that is also wrong. I think films are basically meant for entertainment. . . . Having said that, however, I still repeat that in entertaining people it does not mean that you start removing your pants on screen. Because that also will entertain people, but you have to have a certain amount of responsibility; you have to be aware that what you're making is going to have an effect on the minds of people watching, so you should not cross a certain limit. (Interview)

Located as they are within an industry and a filmmaking tradition that is aggres-sively oriented toward commercial success, Khan's and Vaswani's emphasis on social responsibility may seem self-important and out of place. However, what becomes apparent from examining the large volume of state-generated discourse is that cinema has been a consistent feature in discussions about development and modernization in India and that Hindi filmmakers have been interpellated as partners in these projects for decades.[10] As a result of the high rates of illiteracy and the unparalleled popularity of films and film stars in India, the state has viewed film as a pedagogical tool in its modernization agenda. Elected officials and bureaucrats throughout the decades have been exhorting filmmakers to make "socially relevant" films to "uplift" the masses, since the "masses" are perceived as malleable and in need of proper molding. For example, in the fiftieth anniversary celebration of Indian sound films in 1981, the Indian Academy of Motion Picture Arts and Sciences published a commemorative volume (*Fifty Years of Indian Talkies, 1931–1981*) with a section entitled "Greetings from Leaders," which contained official statements about the role of cinema in Indian society. The Chief Minister of Maharashtra, A. R. Antulay, stated,

> The film being the most effective medium of communication, its potential besides providing wholesome entertainment to the masses, lies in its tremendous capacity to create social consciousness among the people about all evils, and this must be harnessed to the maximum benefit of society at large. I am glad that the film industry as a whole is helping every national cause in its own way. (Ramachandran 1981, 8)[11]

A discussion of the power of cinema inevitably led to a discussion of censorship. After stating the importance of self-restraint and self-imposed limits on cinematic expression, Khan shifted his focus to censor boards:

> *Which is why there are censor boards which are meant to view what is shown in a film, and the people in censor boards are selected from various parts of society and they are meant to judge whether anything in the film is offensive to the viewer and should not be watched. And if it should not be watched by a certain section of the audience under a certain age group, then that section should be blocked off by giving it an A certificate or whatever. So I think the system is there. We are not following it, that is another issue.* (Interview)

Khan states that a filmmaker's sense of responsibility is not enough; an external check in the form of the state censor board is also necessary. In the previous section, we encountered Khan's criticisms of the execution rather than the institution of censorship. When I asked Vaswani if state censorship was necessary, he responded by asserting,

> *We've got too many castes, too many communities, too many idiots writing too many letters to too many newspapers for the government to abolish censorship totally; it will never happen. It can't happen. The uproar that is created because* Bandit Queen *is banned is nothing compared to the uproar that would be created if Hindus started burning down Muslims' houses just because* Bandit Queen *showed something wrong. The government can't take that risk. . . . We are not a country of logic and rationale. We are not a country where sense and common sense take precedence. We are a country which is emotional.* (Interview)

Vaswani's resigned and hyperbolic explanation for the necessity of censorship points to India's sociocultural diversity, its history of communal conflicts, and the hypersensitivity and emotionality of its citizens. His statement that films can incite violence is akin to the Indian state's understanding of media effects and influence as acting like a hypodermic needle. In this top-down causal view of media influence, cinema, and audiovisual media in general, can "inject" their messages into viewers, directly influencing behavior and shape attitudes and subjectivities. Therefore, a film is evaluated according to the positive or negative effects its main theme seems likely to have on viewers, and thus on society.

Hence, much of the discourse about film in India communicates that it is a powerful tool that can be used for good, but can be very dangerous in the wrong hands. This perspective provides the continued justification for film censorship. The website of the Central Board of Film Certification unequivocally asserts this viewpoint, quoting the Supreme Court of India:[12]

> Film censorship becomes necessary because a film motivates thought and action and assures a high degree of attention and retention as compared to the printed word. The combination of act and speech, sight and sound in semi darkness of the theatre with elimination of all distracting ideas will have a strong impact on the minds of the viewers and can affect emotions. Therefore, it has as much potential for evil as it has for good and has an equal potential to instill or cultivate violent or good behaviour. It cannot be equated with other modes of communication. Censorship by prior restraint is, therefore, not only desirable but also necessary. (Central Board of Film Certification, n.d., "Background")

The National Film Development Corporation's[13] website displays a similar anxiety about moving images in its explanation of why film censorship is necessary in India:

> While the media in our country is free, it is considered necessary in the general interest to examine the product before it goes out for public consumption, because of the effect that the visual medium can have on the people, which can be far stronger than the influence of the printed word. . . . Film censorship ensures that the people do not get exposed to psychologically damaging matter. (National Film Development Corporation, n.d.)

Both sets of statements present the disproportionate power of images as compared to text as a rationale for film censorship. These statements also present film viewing as a passive reception of images, in which viewers either are empty vessels, to be filled by the messages from the movie screen, or contain latent impulses that may be aroused. Such an idea of viewership echoes early Frankfurt School arguments about the manipulative power of the culture industries. Implicit in these statements is the role of literacy in determining the affective impact of film as a medium. In state discourses, the power of the filmic image is magnified because of the high rates of illiteracy in India. Illiteracy or the lack of a formal education signals to government functionaries that vast portions of the populace—the "masses"—are incapable of distinguishing the difference between filmic representations and reality and therefore are easily swayed or manipulated by film images. It then becomes the state's responsibility to ensure the production of films that engender positive or beneficial effects, as well as prohibiting those which can be damaging.

Members of the older generation of the film industry explicitly articulated the hypodermic view of film influence when discussing film censorship with me. The late Hrishikesh Mukherjee, a successful and respected director in the 1960s and 1970s who was the chairman of the Censor Board in the early 1990s, explained to me why he believed censorship was necessary in India:

> You see, Tejaswini, we are living in a society where most of the adults also are at the kindergarten level of intelligence. Do you know about threshold theory?[14] Professor, I forget his name now, in his research, he said that 20 percent of the people who never commit adultery or murder or theft, whatever film they see their whole life, they will never do anything wrong. Another 20 percent of the people will do those things whether they see a film or not. They will steal; they will murder; they will rape. What about the 60 percent of people in between? He called them "threshold people." They get terribly influenced. That was his research. They follow everyone. So 20 percent, whatever you show them, they will remain honest and remain virtuous. Twenty percent, whatever you show— all films of Christ and religious leaders—they will still rape, steal, and murder. But the 60 percent you have to protect. (Interview)

While Mukherjee distinguished between segments of society for which film censorship would or would not make a difference in the constitution of their subjectivities, B. R. Chopra, a highly regarded producer and director whose career stretched from the 1950s until the 1980s, was more categorical in his arguments for censorship. He stated unequivocally,

> Censorship is necessary because we are still a backwards society. The majority of people are in villages, and some of them are uneducated. So according to me they [filmmakers] should not have the complete freedom to make it. Although there is no censorship in America, the complete freedom also is not there. You don't see a bedroom scene in a good movie there. I feel that in India, we need some kind of restrictions. (Interview)

Like those of state discourses, both Chopra's and Mukherjee's characterizations of Indian audiences point to their lack of formal education as a reason for their infantilism and backwardness as well as their vulnerability to the screen image. These filmmakers' perceptions are also grounded in long-standing government discourses in India which designate the vast majority of the population as "backward" and in need of "upliftment" or "improvement" (Ganti 2000).

All of the aforementioned comments emerge from the political discourse produced by the postcolonial Indian state, according to which the majority of the populace is not quite prepared for the rights and responsibilities of citizenship. Thomas Hansen points out that after Independence the national leadership produced a more openly paternalist discourse in which the "ignorance and superstition" of the masses were the main obstacles to national development (1999, 47). Therefore reforming social habits, "civilizing" the Indian masses, and inculcating the values of an Indian modernity became the task of state institutions, the political elite, and the social world of the middle class they represented.

The link between social reform and censorship was made explicitly by critically acclaimed and internationally renowned actor Shabana Azmi, who put a more unconventional spin on her support for film censorship:

> I am saying something very unfashionable, which is that I do think there is a need for censorship. I don't think that there are absolutes in freedom. . . . For instance, if I was on the Censor Board, I would hack a lot of things that have to do with the subservience of women, or in the dialogue suggesting that women need to be put into subservient positions. That's the kind of thing I would come down very heavily on, and not so much explicit nudity. Because I think that is not so much a problem as the kind of values with our society. So firstly I am in favor of censorship, but I do believe that the Censor Board needs to work up its guidelines more carefully, more clearly, that you need to involve women, and people from all sections of society—housewives, specialists, people in academia, sociologists, etc. (Interview)

Although the tone of Azmi's comments is different from the previous statements endorsing censorship, her belief that representations of women have a powerful impact resonates with state discourses about film's potential as a tool for social change.

Other filmmakers articulated the relationship between censorship and social change in a less instrumental fashion. Subhash Ghai, a highly successful contemporary producer and director, used the metaphor of policing to discuss why censorship is necessary:

> I think it's working all right. There's a lot of hue and cry about censors that I've been hearing for the last thirty years. I don't think you'll like a policeman stopping you on the road, but the policeman has to be there, the traffic cop has to be there. Nobody likes red lights, traffic lights, but you need to have them for the traffic to go smoothly for everybody. So you need a Censor Board for your society to go smoothly. Let them [the populace] develop themselves, if they want to develop their tastes, values, or change of fashions, let them change it and cinema will present and the Censor Board will also accept it. (Interview)

Unlike Azmi, who viewed censorship as a method or instrument to bring about social change, Ghai argued that censorship practices respond to social change—once society changes, then censorship norms can change. Ghai's statements present censorship as a quasi-Durkheimian institution necessary for the trouble-free functioning of society. Ghai's traffic police are the ones who will keep Vaswani's emotional hordes in check.

Ghai acknowledged that categories such as "obscenity" are not absolute and that they are shaped by cultural norms and expectations. But he also asserted a rather broad definition of obscenity and endorsed the existence of the Censor Board:

> You see, obscenity, when you define obscenity, it is very much relative to the aesthetic sense of the society. What is obscene for you may not be obscene for me. Like going into beaches with the swimming costume is quite obscene to the rural people of India. But it is a very healthy kind of thing in a Western country to go into beaches with swimming costumes. But then, if it is offensive to the mind of the people, then it is obscene, that's how I define it. So the Censor Board does its job, okay, and it should be there and I don't agree with those people who say there should be no Censor Board. (Interview)

The perspectives presented thus far explicitly articulate film as a tremendously powerful medium and coincide with the Indian state's discourses about socio-economic development and media influence. The focus of this particular strand of discourse surrounding censorship is upon the vulnerable, emotional, backward, and immature audience—the objects of censorship—who need to be shielded from stirring, provocative, or titillating images.

Other filmmakers were more conflicted about their support for censorship. I would like to conclude this section by discussing comments on censorship from Ramesh Sippy, the director of *Sholay,* one of the most significant and successful films in Hindi cinema. During our interview, he discussed censorship and its role in India at great length. Sippy described what he felt were the two sides of the debate about censorship, and in the process articulated the ambivalence that typifies many Hindi filmmakers' attitudes about censorship. In response to my question about whether censorship was necessary, Sippy said,

> There's always a hue and cry in this country about censorship. On the one hand, I don't think I would ever like to be a censor, on the board of the censors. The industry is always up in arms that they're overdoing their role, and there are critics who very strongly feel that they're not playing their role as strongly as required. I don't know, maybe that's healthy. If you go into an overdrive on censorship, you'll be curbing any creativity, there's no question about it. On the other hand, if you give a total free hand, do we have a society mature enough to handle the kind of material that may be doled out in a totally free atmosphere? (Interview)

Unlike the other filmmakers quoted thus far, Sippy raises the issue of freedom of expression, but still locates it within a developmentalist paradigm when he questions the maturity of Indian society and expresses anxiety about the impact of freely circulating images.

However, Sippy answered his own question by locating censorship within the context of social change:

Personally I feel it's a constant change, and therefore one should view it with society's present view of things, ever-changing present view, it's always a changing view. I get these kinds of things when I go either for a chat show or a something else with people saying that "Oh, in the old days, the films were so nice and neat and clean and all that," but then in the old days the role of the woman was locked in the house; she was locked up in the house; do you think those days should come back? No, they shouldn't. You have the freedom today, you're sitting here and talking, isn't that a wonderful thing today that you're able to do this? So that's part of the freedom movement, so you must not curb what is happening. Yes, when it is in excess, criticism is important. (Interview)

In addition to criticizing unexamined nostalgia for older films, Sippy locates changing norms of censorship within changing norms of gender roles and relations. He draws a correlation between freedom of expression and greater social freedom for women. However, Sippy seems to imply that greater freedom for women can lead to some form of excess within cinema. In his next comments, it becomes clear that the "excess" refers to sex and violence, but Sippy posits the audience, via the medium of the box office, as the ultimate censor:

Ultimately, the audience themselves reject what is in excess and we have seen it time and again, an excess of sex and violence films have failed miserably at the box office. You will never find examples of sex and violence encouraging films to run. Because an action film will have action in it, you cannot prevent action, it's got to be an action film. But whenever it's in excess, people reject it—both sex and violence. (Interview)

Sippy went on to lay out the two sides of the censorship debate in India:

When we have gone the democratic way, I think it would be wrong to start curbing anything—there is no censorship on books, there is no censorship in art or painting, now just to say that because the mass of audience does not see all that, and therefore a mass media should have censorship, is not fair. But one can still understand the point that one cannot allow it to go berserk either. (Interview)

While Sippy acknowledges the apparent contradiction of state censorship in a democracy, seemingly criticizing the singling out of cinema as compared to print and other visual forms, he returns again to the anxiety about unconstrained media circulation. He offered an expanded list of ratings categories as a potential solution to the extremes of absolute freedom and censorship:

Therefore, of course, on the one hand you could have a grading in censorship like they have in the West, a much wider grading—you have from a very general audience, universal audience, to certificates of 12 years old, 15 years old, 18 years old, and X-rated films. Again, for this, unfortunately, you need a more educated audience. That's why I said as awareness comes in, these things will change. I think awareness should grow; people should be more exposed to, rather than kept away from, aspects of life, which gives them an opportunity to build their own thinking process. (Interview)

The paternalist and developmentalist attitudes toward audiences present in previous filmmakers' statements are present in Sippy's comments as well. Since, according to Sippy, the majority of audiences in India are uneducated or poorly educated, an elaborated system of ratings would not succeed in guiding and disciplining viewers. However, Sippy predicts that audiences will eventually become more aware and enlightened.

Part of the reason for audiences' poor power of discrimination (aside from a lack of formal education), according to Sippy, has been the generally repressed nature of Indian society. He asserted,

> *Because we've lived in a society which is very isolated and sort of kept in wraps, you find a lot of issues never discussed. Is that building a healthy society? In my opinion, no. On the other hand, aping the West or going entirely the other way is not necessarily the best alternative. Being overclothed is as foolish as being unclothed. You can't say that on the other hand, if you have freedom, you go around naked; no, that's not correct. That's equally wrong.* (Interview)

What is remarkable is how a discussion of film censorship developed into a discussion about the West and India's relationship to this vague, broadly conceived entity. Discussions about censorship were frequently organized around comparisons between India and the U.S. or Indian cinema and Hollywood, a point that I will discuss later in relation to the system of film ratings.

That Sippy used "clothed" and "naked" as metonyms for India and the West, as well as a metaphor for the tension between censorship and free expression, also points to how the discourse about censorship by mainstream Hindi filmmakers is primarily structured around the representation of bodies, sexuality, and sexual behavior. However, examining the statements presented thus far, what is striking are the oblique rather than explicit references to nudity and sexual behavior: from Aamir Khan's statement "In entertaining people it does not mean that you start removing your pants on screen" to Subhash Ghai's invocation of "swimming costumes" and B. R. Chopra's reference to "bedroom scenes," Hindi filmmakers allude to the object of censorship rather than addressing it directly. Such allusions are a part of the discourse around "vulgarity" that is central to Hindi filmmakers' relationship to censorship, which I will discuss further in the following section. I also examine the perspectives of filmmakers who are critical of film censorship and reveal that their criticisms are based much less on a right to free speech or expression and more on the redundancy of the practice. Rather than being concerned for a vulnerable audience, this strand of discourse emphasizes the filmmaker as a morally upright and respectable subject.

Regulating the Self

A small number of filmmakers I spoke to did criticize censorship, but not because they felt that it impinged upon their rights as citizens in a democracy. Rather, they felt it was either redundant, because of their own ethical or moral sensibilities, or irrelevant, because of the altered media landscape of the late 1990s. Shahrukh Khan, one of the biggest stars of Hindi cinema since the mid-1990s, discussed how he, as an actor, already operated with a set of internal checks and boundaries that he characterized as "self-censorship," thereby implying the redundancy of state censorship. He stated,

> *I really can't comment on what I think about the censorship in India, because when I do a film, I work like six months or eight months, and I would love every shot to be in the film. I personally disagree with certain aspects of Hindi films. As an actor, there's a self-censorship—that I'll not do these roles. Some of them include certain things that other actors would do, but I don't do. I don't kiss my heroines, I don't try to—I've got some standards of vulgarity. . . . I don't do certain kinds of films. Mainly because I don't even understand them. I don't do absolutely senseless films. . . . There are certain things in films that I would not do, which I personally feel are undesirable. A lot of my censorship is actually geared toward the fact that when my children see this film ten years from now,[15] they should not, I should be able to see it with them, without having to give an excuse why I did it: ki, "Look, I had to do this for money, son." I don't want to give them any excuses for that. So I have that kind of self-censorship, and then you find your own level. I choose the kind of directors who think alike.* (Interview)

Khan's comments can also be interpreted as a way of asserting distinction and difference within the film industry—that with his standards and his choices among films and directors, he does not represent the norm within the industry, the filmmakers who need state censorship. Khan continued his discussion of censorship by noting that viewers can opt not to see a film as well as shifting the burden of responsibility for film choices onto them and the state. He asserted,

> *If the censors have passed a film, we are not forcing you to go and see the film. You want to go see it, see it. You don't want to see, don't see it. My logic is very simple. Some people tell me, "Shahrukh, that film was so violent, how can you do it?" I said, "With an Adult certificate, why did you take your kid for it?" "Ramjaane is so violent my kid got so scared!" "So why did you take him there? It was adults!" So he says, "No, but you know, they get access." That's not my problem. That's not my problem if they get access, then the government has to look after access. They say it is a bad impression on children. They give an A certificate; then why do they let kids get into it? They should have better ways of pulling them back.* (Interview)

Khan criticized the paternalist ideology behind film censorship, drawing an unusual analogy between film-viewing and footwear:

> *I think as long as we take ourselves too seriously about entertainment, we're going to have these problems. There will be always somebody who is not going to be happy. You can't please everybody. . . . I mean, it's not even coming on TV [so] that you have to see it. Even if it's on TV, switch it off. It's your control. I'm*

sure, if I had a kid and I didn't want him to see something, I'd tell him, and hopefully he'll listen to me. If he doesn't, then my upbringing of the kid is wrong; I can't complain that the film is wrong. It's like, instead of covering your own feet with shoes, so that dust doesn't get onto your feet, you cover the whole world with leather. I think the logic is that you cover your own feet with shoes, and take it from there. Please don't try to cover the rest of the world. The world is going to be there; how many things are you going to stop? Are you going to stop the bombings? Are you going to stop killings? They are as vulgar and obscene as naked women. We're free to do what we do, and nobody is forced to see us, if they don't wish to. (Interview)

The agency accorded to viewers in Khan's comments stands in stark contrast to the vulnerability, sensitivity, and infantilism ascribed to them in the previous section. But, although he derides the practice of censorship, Khan still expresses a concern with vulgarity.

Like Khan, producer Mukesh Bhatt discussed censorship in terms of redundancy and an internalized check on vulgarity as well. He asserted,

As a producer, see, when I think of making a project, a film, one thing I'm very conscious about is that I don't want to make any film which is embarrassing, in terms of vulgarity. I would not like to make a film which I cannot see with my mother or my wife, or my sister or my daughter. But, at the same time, I see that's why I say censorship is inside me, so I don't need an outside guy to faff around! And meddle with my film! (Interview)

What is apparent in both Khan's and Bhatt's statements is that the category of vulgarity is integrally connected to the social context of reception and the social relations of viewing. Vulgarity refers to images and dialogue that would be difficult or inappropriate to view and hear in an intergenerational or mixed-sex setting. Most often, it means expletives and double entendres in dialogue, a fetishistic display of scantily clad women's bodies, and sexually suggestive dance movements in song sequences. Vulgarity is explicitly mentioned in one of the Censor Board's twenty-two guidelines; number seven states, "Human sensibilities are not offended by vulgarity, obscenity or depravity" (Ministry of Information and Broadcasting [MIB] 1992).

However, Dalip Tahil, a stage and screen actor, argued that the censors' practice of mandating cuts in films actually increased rather than reduced their level of vulgarity. He exclaimed,

They try to cut up a film, and when they cut it up it makes no sense to the audience. Basically the essence of the violence is there. They're saying, "Oh, cut this here, don't say this, don't say that!" They cut a particular point so that they have their formality of having done their job, but they have not served any purpose, because they have not taken all the violence out of their film, they have not taken all the sex out of that film. It is worse to have implied vulgarity and double entendre in terms of words that sound cheap and vulgar, rather than have proper sex if it has to be shown, between a man and a woman. I mean, you see, censors have also been involved in trying to convolute the public's mind. They have these jhatkas [gyrations] and you have these double entendres. That's what degrades you. It is less degrading to show sex than to have all this stuff that the censors jump onto. (Interview)

Unlike Tahil, who held the practice of censorship responsible for the "degrading" nature of Hindi films, director Mansoor Khan pointed out that he could empathize with the censors, given the vast number of films that they had to see, especially ones that he characterized as "crass," which involved gratuitous dance sequences made by filmmakers who lacked "finesse." Khan explained,

You see, sometimes I can see the good intentions of the censors, you know? I mean, they see all these crass films with phenomenal pelvic movements, for no good reason! I mean, you can have it if it's an art form, but you don't do it in the middle of the square like that. . . . See, there's no finesse in what they're doing. You can have anything, but you must know how you're doing it or what. So I can see where the censors are getting frustrated, trying to pin down and saying, "No, not this, but this." So they come up with a ridiculously hard-line thing like "No close-up shots of these parts," whereas you may need a close-up shot of that part because that's part of your suspense, you know? I mean, that freedom should be given to the director. If he really knows what he's doing . . . so that gets very difficult. (Interview)

Khan distinguishes between directors who know their craft and those who do not, suggesting that censorship is only necessary for the latter, but acknowledging the reality of the system, in which even the good and tasteful filmmakers bear the burden of absurd censorship policies. Like Shahrukh Khan, Mansoor Khan represented himself as different from the norm within the film industry. "I've been lucky because I've selected subjects where I've never had to enter these controversial things. Either national-wise, communal-wise, you know, or sex-wise. Or violence-wise" (interview).

While Mansoor Khan posited crass, vulgar filmmakers as the source of the film industry's problems with the censors, Mukesh Bhatt argued that the average age of the members of the Censor Board and its examining committees was the main problem. As they were much older than the average filmgoer, censors were not in tune with contemporary social trends or filmmaking. He stated vehemently,

Some senile old fifty-five-year-old . . . You can't keep them in the censor board, sorry. You have to have people of today! To judge films of today . . . you can't have people of yesterday to judge films of today. Like tomorrow, after twenty years, I cannot judge my son's film! When he grows up and is 25 or 26, and I'm 55 or 60, the whole vision of the man is going to be different! The world is going to be different! So we have to grow with the world! . . . We are going into the space age, you can't talk about bullock carts! When you're making progression in terms of social taboos like sati and all that . . . and not having those ghoonghats, there's nothing wrong, the ghoonghat is out. . . . My daughter roams in jeans . . . tomorrow my daughter-in-law will roam in jeans in front of me and there's nothing wrong in it! What are you holding on to that sari for? What nonsense! . . . As long as she doesn't wear clothes which are very embarrassing to society, she wears jeans or she wears salwar kameez, it's beautiful! So I feel you should grow with the times. And that's not happening. (Interview)

Like Ramesh Sippy in the previous section, Bhatt asserts links between gender, social change, and censorship. Clothing is once again articulated as an index of tradition, social change, propriety, and ideal behavior by kin.

While Shahrukh Khan and Mukesh Bhatt saw censorship as redundant, others in the film industry saw it as irrelevant. Many filmmakers asserted that censorship was pointless because of the vastly altered media landscape of post-liberalization India. In 1991, structural adjustment policies mandated by the IMF set the stage for the entry of satellite television by reducing red tape and providing more incentives for multinational companies to set up their operations in India. Satellite broadcasting radically changed the nature of Indian television.[16] In 1992, Indian viewers had only the single-channel state broadcasting network; now they can choose from among ten to fifty channels, depending on the cable operator. The presence of foreign programming via satellite television meant that audiences could view images on television that might have been prohibited in the cinema hall. This irony did not go unnoticed by members of the film industry. Actor Dalip Tahil asserted,

I think censorship is completely redundant. Today, from any point of view, I mean I just cannot understand why you need to have this school teacher ma'am kind of attitude. . . . Why should you go sit and moralize, "You shouldn't see this; you shouldn't see nudity." Hey! I mean, everybody is seeing it on television; you're making a joke of it; you're making a fool of yourself as a censor board. You want to censor feature films, but you can't censor television. You can't censor what the public is seeing. There's satellite, and in the age of satellite, if you want to see a nudie porno film, you can see it at home in the evening today—in any major metro. I mean, outright, a sexual film—the act. So what are you hiding? Violence? You want to see violence? I mean, you call Indian movies violent? They're caricatures compared to what people see on television. I mean, that's like, solid, hundred-million-dollar-backed violence, which really looks like complete violence! (Interview)

Actor Sanjay Dutt characterized film censorship in the era of satellite television as "hypocrisy," and exclaimed,

See, I'll tell you, censorship is a piece of crap, it's bullshit, according to me. On TV today you're seeing everything. Everybody's house has got a cable and everybody is seeing the satellites, and we're advancing . . . you know, it's '96! And yet you have a Censor Board. What is this, it's hypocrisy again: "Picture mein voh kaat do, bahut lambha khoon ka shot hai!" [*Cut that out of the picture—that is a very long shot of the blood!*] *But you're showing BBC, you're showing hundreds of people dying in Bosnia every day, or in Lebanon. But out here . . . "Voh kya hai, voh kamar se kuch zyaada pakad liya, voh thoda kum kardijiye."* [*What's this? He's grabbed her waist for too long, please reduce it some.*] *Arrey! you're seeing MTV and Channel V and all that shit. Basically it's hypocrisy.* (Interview)

Both Tahil's and Dutt's criticisms are less concerned with the principle of censorship and more with the efficient execution of it. They do not see the point of censoring films when audiences are faced with a televisual onslaught of previously taboo images. However, it is unclear whether either actor thought that censorship had been relevant and effective prior to the arrival of satellite television. Of course, their arguments could just as easily support censoring satellite television.[17]

Dutt and Tahil both considered the U.S. system of film ratings a more suitable option than the current censorship regime. Unlike Ramesh Sippy, who felt that Indian audiences as a whole were not prepared for such a ratings system, Tahil discussed ratings specifically in terms of parents, children, and responsible choices:

> *You write there, "For the parents," "Parental Guidance required," "Suitable for the age of 12 and over," "Suitable for 18 and over," "Suitable for nobody, 80 and over." [laughs] . . . You categorize it, then the choice is up to people, parents and people to go and show their children what they have to show. Say it in Hindi, "Ke isme phalana phalana hai, maar peeth hai, sex hai. Chote bache ke liye accha nahi hai, mat dikhao." [This film has this and that—violence, sex; it is not good for young children, don't show it to them.] You tell parents that in every language in the country, and parents will take their own decision. Parents the world over are the same. I can't think of any mother or father who will say, "Come, six-year-old child, I want to show you gore and murder and complete sex." Who's going to show that to their kid? Nobody is!* (Interview)

Since ratings do exist in India—U, UA, and A, albeit two fewer than the G, PG, PG-13, R, and NC-17 assigned by the Motion Picture Association of America (MPAA)[18]—it becomes apparent that what Tahil and Dutt are objecting to is the bureaucratization and paternalism inherent in the Indian censorship process, in which a group of reviewers located in structural opposition to the film industry mandates changes and deletions in films. The paternalism of mandating cuts to a film that is issued an A or adults-only rating was criticized heavily by many filmmakers as well as some members of the Censor Board (see below).

When I asked Dutt whether he thought a time would come when the state did not involve itself in censoring films, he replied in the negative, as he did not believe that the Censor Board would give up its power so easily. He also characterized the censors as cinematically illiterate and drew analogies between filmmaking and other professions.

> *See, I'll tell you, I feel one thing: when somebody has power in their hands, he can't let go of that power. Censor Board has power, basically. Why should they let it go? People have to stand there and ask, "Pass kar do yey picture" [Please pass this picture]. And I want to say one thing is that on the Censor Board, you have people like doctors and social workers and this one and that one, who don't know a shit about our films, trying to tell us what to do. Would they like it if the doctor, if I come and say, "Why are you making an incision on the stomach, you make one on the face?" Or "You made a six-inch, make it an eight-inch incision"? He'll kill me! I mean, the Censor Board should be within the family, there should be people from the industry, producers, directors, actors, who should sit on the board and okay, fine, it is fair enough then. I'm also not saying let the hero take his pants off and show his ass. I can understand that stuff.* (Interview)

Notice that Dutt never actually endorses a censor-free scenario, but simply one where filmmakers participate in the process. Like other members of the film industry quoted in the previous section, Dutt also identifies nudity as the line he draws in the sand delimiting acceptable images. What is interesting is that despite the participation of members of the Hindi film industry in the censorship process—the chair of the Censor Board in 1996 was veteran producer-director Shakti Samantha[19]—Dutt constructs a completely oppositional relationship between filmmakers and censors.

However, the relationship between filmmakers and censors is more complex than Dutt describes it as. During my interview with Pamela Chopra, the wife of Yash Chopra—one of the most successful producers and directors in the contemporary industry—she revealed that she was on the Censor Board herself. We were talking about Shekar Kapur's film *Bandit Queen* about the dacoit Phoolan Devi, which had been mired in controversy for its expletive-filled dialogue and a scene of full frontal female nudity. Released on January 28, 1996, it was banned by the Delhi High Court on March 8 after a member of the Gujjar caste filed a lawsuit against the film and its makers, arguing that it defamed his community. The Supreme Court lifted the ban on May 2, 1996. Though Chopra indicated that she was not particularly impressed with the film, she did not approve of the obstacles the film faced in order to be released. She then began talking about censorship in a more general vein:

> *I'm on the Censor Board myself, but I don't agree with the censor guidelines in any way. I think they are really stupid. I mean, if you made a film for adults, once you put an "Adults" certificate on it, then you have no right to cut anything from it then. It's stupid. Who are you trying to protect? Are you trying to say that a 21-year-old, or an 18-year-old man or a woman, are not old enough to be able to accept all that is implied in a film? If he's old enough to vote, and decide who's going to govern them, then they jolly well have the right to decide what they can and they want to see. It's so silly!* (Interview)

While Chopra's analogy between electoral democracy and film-viewing appears as a familiar trope in mainstream Indian media discourses about film censorship, it was not commonly articulated amongst the filmmakers I spoke to, who, if critical of state censorship, criticized it as ineffective, irrelevant, or redundant.

During the first months of my fieldwork in 1996, *Bandit Queen* was mentioned frequently during discussions about censorship as an example of a film in which the subject matter and the dictates of realism necessitated language and visuals that would normally never be heard or seen in a Hindi film. Many of the filmmakers I spoke to praised the film for its authenticity and decried the ordeal that Shekhar Kapur underwent with the Censor Board to release the film. However, some filmmakers qualified their criticism of the Censor Board by stating that the release of *Bandit Queen* set a precedent that could be troublesome, inviting copycats or providing justification for filmmakers with less than noble intentions. Screenwriter Honey Irani (who turned director in 2002) described her attitudes toward censorship, specifically citing the case of *Bandit Queen*:

> *I definitely think that censorship is there for a certain amount of things. Vulgarity shouldn't be shown, or this shouldn't be shown, or that shouldn't be shown, but the thing is that a film like* Bandit Queen, *now that whole film needs that, okay? I also understand the trauma of the censorship people, because they are not against* Bandit Queen, *they are against the other* Bandit Queens *that will be made. So I can see their trauma also, ki, okay you're right, because then the producer will say, ki, "If you can pass* Bandit Queen, *what is wrong with my film bhai?" Every filmmaker feels that he's made a great film, so he can get away with murder! So you have to draw a line somewhere. . . . I'm all out for Shekhar Kapur, but unfortunately, yes, I'm also worried about those directors and producers who'll get carried away.* (Interview)

Her anxiety about filmmakers who would get "carried away" demonstrates how much of the discourse about censorship presented in this section is centrally concerned with the subjectivities, sensibilities, and conduct of filmmakers rather than audiences, as it was in the previous section. The filmmakers who criticize state censorship have a Foucauldian notion of governmentality (1991), seeing it in terms of "the conduct of conduct" and self-regulation. A significant feature of their discourse is the figure of an undisciplined, errant filmmaker who is unable to censor or regulate himself. In the following section, I discuss how Hindi filmmakers represent the film industry as a whole as an errant, libidinal institution that is incapable of self-regulation.

Regulating the Industry

Many Indian filmmakers identified the American system of detailed ratings as a model to be emulated. But when I asked them if the Hindi film industry could regulate itself like the American one, most said it could not. Whether the filmmakers were in favor of or critical of censorship, they were unified in their skepticism that the industry could restrict its own representation of sex and violence. The main differences articulated between the two positions had to do with how the industry was represented as a whole and which institution was the more effective regulatory mechanism—the state or the market.

Aditya Chopra, Yash and Pamela Chopra's son, directed the 1995 box-office blockbuster *Dilwale Dulhaniye Le Jayenge* (The One with a True Heart Takes the Bride) and is one of the most commercially savvy and successful producers in the Bombay industry. He was very conflicted about the issue of censorship. He said,

> I feel self-censorship is the best form of censorship, but then I feel there will always be people who will take advantage of it. You don't know, actually, if it will work, because, you see, it's the best if everyone thinks correctly, if everyone thinks positively, if everyone has this social obligation to the audience, then there's no better form. But I don't know, I don't know if it's bound to work here. Because nobody really works together, nobody comes together, they all think separately, and they all have their own personal biases, personal thoughts. I don't, I don't know, I'm confused about this issue of censorship as to how it should work, how it should . . . I don't know, I really don't know. (Interview)

Chopra points out the discrepancy between the ideal and the real: self-censorship is the ideal in his view, but he acknowledges that it is only possible if every filmmaker is aware of his social responsibility to the audience. The reality, according to Chopra, is that filmmakers are not a unified community and they do not think about their social obligations. The implication is that some sort of neutral, outside body is required to regulate the film industry.

Another important observation regarding the nature of the film industry was made by Punkej Kharabanda, who at the time of my fieldwork was Sanjay Dutt's manager. He stated bluntly, "The film industry will never be able to censor itself, that much I can assure you, because there's so much rivalry, so much of infighting, that they would always try and screw the other person's film. It's not a very united industry that way" (interview).

While Chopra and Kharabanda said that the film industry was unable to regulate and censor itself because of its disunity and competitiveness, other filmmakers blamed its lack of self-control, self-discipline, and maturity. When I asked Aamir Khan whether it would be possible for the industry to regulate itself, as happens in the U.S., he retorted,

> Right now no, I don't think that we are that balanced a society to apply self-censorship to ourselves. I think most of us would just end up exploiting that. So I don't think we are ready for self-censorship yet. First we have to improve as human beings and then maybe we can do that. (Interview)

Shabana Azmi, in response to my question about whether an American style of ratings and self-censorship would be preferable, replied with some skepticism,

> If the film industry shows that kind of responsibility, which it hasn't shown so far, if the film industry gets up together, lobbies and creates that kind of responsibility, then of course that's the best form of censorship, absolutely. (Interview)

Subhash Ghai, however, argued that without state censorship, filmmakers would go "berserk." He asserted unequivocally, "There has to be a law, and implementation of the law. There has to be, otherwise we will make pornos, nothing else. The people will go berserk" (interview).

These assertions that filmmakers are not capable of regulating themselves point to the main source of anxiety about a censor-free scenario, which is other filmmakers. Sachin Bhaumick, a top screenwriter who has worked in the industry for the last forty years, argued the need for state censorship by describing the majority of filmmakers as opportunistic, money-obsessed men:

> Censorship in India is absolutely necessary. Really, if there's no censorship, this country can go to [the] dogs. There are mainly do-number ke aadmi [unscrupulous men] who put money into pictures to make their black money white. Not all, there are good producers, but there are a lot of bad producers who want lots of vulgarity to run their pictures. And so that is one thing, if there is no control, it will be very ridiculous. There should be control in India. Democracy doesn't mean that you can do anything. There is no Censor Board in Hollywood, there is no government rule, they have their own style of censoring, they give ratings. Here it is better that government should be censoring, otherwise it would be difficult, because 50 percent of the people are crooked, do-number ke aadmi, who are making pictures. They've got illegal money. They want to put in films, thinking if you put in films, you'll get two—three heroines also in your bed, with that type of thinking they come to the film industry. So they don't understand culture, they don't understand anything, they just want to make money. (Interview)

Bhaumick made more explicit what other filmmakers were hinting toward in their discussions of censorship. State censorship is not just a way of protecting audiences from unscrupulous filmmakers, but also a way of protecting the Hindi film industry's image by keeping out disreputable operators. As the Bombay film industry is frequently associated with the criminal underworld, promiscuity, and illicit activities like tax evasion and money laundering, many of its members go to great effort to prove their respectability, legitimacy, education, and morality as defined by Indian middle-class standards (Ganti 2000). And their anxiety about other filmmakers is in the end also an anxiety about the market—a fear that audiences, if left to their own devices, would choose to indulge their prurient tastes in cinema.

However, some filmmakers expressed very little anxiety about audiences and the market, arguing instead that the market would do a better job than the censors in filtering out undesirable films. Dalip Tahil also argued that the film industry could not censor itself, stating that filmmakers would make films showing what the "public wants to see." However, he did not advocate state regulation either, but expressed faith in ratings, audiences, and norms of respectability to keep sexual imagery in its place at the margins of society. Tahil reasoned,

> You do your rating. I'm telling you, look, there are sex films being made. See, society has its own controls. You'll never ever, unfortunately or fortunately, you'll

never gain respect being a filmmaker if you make XXX-rated films. . . . There is a bunch of people who want to watch it. What are you going to do about it? I mean there are people who want to watch sex films, and it is made for that market. There are people . . . you have red-light areas, and there are colonies of prostitutes and sex areas in Bombay, who knew about that? This is, it's a choice. You don't want to see it, you don't see it. But it's being made for people who want to see it. [pause] Don't give it a theatrical release, but if you give it a theatrical release, you say okay, there are certain ways you can restrict viewership in terms of certain really bad theaters, but you have the video circuit, so by and large I don't believe in it, I don't think the censors really serve a purpose. (Interview)

Mansoor Khan argued that the industry was incapable of regulating itself, but that audiences, and by extension market forces, were valuable mechanisms to curb the excesses of the film industry. He stated,

See, the industry right now, if you look at it, by and large is only concerned with success. If the industry were to regulate itself, look at it! Okay . . . let's talk about the industry. When all this crass dancing started, what I am trying to say is, when you look at the old films, it used to be so exciting to watch, but it was not crass, it was not vulgar! It was so energetic. So you can have that, you know. You've got to work hard at that, you know, and you've got to be doing it without an ulterior motive. You can make people excited by energetic dancing. You don't have to be vulgar. But it is definitely out of lack of thought, and lack of preparation that everybody was doing the same thing. So the industry never censored themselves, they never said, "Let's stop it!" It's only when there was a revolt from the audiences, and then when a film like Hum Aapke Hain Koun![20] *worked, then they said, "Oh shit!" Something happened, so it was not their own thinking which was working. It was some feedback, and somewhere, a public opinion was formed, and the producer said, "Okay, we shouldn't do it," and they started backing away and that was a form of censorship.* (Interview)

Khan's statements invert some of the arguments made by filmmakers in a developmentalist vein. While the rationale offered for censorship is that it will protect audiences from harmful, disturbing, or titillating images, here Khan posits audiences as the saviors of filmmakers, in that they rein in or curb the filmmakers' excesses.

That filmmakers cannot regulate themselves and their peers is an ironic assertion, since the process of making commercial cinema, as I have discussed elsewhere, involves a great deal of self-censorship (Ganti 2000). There is an important distinction, however, between formal censorship and creative decision making. Censorship is concerned with effects on the audience and is motivated by a paternalist discourse; it constructs audience taste and desire as things to be surmounted and disciplined. But aesthetic, narrative, and other creative decisions made in producing a film construct audience taste as providing the foundation and reason for those decisions (Ganti 2002). Members of the Bombay film industry are therefore constantly negotiating between these two poles in the course of making films.

Eliciting Hindi filmmakers' attitudes regarding state censorship and possible alternatives to it yields information and insights into the self-representation of the Bombay film industry—as a licentious, libidinal, unruly social world. However, the typicality of this social world is an abstraction, since each filmmaker asserts an individual identity and sensibility, distinct from what she or he considers the norm. All the industry members I met represented themselves as more responsible, respectable, educated, cultured, and professional than the "typical" Hindi filmmaker. Therefore, even if individual filmmakers believed that they themselves did not require state regulation or censorship, they maintained that the industry as a whole did, because of those "other" filmmakers who had neither the capacity nor the desire for self-regulation.

x x x

I have discussed how much of the Bombay film industry's discussion of state censorship is couched in a developmentalist idiom according to which audiences, Indian society, and even the film industry are not sufficiently developed to do without censorship. A clear evolutionary logic undergirds filmmakers' discussions of censorship; the existence or absence of censorship is integrally connected to how mature or "developed" a society is. Even those who disagree with the practice of state censorship still endorse the idea of limits and boundaries. For filmmakers, self-restraint, self-control, and self-discipline are crucial elements of modernity, a state which they are striving for but which, in their view, neither the film industry nor their audiences have yet fully achieved. Both the Indian state's rationale for continuing censorship and filmmakers' overt or tacit support for the practice reveals how censorship is about the fashioning of selves and the creation of rational, modern subjects. Therefore, the discussions and debates about film censorship are significantly debates over citizenship, the expectations of the state, and the nature of modernity in contemporary India.

However, the practice and discussion of film censorship in India concerns questions not only of citizenship and subjectivity, but also of the constitution, mediation, and regulation of social relations: between parents and children, men and women, filmmakers and audiences, filmmakers and the state, and filmmakers and their peers. Discussion about film ratings and vulgarity is crucially about gender relations, intergenerational interactions, and norms of propriety. The paternalism that filmmakers express toward their audiences recasts an economic exchange (seeing a film) into a social one, so that filmmakers articulate a responsibility not to offend or corrupt the moral sensibilities of their audiences. Filmmakers' criticism of the ambiguity of censorship guidelines and their erratic application is a call for consistent and equitable treatment by the state. The contention that the film industry cannot censor itself is a commentary on working and social relationships within the industry, a claim that jealousy, competition, and partiality would impede any attempt at reform.

Thus the debates and discussion about censorship are not merely restricted to questions of artistic freedom and the ideology of free, rational subjects, but more importantly are about mediation as a constitutive process in social life (Mazzarella 2004, 345).

Epilogue

Given that the interviews quoted here were done in 1996, readers may wonder what sort of changes have occurred in the censorship regime as well as in film-makers' attitudes toward the practice. In an interview with director Vikram Bhatt in 2006 in New York, I asked him about his views on censorship. His perspective was not very different from those I had heard ten years before: he felt that some form of censorship was necessary and advocated a consistent system of ratings, with filmmakers in charge of editing their own films to fit the parameters of a particular rating. The Censor Board's role would be to rate the films but not to ask for specific cuts, since, in Bhatt's words, "Sometimes you can change the entire meaning of a film by taking some things out. . . . What is unimportant to the Censor Board may be very important to the maker, because that's why he has it in the first place" (interview). Bhatt also felt that the censors had become much more lenient than in the past, but that guidelines were still too often inconsistently or idiosyncratically applied. He stated,

> People are more liberal, but you're still dependent on how liberal or not liberal is the person viewing the film. And how can five people from different walks of life decide for the entire nation? Because everybody has their own moral paradigms, parameters. I might find something okay; you might find something not okay. So does a film's fate depend on who comes to see it on that day? I think it's a very faulty system of censoring a film. (Interview)

While filmmakers are critical of this system of censoring, the Censor Board has sometimes recently seemed more predictable and systematic than the general public. Since May 2006, when controversies erupted in India surrounding the release of the Hindi film *Fanaa* (Destroyed in Love) and the Hollywood film *The Da Vinci Code*, filmmakers have been discussing in the mainstream and trade press the problem of "super censorship." Super censorship refers to efforts by organized nongovernmental groups to prevent films that the Censor Board has approved from being shown in theaters. Frequently the protests have to do with the content of the film; in the case of *The Da Vinci Code*, Christian groups in India argued that the film was blasphemous and offensive to Christians and demanded that it not be released.[21] However, in the case of *Fanaa*, the contro-versy was unconnected to the film's content. Rather, political groups in Gujarat were outraged that the lead actor in the film, Aamir Khan, had expressed solidar-ity with groups protesting the construction of the Narmada Dam and told the media that those displaced by the dam must be rehoused. Members and officials of the Bharatiya Janata Party (Indian People's Party) called Khan anti-Gujarati and antidevelopment and threatened violence at showings of *Fanaa*, and therefore both exhibitors and distributors chose not to release the film in Gujarat.[22] *Parzania*, a 2005 film about the anti-Muslim riots and violence that engulfed Gujarat in 2002 after the Godhra incident, was also not released in Gujarat because exhibitors feared reprisals by BJP and Bajrang Dal activists.

That films in recent times have sparked controversy after being cleared by the censors is a point of continual frustration and anxiety for filmmakers, since censorship is supposed to prevent such imbroglios. Censors are supposed to be the mediators between the film industry and the public. In current discussions about super censorship, the Censor Board's certificate becomes a shield, an index of propriety, and a legal position with which to fend off the unpredictable and potentially hysterical public. Rather than calling into question the edifice of film censorship, the recent controversies appear to be validating the entire apparatus. They seem to reinforce the state's and filmmakers' belief that audiences in India are ultrasensitive, emotional, and not quite developed. Such controversies also reinforce the state's belief in the importance of censorship, and the film industry's belief in that of the Censor Board. Since February 2007, various industry groups have been decrying the practice of banning or disrupting film screenings and have been calling upon the Censor Board to protect the exhibition of films that it has certified. It is tremendously ironic that an institution which at its core is a form of restriction and regulation is now being called on to defend the unfettered circulation of films.

Notes

Fieldwork upon which this article is based was made possible by an American Institute of Indian Studies Junior Fellowship in 1996. I would like to thank all of the people in Bombay who were so generous with their time and helped make my research possible. Additionally, I am very grateful to the following people whose interviews and conversations made this article possible: Shabana Azmi, Mukesh Bhatt, Vikram Bhatt, Sachin Bhaumick, Aditya Chopra, B. R. Chopra, Pamela Chopra, Madhuri Dixit, Sanjay Dutt, Subhash Ghai, Sutanu Gupta, Honey Irani, Aamir Khan, Mansoor Khan, Shahrukh Khan, Kiran Khanna, Punkej Kharabanda, Hrishikesh Mukherjee, Ramesh Sippy, Dalip Tahil, and Viveck Vaswani. I would also like to thank Vipul Agrawal, Raminder Kaur, William Mazzarella, and Srirupa Roy for their comments and feedback on various drafts of this article, as well as expressing my tremendous gratitude for Raminder Kaur's and William Mazzarella's endless patience and understanding! An earlier version of this article was presented at the 101st annual meeting of the American Anthropological Association in 2002.

　　1. Encouraged by promises from the Minister of Information and Broadcasting that the system needed to be and would be reformed, Anand conducted a review of the process, anticipating that Parliament would pass a new cinematograph act. During his

brief tenure, he researched the censorship practices of a variety of Western countries and traveled to all of the major filmmaking centers in India, soliciting opinions and suggestions about the censorship process from officials in the nine regional censor boards.

2. These recommendations included fiscal autonomy for the Censor Board, doing away with political appointees, ensuring that half the board was aged between 20 and 25, and rating rather than censoring films: classifying them as "universal," "adult," or "parental guidance necessary" rather than mandating cuts. Currently the board both assigns ratings and mandates cuts, even to films given an A rating, which are ostensibly for adult audiences (no one under 18 admitted). For a detailed textual analysis of censorship in Indian advertising, see Chowdhry's chapter in this volume.

3. K. Ahmad Abbas, a noted screenwriter, director, journalist, novelist, and short-story writer, who in the late 1930s was working as a publicist for Bombay Talkies (a leading studio), wrote an open letter to Gandhi that was published in the magazine *Filmindia* in October 1939. In the letter, Abbas presents a narrative of improving standards in cinema connected to the increased interest that "honest and socially conscious people" are taking in the medium, whereas a decade earlier good films were not produced because "educated and 'respectable' folk" viewed films as "evil and loathsome." He asserts that such prejudices are breaking down and argues,

> The "cleansing" of the Indian films will be in direct proportion to the number of honest and responsible people who are able to take the place of ignorant profiteers who dominated the industry for so many years. We want more decent people to take interest in this industry, so that it becomes an instrument of social good rather than a *tamasha* [spectacle]. (quoted in Bandyopadhyay 1993, 145)

4. For example, two rulings in 1949 simply stated,

> *Matlabi*—Hindi. Jagriti Pictures. Rejected. This is a sloppy stunt picture, not suitable for public exhibition.

> *The Madonna's Secret*—English. Republic Pictures. Prohibited as this is a crime picture without any relieving feature. Trailer is also banned. (quoted in Barnouw and Krishnaswamy 1980, 140)

5. The 1991 act states that the Board of Film Certification shall ensure that
   (i) Anti-social activities such as violence are not glorified or justified

   (ii) The modus operandi of criminals, other visuals or words likely to incite the commission of any offence are not depicted.

   (iii) Scenes:

   (a) showing involvement of children in violence as victims or as perpetrators or as forced witness to violence, or showing children as being subjected to any form of child abuse;

   (b) showing abuse or ridicule of physically and mentally handicapped persons; and

   (c) showing cruelty to, or abuse of, animals, are not presented needlessly;

   (iv) Pointless or avoidable scenes of violence, cruelty and horror, scenes of violence primarily intended to provide entertainment and such scenes as may have the effect of desensitising or dehumanising people are not shown;

(v) Scenes which have the effect of justifying or glorifying drinking are not shown;

(vi) Scenes tending to encourage, justify or glamorise drug addiction are not shown;

(vi-a) Scenes tending to encourage, justify or glamorise consumption of tobacco or smoking are not shown;

(vii) Human sensibilities are not offended by vulgarity, obscenity or depravity;

(viii) Such dual meaning words as obviously cater to baser instincts are not allowed;

(ix) Scenes degrading or denigrating women in any manner are not presented;

(x) Scenes involving sexual violence against women like attempt to rape, rape or any form of molestation, or scenes of similar nature are avoided, and if any such incident is germane to the theme, they shall be reduced to the minimum and no details are shown;

(xi) Scenes showing sexual perversions shall be avoided and if such matters are germane to the theme, they shall be reduced to the minimum and no details are shown;

(xii) Visuals or words contemptuous of racial, religious or other groups are not presented;

(xiii) Visuals or words which promote communal, obscurantism, anti-scientific and anti-national attitudes are not presented;

(xiv) The sovereignty and integrity of India is not called in question;

(xv) The security of the State is not jeopardised or endangered;

(xvi) Friendly relations with foreign States are not strained;

(xvii) Public order is not endangered;

(xviii) Visuals or words involving defamation of an individual or a body of individuals, or contempt of court are not presented;

(xix) National symbols and emblems are not shown except in accordance with the provisions of the Emblems and Names (Prevention of Improper Use) Act, 1950 (12 of 1950).

6. When this chapter was written, no conclusions had been reached; the Ministry's recommendations had to be debated and passed by Parliament.

7. "Mrs. Kapoor" is a pseudonym, since censors' identities are not supposed to be public information. For greater detail about Indian censorship practices from the perspective of censors, see Mehta 2001.

8. Many filmmakers initially interpreted and characterized my research project as that of trying to understand the effect of cinema on the "masses" and were perplexed

by my extended focus on filmmakers.

9. This film, starring Shahrukh Khan, Juhi Chawla, and Nana Patekar and directed by Aziz Mirza, was produced by Vaswani. It is the story of a small-town man who comes to Bombay with big dreams and aspirations to succeed.

10. The state has also treated cinema as a problem warranting a number of government commissions, inquiries, and symposia. Examples include the 1951 Film Enquiry Committee, the Sangeet Natak Akademi Film Seminar of 1955, the Khosla Committee on Film Censorship in 1968, the Symposium on Cinema in Developing Countries in 1979, the Working Group on National Film Policy in 1980, and the National Conference on Challenges before Indian Cinema in 1998.

11. Even prior to Indian independence, one comes across similar statements. For example, Sarojini Naidu, a member of the Indian National Congress, declared in an interview in *Filmindia* in January 1943,

> Cinema can do to a whole people what a loving and devoted wife [can] do to an erring husband. To root out superstition, to make people rational and make them better informed, and to give them useful entertainment. . . . If Indian Film Industry is to justify and fulfill its purpose, it must plan on sound principles, and we must all help it do so. (quoted in Kaul 1998, 51)

12. After some searching, I found that the statement is taken from the Supreme Court's judgment dated March 30, 1989, in a civil appeal relating to censorship of the Tamil film *Ore Oru Gramathile*.

13. The National Film Development Corporation (NFDC) was created in 1980 by the merger of the Film Finance Corporation and the Film Export Corporation. Of all the film-centered institutions set up by the Indian state, the NFDC is the most significant in its mandate—to promote the cause of good cinema in India—and its activities. Its main task is to finance and produce low-budget films of "high artistic content."

14. Threshold theory is attributed to British clinical psychologist Hans Eysenck (Bose 2005, 122).

15. At the time of the interview, Khan did not actually have children.

16. Television did not become significant in India until the mid-1980s. The first telecast was made in September 1959 as a UNESCO-sponsored pilot educational project, and the initial range of transmission was only forty kilometers. Educational programs were broadcast for twenty minutes twice a week beginning in 1961, and throughout the 1960s various pilot educational projects were attempted, but no systematic program of television broadcasting. It was not until 1976 with the formation of Doordarshan, the state-owned single-channel network, that television programming was broadcast to a wider (but still small) audience. Color broadcasting as well as national transmission via low-power transmitters and satellite began in 1982 when India hosted the Asiad Games. Commercial sponsorship of programs began in 1983, as did the first major expansion of Doordarshan's network. Cable broadcasts began unofficially in India in 1984, first in tourist hotels, then in apartment blocks, and finally in individual homes. At first the cable networks were fed by videocassette players, linked centrally to the cable network. By May 1990, 3,450 cable TV networks existed in India, primarily in the four major cities of Bombay, Calcutta, Delhi, and Madras. By 1991, cable networks were equipped with satellite dishes and had gained access to

STAR TV, the BBC, and CNN. The rapid spread of this unauthorized cable network with satellite access was one of the main reasons for the changes that occurred in the Indian television landscape in the 1990s.

17. In 2006, the Ministry of Information and Broadcasting drafted the Broadcast Services Regulation Bill, which sought to create the Broadcast Regulatory Authority of India for the purpose of regulating broadcast media. One of the tasks of such an agency would be to implement a content code on television and radio akin to the guidelines for film certification listed in note 5. At the time of writing this article, no conclusions had been reached; the Ministry drafted a 2007 version of the bill, which still had to be debated and passed by Parliament.

18. There is a fourth Indian rating, S, but it is extremely uncommon and not part of the daily practice or discourse of censorship. The voluntary American film-rating system was originally instituted in 1968 by the MPAA, the National Association of Theater Owners (NATO), and the International Film Importers and Distributors of America (IFIDA) as a way to deter U.S. government censorship.

19. Subsequent chairpersons have included Asha Parekh (actress), Vijay Anand (director), Anupam Kher (actor), and Sharmila Tagore (actress).

20. *Hum Aapke Hain Koun!* (What Do I Mean to You) was written off after preview screenings as a huge flop waiting to happen. With its fourteen songs, minimal plot, lack of a villain, lack of violence, and 195-minute running time, *Hum Aapke Hain Koun!* broke with the then-dominant norms of filmmaking. It was dismissed by the film industry as a "wedding video" because of its elaborate depiction of North Indian Hindu wedding rituals and its presentation of an extended family that was unusual in Indian film: one free of conflict, tension, and jealousy. The industry was stunned when it went on to become one of the highest-grossing Indian films of all time. Its tremendous success gave an enormous boost to the film industry and ushered in a new era of Hindi filmmaking focusing on wealthy, happy extended families.

21. The Supreme Court of India ruled that it was absurd to ban a work of fiction, especially when Christian-majority countries throughout the world, including Italy, France, and the United States, had no objection to the film. Nonetheless, seven states—Andhra Pradesh, Goa, Kerala, Meghalaya, Nagaland, Punjab, and Tamil Nadu —banned its exhibition, even though it was never planned to be released in some of them.

22. Members of the Bombay film industry came out in support of Khan and his right to express his opinion; they expressed outrage at this attack on civil liberties. Filmmaker Mahesh Bhatt even filed a case with the Supreme Court urging it to rule that the film had to be released in Gujarat. The Court threw out the case, but did state in its judgment that the state needed to provide police protection to those exhibitors and theater owners who requested it. One theater in Gujarat started screening the film, but a young man immolated himself in protest, whereupon the producer and distributor of the film, Yash Chopra, requested the theater owner to stop screening it.

References

Interviews (all by author)

Azmi, Shabana. 1996. August 14. Bombay.

Bhatt, Mukesh. 1996. October 10. Bombay.
Bhatt, Vikram. 2006. January 5. New York.
Bhaumick, Sachin. 1996. October 15. Bombay.
Chopra, Aditya. 1996. April 2. Bombay.
Chopra, B. R. 1996. August 14. Bombay.
Chopra, Pamela. 1996. March 26. Bombay.
Dixit, Madhuri. 1996. November 25. Bombay.
Dutt, Sanjay. 1996. May 6. Bombay.
Ghai, Subhash. 1996. December 10. Bombay.
Gupta, Sutanu. 1996. November 21. Bombay.
Irani, Honey. 1996. May 5. Bombay.
Khan, Aamir. 1996. March 23. Bombay.
Khan, Mansoor. 1996. April 5. Bombay.
Khan, Shahrukh. 1996. March 20. Bombay.
Kharabanda, Punkej. 1996. April 17. Bombay.
Mukherjee, Hrishikesh. 1996. November 7. Bombay.
Sippy, Ramesh. 1996. July 8. Bombay
Tahil, Dalip. 1996. April 5. Bombay.
Vaswani, Viveck. 1996. April 19. Bombay.

Published Works

Bamzai, Kaveree, and Sandeep Unnithan. 2002. "Is Sex Ok?" *India Today*. August 5.
Bandyopadhyay, Samik, ed. 1993. *Indian Cinema: Contemporary Perceptions from the Thirties*. Jamshedpur: Celluloid Chapter.
Barnouw, Erik, and S. Krishnaswamy. 1980. *Indian Film*. New York: Oxford University Press.
Bose, Derek. 2005. *Bollywood Uncensored: What You Don't See on Screen and Why*. New Delhi: Rupa.
Central Board of Film Certification. n.d. Website. http://www.cbfcindia.tn.nic.in/, accessed June 10, 2005.
Chatterjee, Partha, ed. 1998. *Wages of Freedom: Fifty Years of the Indian Nation-State*. New Delhi: Oxford University Press.
———. 2004. *The Politics of the Governed: Reflections on Popular Politics in Most of the World*. New York: Columbia University Press.
Foucault, Michel. 1991. "Governmentality." In Graham Burcell, Colin Gordon, and Peter Miller, eds., *The Foucault Effect: Studies in Governmentality*. Chicago: University of Chicago Press.
Ganti, Tejaswini. 2000. "Casting Culture: The Social Life of Hindi Film Production in Bombay." Ph.D. diss., New York University.
———. 2002. "'And Yet My Heart Is Still Indian': The Bombay Film Industry and the (H)Indianization of Hollywood." In Faye D. Ginsburg, Lila Abu-Lughod, and Brian Larkin, eds., *Media Worlds: Anthropology on New Terrain*. Berkeley: University of California Press.
Gupta, Akhil. 1998. *Postcolonial Developments: Agriculture in the Making of Modern India*. Durham, N.C.: Duke University Press.
Hansen, Thomas. 1999. *The Saffron Wave: Democracy and Hindu Nationalism in Mod-*

ern India. Princeton, N.J.: Princeton University Press.

Indian Institute of Mass Communication and Directorate of Film Festivals. 1979. *Symposium on Cinema in Developing Countries*. New Delhi Ministry of Information and Broadcasting.

Kaul, Gautam. 1998. *Cinema and the Indian Freedom Struggle*. New Delhi: Sterling.

Mazzarella, William. 2004. "Culture, Globalization, Mediation." *Annual Review of Anthropology* 33:345—67.

Mehta, Monika. 2001. "Selections: Cutting, Classifying and Certifying in Bombay Cinema." Ph.D. diss., University of Minnesota.

Ministry of Information and Broadcasting. 1992. *The Cinematograph Act, 1952: Cinematograph Certification Rules, 1983 and Certification Guidelines*. March 3. New Delhi: Directorate of Advertising and Visual Publicity.

Nair, Sunil. 2002. "X-tra Special Halls for X-Rated Films: Censors Want It!" *Indian Express*. June 17.

National Film Development Corporation. n.d. Website. http://www.nfdcindia.com/index.php, accessed June 10, 2005.

Rajadhyaksha, Ashish, and Paul Willemen. 1999. *Encyclopaedia of Indian Cinema*. Revised edition. London: British Film Institute.

Ramachandran, T. M., ed. 1981. *Fifty Years of Indian Talkies, 1931–1981: A Commemorative Volume*. Bombay: Indian Academy of Motion Picture Arts and Sciences.

Raman, Anuradha. 2005. "Cuss & Tell: Filmmakers May, but Will Parliament Approve the I&B Ministry's Changes to Censorship Guidelines?" *Outlook*. September 12.

Rangoonwalla, Firoze. 1983. *Indian Cinema, Past and Present*. New Delhi: Clarion.

Anxiety, Failure, and Censorship in Indian Advertising

Angad Chowdhry

As commentators have suggested (Breckenridge 1995, 6–7), the explosion of the Indian middle classes and the advent of consumerism have created an anxiety that is being addressed by a variety of specialists. The category of "consumer" is contingent on people's being addressed as such by the Indian mass media. Advertising is one of many means by which audiences are invited to recognize themselves as both consumers and individuals. This is not a new phenomenon, though certain dimensions of it have changed over the last century. In Nehruvian India, product advertisements were "remedial" rather than "aspirational" (Inden 2004). These advertisements projected deficiencies onto their addressees.[1] More recently, advertising in India has been seen as agentive in transforming citizens into consumers (Mazzarella 2003). However, despite the critical appraisals, most producers of advertisements assume that ads "work" in some way or another. They assume that an ad works when it causes products to fly off the shelves (the *telos* of all successful advertising) and lends them particular associations in the consumer's mind. This working can only be recognized retroactively, on the basis of evidence assembled by quantitative and qualitative research agencies. A fair amount of reification takes place in both kinds of research. In quantitative research the tabulation of numbers is seen as indicative of broader social trends; in qualitative studies the consumer, a figure produced out of processes of substantiation and rhetoric, is assumed to already exist.

It is impossible to prove that a short advertisement can cause a consumer, who might have glanced at it while flipping pages or channels, to go out and purchase a product. Nevertheless, in this chapter, I argue that advertising censorship is predicated on the assumption that it can. It is around this "immanent void" (or "null hypothesis" [Hobart 2001b]) that anxieties are articulated by the censors.[2]

Advertising Standards

If cost is the criterion, ads must be regarded as among the most important elements in the economy. Ads are also in a central structural position in the economy, overlapping both the means and relations of consumption. The major problem of the capitalist economy since the 1920s shifted from production to consumption. . . . When an individual watches a TV ad the health of the economy is at stake.

—Mark Poster, *The Mode of Information*, 47–48

The Advertising Standards Council of India (ASCI), established in Mumbai in 1985, describes itself on the home page of its website as a "self regulatory voluntary organisation of the advertising industry" and states that it and its Consumer Complaints Council (CCC) process complaints that are "received from Consumers and Industry, against Advertisements which are considered as False, Misleading, Indecent, Illegal, leading to Unsafe practices, or Unfair to competition, and consequently in contravention of the ASCI code for Self-Regulation in Advertising." Complaints may be filed by other agencies, "consumers," or "consumer activist groups." They are discussed in the meetings of the CCC and either upheld or not upheld. If they are upheld, then the agency that produced the advertisement is informed, and the product is usually withdrawn or modified.

I arrived at the ASCI's doorstep in 2005, a few hours before my scheduled meeting with ASCI representatives. Outside the office, Mumbai was waking up with ritualistic flair. Fried foods, tea, and newspapers were being sold and consumed rapidly while I waited for my appointment. This was the first of many meetings I was to have with representatives of the ASCI. Formal interviews with one representative of the ASCI were followed by hours of poring over the organization's extensive archives. I was not able to attend any of the meetings in which decisions were made. Instead, accounts of them were provided to me. ASCI members seemed to take their business extremely seriously, almost as if it was a moral crusade for the making of a modern India.

The process of decision making at the ASCI was extremely disciplined yet maddeningly paradoxical. Each decision about an advertisement was made long after the advertisement had ceased to appear on television or in newspapers. Any dangers that the advertisements were deemed to have posed would already have been unleashed.[3]

For more than twenty years, the ASCI has reached decisions about the effects an advertisement may have, guided by an occasionally modified "code for self-regulation." The code's four provisions concern themselves with different aspects of advertising. The first requires that advertisements be truthful and honest; the second that they not offend standards of public decency; the third that they not promote harmful products, particularly those that might endanger minors; and the fourth that they observe fairness in competition.

Because of the continuously changing, contextual nature and huge number of advertisements at any given time, the code, in order to be effective as a means of evaluation, has to be fairly flexible and broad. This flexibility is accomplished by means of abstractions ("generally accepted standards of public decency"), as well as the slippery imagining of effects; it forbids

> the indiscriminate use of Advertising in situations or of the Promotion of Products which are regarded as Hazardous or Harmful to society or to individuals, particularly minors, to a degree or of a type which is Unacceptable to Society at Large. . . . No advertisement shall be permitted which . . . Tends to incite people to crime or to promote disorder and violence or intolerance. (Advertising Standards Council of India [ASCI] 2005a)

It also requires that "advertisements addressed to minors . . . not contain anything, whether in illustration or otherwise, which might result in their physical, mental or moral harm or which exploits their vulnerability." The child, represented as vulnerable and innocent, occupies a privileged space in official discussions about censorship, media effects, and self-regulation (Barker and Petley 1997). The child's agency and inclinations are, as we shall see below, imagined in very particular ways.

Untangling Childhood

In order to understand the significance of the ASCI and to untangle its workings, this chapter focuses on its rhetorical deployment of childhood. It examines the figure of the "innocent child" and its relationship to the market, in order to demonstrate that the ASCI performs the meta-function of regulating failed and successful interpellations in order to produce a contemporary subject that is both resistant to and open to the efficacy of advertising.[4]

Here are two examples of entries in the ASCI archives:[5]

> **Date:** August 2001. *ICIC asset management* **Visuals:** girl goes to school, unhappy. The father sneaks in to pacify her. **Complaint:** Suggests school is a place to be feared. The complainants two and half year old daughter was just started going to play school this June, was very enthusiastic and after seeing the ad, she has started fearing the school and wants her mother (complainant) to stay with her in the classroom. The complainant strongly feels that this ad has negative influence on her daughter.

> **Date:** February 2002. *Berger Paints.* **Visuals:** the TVC [television commercial] shows children throwing Holi [festival] colours on a boy, who runs up to his house and retaliates by throwing paint (Berger apparently), at the boys standing below. The next day in the class, the boys are shown with the long lasting paint still on their faces which is again shown even when they graduate "several years later." The ad will encourage boys to use toxic paints during Holi which can result in blindness and skin rash.

The first complaint includes a personal statement by the complainant about the influence this advertisement has had on her daughter. Childish enthusiasm has been transformed into fear. The decision of the CCC was that this advertisement was "not likely to give rise to such a degree or feeling of fear as to be harmful to children in general," even though the complainant had said that such harm had already occurred.[6] In the second complaint, the CCC's decision was different. It felt that the advertisement "featured a dangerous act, likely to encourage minors to emulate such acts in a manner which could cause harm or injury." The actual effect or influence of the advertisement is not evident; what is evident is that someone is naming something as effect or influence in a particular situation for a particular purpose. When it was the consumer herself who pointed out the presence of an effect, her complaint was dismissed.

> **Date:** October 2004. *MET Life Insurance.* **Visuals:** TVC shows "people falling off buildings appearing to be enjoying themselves and having huge smiles on their faces." On seeing this Ad, the Complainant's 5 year old son has been insisting that he too wants to do the same. (One similar complaint received against the TVC) **CCC:** ad showed dangerous practice, TVC suspended.

Two of these complaints (those against ads for ICIC Asset Management and MET Life Insurance) refer to a child who has been interpellated by the advertisement. The difference between the two complaints is that in the former the child is already scared, the effect has already happened, but in the latter the child is "insisting that he too wants to do the same." In the first case, the child had been "enthusiastic" but is now frightened of school—the advertisement becomes, retroactively, the cause of the transformation. Here, the parent is representing something (fear) as the advertising's effect. In the second case, however, the parent is suggesting that the effect will take place in the future; the child will jump off a building. Censors necessarily imagine the future as a time of all kinds of dangers, and it would appear that the potential for peril in the future has more power over censorship decisions than an event in the past.

> **Date:** November 1995. *Parry lacto king chocolate.* **Complaint:** The ad is totally misleading, i.e. calling the consumers to collect wrappers from even roads or footpaths. This shall lead to seriously unhealthy situations especially among children. They may run into the street in the event they see a wrapper there and may be run over by moving vehicles (dangerous). They may search for wrappers in the wayside dustbins and sweeping, which shall definitely causes serious unhealthy situations and even quarrels among the children. **CCC:** Encouraged children to indulge in dangerous practices. The ad has been modified.

In my discussions with the General Secretary of the ASCI,[7] he indicated that advertisements inviting children to think of themselves as consumers were of great concern. Such an advertisement can transform the child into a certain kind of person, one who charges toward discarded wrappers, fights with other children, and runs into traffic. The transformation of the child into someone guided by the injunctions of the advertisement poses a major problem for the ASCI. The child's response to the advertisement is represented as mimetic—the advertisement will cause the child to perform the act that the advertisement represents. However, the ASCI considers dangerous only those advertisements whose content will lead children into danger when they repeat it.

> **Date:** September 2001. *Cadbury*. **Complaint:** As per complaint (from a member of a Medical Profession), the TVC features a free "sharp shooter" offer with Cadbury's Milktreat. It shows children using the "sharp shooter" to choke an adult, causing him to "fall unconscious." This Ad is dangerous, and there ought to be strict warnings about the dangers of life threatening toys promoted to children. **CCC:** Ad featured a dangerous act which could result in an injury. Ad campaign concluded.

This complainant says that the representation of a child shooting an adult would cause children to imitate the act. However, there are multiple reasons why this might happen, none of which are discussed: children will repeat the act because they recognize it as dangerous; children want adults to suffer, and the advertisement shows one way in which they can achieve this; children will repeat the act because they cannot distinguish between represented humor and danger; children only want chocolate, and killing an adult is just one more way of getting it. Whatever the correct reading may be, from these decisions it is possible to conclude that the ASCI feels a need to regulate such advertisements because it does not believe that children recognize them as humorous or informational, and will repeat many unsafe actions. It imagines children as entities that understand advertisements as commands that might transform them into something dangerous. If advertisements represent themselves as aspirational, motivational, and informational, then any misrecognition of them as orders that threaten the lives of children or adults must be imagined as failures. Such failures produce a "surplus of meaning" that cannot be accounted for and that will be actualized in the future—that is, it "could result in an injury." Such an advertisement, according to the operative assumptions of the ASCI, should be addressed to one who will not misrecognize it as something other than the producer intended. By this standard, the good consumer is the consumer who is fully and successfully interpellated by the producer's message.

> **Date:** December 2003. *Dabur*. **Visuals:** "the grandson standing on the sloping tiled roof, in heavy rain, holding the TV antenna in his hand, because his grandmother wants to watch the TV serial 'Ramayan.'" The ad is dangerous for children as they have a tendency to imitate and copy what they watch on television. Seeing this Ad, a child might try to hold the TV antenna and stand on the roof of the house. This might prove fatal and extremely dangerous. **CCC:** Ad featured a dangerous act which was *likely to encourage minors to emulate* it in a manner which could case harm or injury. Ad showed a dangerous practice. TVC modified. [Italics added]

Date: December 2003. *Daewoo fridge.* **Visuals:** "an old gentleman opens the door of Daewoo fridge then he enters the fridge sits inside then shuts the door. After few seconds he opens the door from inside the fridge extends his hand and takes a newspaper and shuts the door again." Voice over (in Hindi): fridge has anti ageing technology but only for your food. This act if copied/ attempted by a child might have fatal consequences. *Children have a tendency of imitating whatever they see.* The commercial might influence the children to do the same. (One similar complaint received against the TVC). **CCC:** Visual sequence of an "old man entering and remaining inside the fridge" manifested a disregard of safety. Modification of the TVC under consideration by the Advertiser. [Italics in original]

In earlier examples, it was assumed that children would repeat actions they saw in advertisements. In the examples above, the child is represented not only as a mimetic automaton capable of repeating dangerous acts, but also as someone who is capable of recreating the situation represented in the advertisement in order to perform a dangerous act. Thus the child is not merely an ideologically duped performer, but the orchestrator of its own destruction. What is implicit in these complaints is the way the child's capacity for recognition and re-creation is imagined. For instance, would the child repeat the actions of the first advertisement if it recognized that in 2003 *Ramayana* could not have been on television? Would it repeat them if it wasn't raining? Would it repeat the actions of the second advertisement even though the primary actor in it was an old man who could read a newspaper? Since the first ad features a broadcast of *Ramayana* and the second an old man reading, they offer few features with which a child can identify. Following the first complainant, we could say that children "have a tendency to imitate and copy what they watch on television." But this does not explain how the child isolates, from all of the possible representations and readings latent in the advertisement, the most dangerous acts in order to repeat them. In other words, it is imagined that children mimic television advertisements selectively, not blindly. The part of the child that is in need of protection is the part that is seduced by danger. Since the ASCI strives only to prevent the child from that seduction, it is clear that other effects the ad may have are not only expected but actively encouraged. In repressing some of advertising's effects and not others, the ASCI seems to suggest that the only possible responses to advertisements are endangerment and consumption.

The ASCI's chosen method of preventing this selective mimicry and its "dangerous rationality" is the warning.

Date: February 2003. *Mountain Dew.* **Visuals:** a man chasing a cheetah and pulling out a can of Mountain Dew by putting his hand deep inside the animal's throat. He then says "bad cheetah, cheetah bhi peetha hai" ["bad cheetah, the cheetah too drinks"] **Complaint:** complainants son aged 4 years attempted to pull out a drink can from a dog's throat. Ad features dangerous act which is likely to encourage minors. **CCC:** Ad featured a dangerous act, which was likely to encourage minors to emulate such acts in a manner which could cause harm or injury. TVC modified by *running a warning before the ad, advising against "attempting the performance" shown.* [Italics added]

Date: September 1997. *ITC Wills* on ESPN. **Visuals:** Indian cricket star Venkatesh Prasad running on railway track in front of advancing train. This is dangerous for children to watch. Most of the members of the cricket team are idols of the young throughout the country. This latter might try and emulate Prasad and run on a railway track. The commercial does not contain warning. **CCC:** a caution is clearly stated in the ad. Not likely to lead to dangerous practice.

The ASCI seems to imagine that unless children are explicitly warned against doing so, they will repeat actions that are potentially harmful to them. However, it believes that warnings override their impulse toward selective mimesis and keep them safe from harm, because children will listen to orders. If there were no warning, then, according to the ASCI archives, children might rush into the street, shoot their uncles, jump off buildings, stuff their hands down the throats of dogs, lick poison, or play cricket using gas cylinders for wickets. But if they are given a warning, these impulses will be checked. Representing the advertisement as dangerous makes it no longer dangerous. Who is being reassured by these cautions to avoid danger? It is not possible for young children to read these warnings, which are flashed on the screen before advertisements play, so perhaps the warnings are intended for parents or other potential complainants. Perhaps they have been inserted there to remind viewers that advertisements do have an effect, or that there are indeed some people out there ("children" and other members of the "masses") who require such warnings.

Untangling Youth

Second only to the figure of the child as a figure for concern is that of "youth." The earliest complaint I found concerning youth was laid against the August 8, 1987, Patna edition of the *Times of India*, which had printed an advertisement for a film. According to the complainant, it "was an effort [on] the part of the advertiser to attract [a] crowd to his theatre for an adult film entitled LOVE LOVE LOVE." The advertisement said that this film was a "carbon copy of a blue film." The complainant "felt such advertisements misled the youth and incite them to sexual crimes." The next references to "the youth," "the young," and their sexuality are in three responses to advertisements for Kamasutra brand condoms (sent between April 1994 and March 1995):

> This ad is obscene and vulgar. The sentence written in the ad tends to incite younger minds in the family, where this newspaper reaches, for unwarranted sex.

> The advertisements are very provocative, inductive to younger generation especially teenagers the advertisement states that 'mating has no place or time' and with Kamasutra condoms it is fearless enjoyable irrespective of time and place.

Ad is obscene and vulgar; the newspaper is read by every family member including children. Reading this ad, the younger minds are polluted. It hampers the studies of children and inculcates the feeling of immorality.

[In all three cases] CCC decision/Chapter II: Ad is offensive to generally accepted standards of moral decency.

In each case, the complainant is representing youth as the accidental victim of the ill effects of these representations: "incitement, unwarranted fearless sex, the pollution of minds, the feeling of immorality and loss of studiousness."[8] The General Secretary of the ASCI told me that "advertising is an uninvited guest and visitor in your home. It is thrust upon you, and should pay respect to you as host." This understanding of advertisements as intrusions into coherent and closed social situations is shared by many complainants as well. In 1999, an advertisement showing "two 2 wheelers being ridden side by side with pillion riders playing chess and going over logs of wood in synchronisation" was the subject of a complaint. The complainant argued that "since the advertisement is running without a disclaimer, it might induce the general public to try out activities which might prove to be fatal." In this case the CCC concurred: "Ad without justification encourages negligence and a dangerous practice which could induce vulnerable inexperienced riders to ignore traffic regulation."

The constant fear is that the dangerous practices depicted in the advertisements are repeated either in the mind (in amoral thoughts about sexuality) or in actions (such as driving dangerously). Certain advertisements are always already articulated with a possible future subversion. There is a difference, in these complaints, between the ways in which children perform this subversion and the ways youth do. We could say that what distinguishes "youth" from "children" is the distinct ways in which they "fail" their interpellation (or respond to such failure). The complainants and the ASCI see youth as imitators of not just any dangerous behavior, but of those that promise excitement and adrenaline-fueled fun. For them, danger is almost always articulated with driving a car or other vehicles. Children, even though they will selectively imitate the most dangerous act shown, will never get into a car and drive it recklessly away.

> **Date:** July 1990. *Action Shoes.* **Visuals:** A TV spot for Action shoes shows the young driver of an open convertible car, stopping the vehicle with his shoes just before the car reached a child playing on the road. This was portrayed by the driver breaking the speed of the car by placing his foot on the road so as to create an impression that the shoes he wore were tough enough to break the speed of the car. The complainant, a consumer group, felt that the spot demonstrated a dangerous practice which could be imitated by younger drivers. The advertiser argued that it demonstrated the grip of the shoes.

The consumer group that complained seemed to assume that younger drivers had no understanding of mechanics or physics, which is why they would imitate this action. Whereas children are imagined to be selectively mimetic, with a well-developed sense of rationality, youth are imagined as irresponsibly, even stupidly, mimetic. What we have, then, are two distinct ways in which interpellation and its failure are imagined. For children, the failure produces an action that is difficult to prevent except by warnings; for youth, the failure produces actions that are related to danger, but also to the benefit that this daredevilry provides: fun. For youth the imminence of "fun" is what prevents successful interpellation (as it is imagined by the ASCI).

> **Date:** November 1995. *Bajaj.* **Visuals:** "College Campus ad" DD. The said ad is not in good taste as it shows a man on a bike riding inside a school/college compound, coming right up to the class room, calling a girl student from inside and riding with her out of the premises. Girl students are likely to be carried away by this ad and cases of leaving the classroom to join boyfriends is likely to increase. . . . **CCC:** Likely to cause grave or widespread offence and might erode community values by exploiting the vulnerability of children (students). TVC withdrawn.

This case and others like it suggest that youth require their transgressions to be communal, distinct from the individual mimicry of the child. If an advertisement fails, it fails for a community of young people. According to these complaints, in order for a youth to imitate a dangerous advertisement, multiple actors need to be involved, a community of advertisement watchers who have all failed their interpellation, misrecognized the intention of the advertisement that addresses them. Such an understanding of this group fits neatly with the representations of youth as consumers employed by most cellular phone, greeting card, and music television companies in India. This production of youth as a community is the result of a successful interpellation, from the point of view of the ASCI. The production of a mob, on the other hand, signals failure. This failure of interpellation, for the ASCI, means that youth wrongly interpret fun and danger. However, another figure sometimes precipitates this failure.

Untangling the Patriarch

> **Date:** January 2002. *TVS scooter.* **Visuals:** The TVC shows a young father performing a variety of unnecessary stunts while riding his motorcycle alongside a school bus carrying his young daughter, presumably to impress the child. Most of these stunts are extremely dangerous and are not really called for, given the condition of traffic depicted in the commercial. Such an Ad is likely to give a wrong and potentially dangerous signal to the riders of motorcycles, *especially the younger generations.* The advertiser needs to put a disclaimer at the beginning to the effect that stunts depicted in the TVC *should not be performed by inexperienced riders.* **CCC:** Ad manifests a disregard for safety and encourages negligence. [Italics added]

> **Date:** May 2003. *Bajaj.* **Visual:** A school going child sitting on the Bajaj two wheeler on the rear seat in a reverse direction doing his home work,

and the father on the front seat, apparently to drop the child at school. **Complaint:** showing a child doing his home work on a running two wheeler and that too by sitting in reverse position, shows a dangerous practice and utter disregard to safety of young children the ad shows the child in a dangerous position and *the same dangerous practice is likely to be imitated by young people.* **CCC:** ad shows dangerous practice and manifested a disregard for safety. [Italics added]

The figure of the father in both of these advertisements suggests that parents perform crucial roles in this process of misrecognition.[9] The failure of interpellation will be more acute because it has been set into motion by a father. The father doing stunts on a motorcycle to impress a child sends a wrong message to motorcycle drivers and manifests a disregard for safety whilst encouraging parental negligence. The move from the singular to the universal (a movement that is required in order for any censorship decisions to be made) requires the presence of both discipline and danger: the father must behave like the child. When children or youth fail in their interpellation (because, as the ASCI believes, they have misrecognized the advertisement's intent), this failure is a cause for concern. It is the misrecognition of the advertisement, rather than the dangerous effects this misrecognition may have, which is the crux of the matter. This is not surprising or indeed unreasonable, considering most censorship councils and advertisers imagine that intention is self-evident and that the addressee of an advertisement will always succeed in recognizing it. Anything that encourages or produces this failure is to be disciplined. To the ASCI, certain representations of family life, or the father, suggest such a failure and, hence, a danger in need of regulation.

> **Date:** February 2003. *Nestle.* **Visuals:** A mother ringing home to find out if her husband has left the house to meet her some place, and the son picks up the phone. Since the father is busy watching some television stuff and has not left the place, the son holding the phone looks meaningfully at his father who promptly brings out a Nestle bar, and the child says to his mother on the phone, that the father has left a long time back. **Complaint:** Ad is actually portraying bribing of a child for telling a lie. Such cheap and morally wrong Ads and have a lasting effect on the psyche of young minds. **CCC:** Portrayal of a day to day family situation in the Ad, which encourages voicing an untruth, even in the context of a humorous situation, could exploit the vulnerability of minors and result in their moral harm. TVC withdrawn.

> **Date:** February 2004. *Bharat Petroleum.* **Visuals:** Two young brothers, the elder brother is angry with mother, and when she calls them he tells the younger brother that she is crazy (making a hand gesture). How can a small child be shown doing this to his mother. It sets a bad example. The ad is in bad taste. CCC: ad is in bad taste which other children could emulate, thereby setting a bad example. TVC modified.

In the first advertisement, the CCC imagines the child addressee as capable of identifying two things that are supposed to be mutually exclusive—family and untruth. Untruth here is mimicked just as dangerous practices were: the child does not repeat the situation shown in the advertisement, but recognizes the untruth at its heart. Similarly, the CCC believes that children will imitate the elder brother's disrespectful act in the second advertisement because they see it as something that is not ordinarily done, but that can be done. The advertisement shows a relationship that is inappropriate, because it violates the image of the child as one who needs to be protected from itself (the Hindi words for "children" and "protection" are *baccha* and *bacha*, respectively) and who accepts regulative discipline. The most threatening advertisement is one whose imitation will disrupt the discipline and regulatory authority that authority figures like parents are assumed to possess.[10] Of course, this is merely suggested, implied, and accidental. There are other situations in which such dangers are not imagined. It is to these situations that we will turn next.

Tangled Successes

In which situations are interpellations imagined as successes, and what do these situations tell us about the imagining of children? Sometimes complaints sent in to the ASCI are not upheld; the advertisement is not considered dangerous to children. The ASCI believes that children will recognize and become interpellated by the advertisement, and any effects it has on them will either be profitable to advertisers or help the children develop into consumers. My reading of the archives suggested that decisions not to uphold a complaint were related to more than just the content of the advertisement.

> **Date:** January 1998. **Complaint:** A viewer in Ambernath, Thane District, wrote in to complain about the advertiser's television spot for their brand of television sets, Onida. He felt the horrible figure of the model, resembling the devil, or a gruesome figure from the planetary world, frightened both young and old. **CCC:** Complaint not upheld: The report (of an independent enquiry) showed that the majority of the children liked the advertisement and were not frightened by it. The council also felt that the character was comical and was not meant to horrify children. [In my reading of the archives, this is the only time the location of the complainant is given.]

> **Date:** May 1990. **Company:** Onida **Complaint:** Man wrote in to say he found the spot frightening each time he saw it as it showed a creature with grey hair, a crawling chameleon and a devil stabbing the Onida television with its tail. **CCC:** not upheld. Already tested complaint. CCC informed advertiser.

The advertisement was meant to be comical. The ASCI believes that children can identify and understand humor, irony, and comic behavior. How can they do so, when these genres are difficult for even youth to grasp? Are we sure that the difficulty is the recognition of comedy, given that these recognitions of comedy have rarely happened before or after the broadcast of this advertisement? My argument here is that it is not whether the advertisement succeeds or fails in interpellating the child that determines whether it requires regulation. If the advertisement addresses the child in a way consistent with the ASCI's imaginings of consumer culture, then its failure is not dangerous or potentially subversive. The ASCI sees no danger in the creation of a new audience, and if consumers complain about it, this only demonstrates that they do not understand what is happening.

> **Date:** April 2003 **Visuals:** "a Fairy inviting a small child for a bath with rose coloured soap in her hand. But as the child approaches, he sees an image of a 'devil' in her. Then another fairy invites him with a 'Hamam' soap in her hand. The child gets up from his dream" **Complainants:** questions—(a) what does the advertiser mean when they portray the Ad in such a mannerwhether Hamam is safe? (b) What would be a normal child's reaction on seeing a rose coloured soap (that too showing a devil)? (c) The timing (late evening) of the Ad on air is just before a child goes to sleep. Should the child go to sleep with such memories? **CCC:** Visuals not likely to frighten children. **Suo Motu complaint:** Advertiser should substantiate the claims. "some soaps can damage/harm your skin," "New Hamam does not contain any harmful substances." **CCC:** decision—May 2003—Not upheld, [advertiser's] claims substantiated.)

In these two sets of complaints, separated by almost thirteen years, complainants suggest that the representations of the devil will frighten people. However, in both cases this possibility was denied, even when, as in my earlier example, the complainant insisted that the advertisement was frightening. In both cases the representation of the devil embodies an emotion associated with a commodity—jealousy and possession are the undersides of consumption for the ASCI, and are implicitly assumed by advertising agencies. In the case of Onida the advertisements suggest that neighbors will be jealous of a commodity in the home of the consumer. The soap advertisement suggests that the differential nature of commodities, when seen as signs, is best negotiated through a strategy of denotation. It is imagined that different brands of soap, like angels and devils, belong to differential sign systems. There are values attached to angels and devils, and when an angel is associated with a product, angelic qualities are supposedly transferred to it. One soap is bad or devil-like, and the other is good or angelic. Advertisements that follow a particular articulation of the market and its affects (such as envy in relation to products) are imagined by the ASCI to be true. Complaints against these advertisements are invariably denied. Perhaps this is because the misrecognition of content implies a misrecognition of the acceptable and imagined structure of commodity signification.

> **Date:** March 1989. "I went against my mother's wishes. I used Libra" said an advertisement for beltless sanitary napkins. The copy continued to describe the product, finally adding "Now my mother uses Libra too." The complainant felt that *in an environment where parents are finding it so difficult to guide*

their children, advertisements like these may encourage them going against their parents wishes on other issues as well. The agency said it was perfectly normal for teenagers to disagree with their parents. In their opinion, the client's superior quality product was a valid reason to do so. **Conclusion:** Complaint not upheld. The CCC found the advertisement did not offend the code in any way. [Italics in original]

Date: May 1995. **Company:** Philips CD system. According to complainant the message of the ad conveys to youth, the following: you have the right to play around all day; if your parents object and there is 'too much order in your life . . . we suggest you leave home.' No ordinary equipment will do for you. (This is an attempt to inflate the self esteem of the purchaser.) If you don't demand this product it shows you must be afraid to "face the music" of parental objections. **CCC:** Ad not considered offensive or objectionable in respect of Code.

By arguing that the quality of a product is a valid reason for teenagers to disagree with their parents, the agency that created the Libra advertisement introduced a product into a system of personal relationships. The complainant is concerned that a product was interfering in the "symbolic" of the family, while the agency believed that a product that performed a role in day-to-day social dynamics was healthily positioned. This was an articulation that suited both the ASCI and the CCC. In the complaint against the advertisement for the Philips CD system, the complainant believed that the ad tells the young consumers it addresses that the CD system will offend their parents, and the only way they can enjoy themselves is to disobey their parents, buy the product, and play it really loudly. Ultimately, the advertisement suggests that the consumer is to blame for a failed interpellation.

The ASCI's relationships with the market and the concept of the consumer have intriguing consequences for the decisions it makes. The complainant quoted below imagines that the advertisement—playing as it does on the insecurities of students who have bad mathematics skills—will produce uncontrollable consumers.

Date: June 1998. *Babool* Chewing Gum. **Complaint:** Ad shows school boy . . . finds maths tough . . . blows Babool chewing gum . . . blows away the imaginary trouble in the shape of various mathematical signs. This implies math problems become easier after consuming big babool. The boy declares I love maths. This propagates an unhealthy practice amongst youngsters who are lured to consume large quantities of gum while they are doing homework. This might result in their physical mental or moral harm and also exploits their vulnerability. **CCC:** product claim as depictednot likely to cause harm to children.

The remark that the advertisement will not cause harm to children is curious. It suggests that either the ad will not turn children into uncontrollable consumers, or it will not harm them even if it does.

Date: July 2003. **Company:** Perfetti Van Melle India Pvt. Ltd. (Marbles). **Visuals:** Two young boys, one of them is shirtless, wearing only his underpants, and facing the camera. His mother asks him, "aap ka kapada kidhar hai?" (where are your clothes?). The boy replies that he has traded his shirt for "Hurricane" and his shorts for "Undertaker." These are stickers given free with the product—marbles. In the next scene the boy is pulling down his underpants, exposing his buttocks. In a surprised tone his mother asks him "what are you doing." He replies "Mujhe Big Show dengga" (It's time for a show). The other boy giggles. **Complaint:** The complainant finds the boy revealing his buttocks highly objectionable. According to him, the advertisement conveys the message that "stripping is worth stickers." **CCC:** Advertisement was not so indecent as to give rise to widespread offence.

The child is once again interpellated as a consumer, and the advertisement is not considered offensive. A consumer is not such a bad thing to become.

✕ ✕ ✕

So what do these interpretations of advertisements tell us about anxiety and interpellation? It is important here to introduce a final term, one that will perhaps unite some of the claims made in the course of this chapter. In Louis Althusser's account of interpellation, we have a hail ("Hey, you there!") that is recognized and then responded to (1977, 245). This response occurs for many reasons. One of them is "recognition"—the subject recognizes that he or she is the person addressed. We can also say that since this hail is generalized, any recognition will necessarily retroactively assume that it was indeed intended for the person in question. The recognition of the hail is merely the assumption that the hail has a *telos*: the subject who (mis)recognizes it. The addressee of the advertisement becomes the person who recognizes that the advertisement is addressing him or her. What does it mean to recognize the hail? Does it testify to a belief in that which is hailing you? In other words, when interpellation fails, when the subject misrecognizes the message, is not the greatest anxiety for a regulatory body the realization that this failure could be a judgment against something far broader than the message which produced this schism? This is what we see in the ASCI's insistence that certain messages are not misrecognized, that their interpellations are always successful, even when complainants insist that they are not. It insists this because a recognition of the lapse, or an affirmation of the failure, will necessarily produce further failure, and this would be a failure that not even a regulatory body can afford.

The broader argument here is that children and youth are, in effect, stand-ins for what censors, along with their set of ideological moorings, imagine their consumers to be. In large part, the pedagogical and paradoxical assumptions on which the censors base their decisions arise out of their belief in the power that they—and indeed the advertisers themselves—attribute to advertising. The ASCI consists not only of moral watchdogs but also of representatives of advertising agencies, the producers of these offending products. Children move from being completely passive (a good metaphor for the efficacy of advertisements) to being selectively passive (discerning consumers) to, finally, being capable of fun on their own terms (consumers who do not consume but celebrate life). Taken together, and read against the growth of India's consumer culture, these moments suggest a highly strategic process in which councils created for the protection of "the consumer" are in fact deeply complicit in its production. One could say that the Council's primary mission is not in fact to protect consumers so much as to protect "the consumer"—to produce and to police the acceptable boundaries of this figure. While interpellation may succeed or fail, the fantasy of a smooth alignment between intended advertising messages and the self-understandings of consumers is what allows the future to arrive—the perfect consumption machine, an advertiser's dream.

Notes

1. For a highly accurate reading of the advertisements of the Congress Party and the India Shining campaign of the Bharatiya Janata Party (Indian People's Party) based on this model, see Inden 2004.

2. Despite studies that focus on the meaningful reception of advertising practices, in my analysis here I am inclined to agree with Baudrillard, who states, "Consumption, in so far as it is meaningful, is *a systematic act of the manipulation of signs, a total idealist practice* . . . which has no longer anything to do (beyond a certain point) with the satisfaction of needs, nor with the reality principle . . . [It is] founded on a *lack* that is irrepressible" (Baudrillard 1988, 22–25, quoted in Hobart 2001b, 197). I take a primarily textual approach. For an analysis of censorship practices in the Bombay film business, see Ganti's chapter in this volume.

3. This imagining of the trauma as having already happened seems consistent with Freud's theory of repetition, in which a defense is built against something that has already happened.

4. By "interpellation," I am referring to the process, first suggested by Louis Althusser (1977), through which "ideology discovers its subject"—a process by which the subject comes into being by recognizing itself in a particular hail. This has been reworked substantially by post-Lacanian theorists, such as Mladen Dolar (1993), for whom the subject is that which fails to become interpellated, and my usage of the term will try and work between the two inflections of it. Interpellation is critical in understanding how the mass media, and censorship in particular, address their audience, how they expect it to respond, and how they deal with the failures of this expected response.

5. I have standardized some punctuation in quotations from the ASCI archives, but have left their wording and capitalization unchanged.

6. The specific instance here will not be made general, and the ASCI does not imagine the transition from the singular to the general, constitutive of public fear (suggested in Massumi 1993), as possible.

7. Interviews conducted in July and August 2005 in Mumbai.

8. In 2001, the complaints offered more sophisticated imaginings of possible forms of sexuality:

> **Date:** October 2001. *Hyundai.* **Visuals:** Ad shows kids getting into stranger's carcharacter role played by film personalitythis could start a precedent in other children thinking that it is okay to jump into the cars of strangers, leading them to become more exposed to child abuse, kidnapping etc. **CCC:** ad apparently addressed to children, encouraged them to converse with apparent strangers and get into the vehicle for the ride which could result in their physical mental or moral harm.

9. Perhaps what fails here is not so much the interpellation per se, but the "dignified" and symbolic authority of the father as an embodiment of the Law in the domestic context. This is particularly worrying to the ASCI since the responsible father is the visual anchor of the authority they are trying to assert vis-à-vis the public space.

10. The irresponsible father—which is the figure of a refusal to bear the burden of symbolic authority—implies limits on the ASCI's own self-imagining.

References

Advertising Standards Council of India. 2004a. *Compilation of Cases Handled by the Consumer Complaints Cell: 1985–1991.* Bombay: ASCI.

———. 2004b. *Compilation of Cases Handled by the Consumer Complaints Cell: 1991–1996.* Bombay: ASCI.

———. 2004c. *Compilation of Cases: April 1996–March 2001.* Bombay: ASCI.

———. 2004d. *Compilation of Cases: April 2001–March 2004.* Bombay: ASCI.

———. 2004e. *On Ads Depicting Women: Complaints That Were Upheld by the Consumer Complaints Council, May 2003–Nov. 2004.* Bombay: ASCI.

———. 2004f. ASCI as Perceived by Our Stakeholders Feedback through ASCI Secretariat. Bombay: ASCI.

———. 2005a. On Ads Depicting Children: Complaints That Were Upheld by the Consumer Complaints Council, April 2003–March 2004. Bombay: ASCI.

———. 2005b. *ASCI at the Cross Roads, January 2005: Concerns and Issues Facing the ASCI in Our 20th Year; Advertising Self Regulation, Self Regulations Codes, ASCI.* Bombay: ASCI.

———. n.d. Website. http://www.ascionline.org/.

Althusser, Louis. 1977. "Ideology and Ideological State Apparatuses (Notes towards an Investigation)." In *Lenin and Philosophy, and Other Essays.* 2nd ed. London: New Left Books.

Barker, Martin, and Julian Petley, eds. 1997. *Ill Effects: The Media/Violence Debate.* London: Routledge.

Baudrillard, Jean. 1988. "The Masses: The Implosion of the Social in the Media." In Mark Poster, ed., *Jean Baudrillard: Selected Writings,* trans. Marie Maclean. Cambridge: Polity.

Breckenridge, Carol, ed. 1995. *Consuming Modernity: Public Culture in a South Asian World.* Minneapolis: University of Minnesota Press.

Dolar, Mladen. 1993. "Beyond Interpretation." *Qui parle* 6(2) (spring–summer): 75–96.

Goodman, Nelson. 1968. *Languages of Art: An Approach to a Theory of Symbols.* 2nd ed. Indianapolis: Hackett.

Hobart, Mark. 2001a. *After Culture: Anthropology as Radical Metaphysical Critique.* Yogakarta: Dura Wacana Press. http://www.criticalia.org.

———. 2001b. "Drunk on the Screen: Balinese Conversations about Television and Advertising." In Brian Moeran, ed., *Asian Media Productions.* Surrey: Curzon.

Inden, Ronald. 2004. "A Campaign That Lost Sheen: Interview with Ronald B. Inden." *The Hindu, Sunday Magazine,* October 3.

Lacan, Jacques. 1962–63. "Le séminaire, livre X: L'angoisse." English translation of the French text edited by Jacques-Alain Miller (Paris: Seuil, 2004). http://www.lacan.com/seminars1b.htm.

Laclau, Ernesto, and Chantal Mouffe. 1985. "Beyond the Positivity of the Social: Antagonisms and Hegemony." In *Hegemony and Socialist Strategy: Towards a Radical Democratic Politics,* trans. Winston Moore and Paul Cammack. London: Verso.

Massumi, Brian. 1993. "Everywhere You Want to Be: Introduction to Fear." In Brian Massumi, ed., *The Politics of Everyday Fear.* Minneapolis: University of Minnesota Press.

Mazzarella, William. 2003. *Shoveling Smoke: Advertising and Globalization in Contemporary India.* Durham, N.C.: Duke University Press.

Poster, Mark. 1990. *The Mode of Information.* Cambridge: Polity.

Nuclear Revelations

Raminder Kaur

Here at Ground Zero, the heart of a nuclear India. A reactor prestigious enough for India to stand up and be counted. A reactor so fascinating that it makes science fiction come alive. . . . And as history turns full circle, maybe this reactor is one more step in the emergence of India as a strong power, taking on the world's superpower on its own terms.

—Royden d'Souza, *Inside India's Fast Breeder*, NDTV, April 2006

More often than not, debates on censorship fall between the supposed opposites of authoritarianism and liberalism, with both polities invoked as ideal types. A focus on nuclear power, particularly as it applies to armament but also in many cases to power stations for civilian use, makes these political dynamics particularly stark. In this chapter, I enquire how debates about censorship of nuclear issues are articulated in public culture along the lines of concealment and calls for more transparency.[1] I then examine the politics of secrecy, which hold an allure irrespective of whether there is something important to be revealed or not. In a sense, what is withheld is produced by what is revealed. Describing this process as "measured revelation," I account for the various strands of Indian public culture which illustrate this dynamic complex.

Secret States and Nuclear "Glasnost"

Patrick Birkinshaw describes countries with vested interests in nuclear power and armament as "secret states" (1990). Robert Jungk concurs, describing the emergence of "garrison societies" in which a "nuclear state must tend towards totalitarianism" (1979, ix). He elaborates,

> If our nuclear power plants are to be well-enough protected to be totally immune to these risks [of radiation], the inevitable consequence is a society dominated by prohibition, surveillance and constraints, all justified by the magnitude of the danger. (1979, viii)

Dhirendra Sharma argues, "Anything connected to nuclear power in this country is a total secret," underlining the fact that there are secrets to be revealed and, in the process, creating some kind of mysterious "rationality" beyond what is known (*Nuclear India* 1992). Similarly, Sukumar Muralidharan and John Cherian point out,

> Institutional processes—and the unwritten rules of national security—make nuclear weapons policy an area of executive privilege, where the Prime Minister is not obliged to seek concurrence from his Council of Ministers, far less the political Opposition (1998)

The topic is so secret that even the Defence Minister, George Fernandes, was kept in the dark about the May 1998 nuclear tests at Pokhran till the very last moment. He stated in early April that "the question of the nuclear option would only be taken up after the National Security Council was constituted and a comprehensive strategic defence review completed" (Muralidharan and Cherian 1998). Some writers maintain that the turn toward authoritarian secrecy is exacerbated by latter-day Hindu nationalist parties:

> Nuclear weaponisation . . . helps in the shift of society towards authoritarianism. That is why the ruling classes of India have been gravitating towards the fascist Sangh Parivar; and Sangh Parivar has resorted to nuclear weaponisation programme to further strengthen reactionary forces—one way to unbridled fascism. (*Indian Express*, November 21, 2001)

Whereas secrecy around nuclear weaponization in this case could lead to "unbridled fascism," Itty Abraham argues that the phenomenon is not exclusive to right-wing parties: it serves a variety of functions, from hiding the level of progress on atomic research from foreigners and Indians alike, to being an intrinsic part of modernity in defining boundaries between the privileged and profane realms of society.[2] According to him, secrecy is a foundational principle in modern India:

> Secrecy is a boundary-producing mechanism, an instrument of modern discipline. Rather than simply seeing it as a furtive condition that keeps information privileged or hidden, it can act to produce a violent rupture between inside and outside, between a space that is privileged and that which is profane. . . . Secrecy . . . becomes a necessary condition for the maintenance of the difference between the modern and everything else. Without secrecy, the singularity of the postcolonial project would become difficult to maintain for those practising, and with most invested in, its performance, and under those circumstances there would be no project at all. (Abraham 1998, 163–64)[3]

The details of secrecy about nuclear power in India are due to a combination of factors. Firstly, legislative acts such as the Official Secrets Act (1923), the Atomic Energy Act (1948, 1962, with amendments in 1986), and the National Security Act (1980) ensure that information on anything to do with nuclear policies and industries is heavily restricted.[4] The Atomic Energy Act in particular provides for "the development, control and use of atomic energy for the welfare of the people of India and for other peaceful purposes and for matters connected therewith" (September 15, 1962). Under this Act, the Indian government has the power to refuse to release information of any kind pertaining to nuclear matters if it deems such material a national security issue.[5]

The control of nuclear matters that the government has ascribed to itself is compounded by the scarcity of independent Indian expertise on nuclear matters outside of the Department of Atomic Energy and kindred organizations. In addition, the term "national security" is bandied around in a very ambiguous and adaptable manner; as the rules of national security are unwritten, it can mean almost anything. Vague as the phrase may be, it still holds powerful currency.[6] Censorship under the pretext of national security is almost unquestioned in India, and state concerns become privatized as individual concerns, especially in light of the threat of terrorism.[7] These anxieties are periodically fueled by the shadow play of enemies of India, such as Pakistan and China (both of which have declared themselves nuclear weapons states), and, to a lesser extent, those countries that India believes opposes its desire to go nuclear.[8] Writing on the pre-1990s American case, Edward Herman and Noam Chomsky instructively observe that

> a constant focus on victims of communism helps convince the public of enemy evil and sets the stage for intervention, subversion, support for terrorist states, an endless arms race, and military conflict—all in a noble cause. At the same time, the devotion of our leaders and media to this narrow set of victims raises public self-esteem and patriotism, as it demonstrates the essential humanity of country and people. (Herman and Chomsky 1988, xv)

Now the bogey of communism has been replaced by the specter of antinationalism and terrorism. Dr. Anil Kakodkar, Director of the Bhabha Atomic Research Centre (BARC) and the Atomic Energy Commission, insists that "nobody should be able to cast an evil eye on India" (Krishnakumar 2000, 18). Recurrent reminders of enemy nations and of antinational elements within India confirm the status of the nuclear enterprise as part of the effort to forge a strong nation, and the nuclear industry's authority to pursue clandestine operations under the banner of national security is guaranteed.

Framing the debate in this way leads critics and activists alike to demand that state authorities be more accountable and transparent. The editor of the current affairs magazine *Frontline* observed, "The Pokhran tests of May 1974 and May 1998, and hawkishness within the nuclear energy establishment, have only reinforced secretiveness and non-accountability on safety issues" (*Frontline* 1999). Even a former intelligence chief declared, "Accountability is the key to better performances of the secret services which worldwide are prone to cover up their failures on the grounds that transparency would jeopardise national security" (*Telegraph*, Calcutta, May 14, 2001).

And the debate goes on. However, it is too simplistic to assert that the state enforces total secrecy on nuclear issues. A democratic state has to be at least somewhat accountable to the populace in order to establish a consensus on having nuclear weapons. This accountability often leads to publicity exercises in which invited members of the public and media are given glowing, even radiant, displays and accounts of the progress of India's nuclear industry. One of the first such publicity exercises was mounted in November 1954 at the behest of Jawaharlal Nehru at the National Physical Laboratory in New Delhi.[9] The National Symposium on Atomic Energy was intended to silence critics such as Meghnad Saha, a physicist and Member of Parliament strongly in favor of hydroelectric plants. It was attended by Nehru and his cabinet colleagues, MPs, bureaucrats, defense officials, industrialists, scientists, and technologists. Even though members of the general public were not present, Salwi argues that "in the present parlance, it can be called an 'open public debate' on the peaceful uses of nuclear energy" (2004, 37).

Strategies of censorship in India have moved away from blatant excision of passages or curtailment of free speech, which are more characteristic of the Emergency years under Indira Gandhi's leadership (1975–77) than of the contemporary period. The critics quoted above overlook the state's need to legitimate nuclear power in the eyes of the general public.[10] So while there is a tendency toward authoritarianism, the government must also demonstrate (or at least appear to demonstrate) democratic accountability. Justice Mathew declared, "In a government of responsibility like ours, where all the agents of the public must be responsible for their conduct, there can be but few secrets" (BCAS Foundation 2005, 1).

By the late 1980s, terms like "glasnost" were being bandied about to refer to the increasing public awareness of the nuclear state. By "nuclear state," I refer specifically to governmental agencies such as the Department of Atomic Energy, but I also use the term in a larger sense to indicate India's nuclear prowess and capability as well as to allude to the nuclear scientific establishment. The nuclear scientists, for reasons of funding and job security, are associated with state authorities and are intimately linked with military and industrial bodies in charge of nuclear research.[11] One report went thus:

> "There is too much secrecy," complains Mohan Parikh [a Gandhian and winner of the Jamnala Bajaj Award for his work on improving farm technology]. "In a democracy, people have to be taken into confidence. But they (the nuclear establishment) do not want anyone to know what is going on," he believes. This obsessive secrecy is a legacy of the old days when reticence was considered a virtue and no attempt was made either to inform the public or refute the various accusations levelled from time to time, say industry insiders.

But all this may be changing. In the last two decades, the DAE has been trying to correct its image and remove the mystique surrounding nuclear energy. "The Department is undergoing a period of glasnost," said the Additional Secretary, N Vittal (Raj 1989, 95).

Indeed, it could well be argued that the relentless accusation of a lack of transparency has compelled the nuclear state to pursue a variety of legitimization strategies in public culture. In this post-liberalization era, to deny the media access to information about and displays of nuclear power altogether would be to invite widespread distrust and critique. There is also the added pressure to assert nuclear capability in public culture in general. Doing so helps to demonstrate Indian's prowess in science and technology and thus the nation's strength. The nuclear authorities have to publicize their efforts, however selectively, and in a democratic nation they must make at least a token gesture toward the freedom of information. More often than not, their publicity is aimed at journalists who are known to be supportive of the nuclear enterprise.

Recently, the ideals of accountability and transparency have been enshrined in the Right to Information Act (2005), which is derived from "our fundamental right of expression under Article 19 of the Constitution of India" (*Right to Know: Citizen's Guide*, 2005, 1). This Act allows Indian citizens to get information on the government's actions and decisions. But information can be denied in certain cases. Although the nuclear industry is not specifically mentioned, one of the Act's provisos alludes to it in saying that there is no obligation to disclose information "which would prejudicially affect the sovereignty and integrity of India, the security, strategic, scientific or economic interests of the State, relation with foreign State or lead to incitement of an offence" (*Right to Know: Citizen's Guide*, 2005, 6). This provision can be interpreted in a number of ways, depending upon the actors and motivations involved.

Thus, information about nuclear power is revealed to the public in a measured way, using narrative, imagery, and performance. By using the word "measured," I am not suggesting that it is a refined or quantitative operation—as M. V. Ramana elaborates, practices of secrecy by the nuclear establishment are never uniform.[12] Nevertheless, what is revealed or becomes public enables one to both support the nuclearization of India and vilify "demons," be they foreign countries or antinational or antidevelopment individuals or groups within the country. The revelations are measured in that, while they are tempered by the strictures of national security concerns, they must try to win over public opinion and seduce audiences by offering grandiose spectacles of the nuclear nation. The disclosures oscillate between the poles of authoritarianism and accountability, offering enough to fetishize nuclear discourse and pacify the majority of audiences but not enough to give the entire game away.

There is another tension to note. On the one hand, as we have seen, there is the powerful idea that nuclear secrets exist, guarded by the authoritarian nuclear state. Activists' focus on "total secrecy" keeps this idea that information is hidden behind the curtain of publicity alive (see Mazzarella 2006). Simultaneously, their appeals also support the idea that the material offered to the public is given in the name of transparency. On the other hand, there is nothing to disclose which is not already known—that is, there is no actual secret behind the state's mask, only a numinous and imaginary secret. What is with-held cannot be separated from what is revealed, and is indeed produced by various modalities of revelation.

Each of these two perspectives, premised upon notions of concealment and the numinous, allows us to see different aspects of a complex situation. In actual practice, we see the articulation of both, often at the same time. The disclosure of information is of vital importance to people directly affected by nuclear projects and to cultures of democracy in general, whereas the allure of a politics of secrecy is present irrespective of whether there is something important to be revealed; it indicates instead our desire for there to be a secret at the heart of the state.

So despite the fact that several authors have assumed that nuclear mat-ters are handled in total secrecy, I note the additional dynamic that censor-ship thrives on a measured revelation of that which it aspires to censor. This dynamic is implicit in discourses of nuclear power in contemporary India and may also appear in other countries with nuclear power. Why measured revela-tion? Herman and Chomsky (1998), discussing news reportage, refer to simi-lar phenomena as instancing processes of "filleted knowledge." They focus on "filleted reports" that are issued in an effort to obscure certain agendas. In this way, consent is manufactured. Herman and Chomsky offer a variation on the Gramscian model that focuses on the emergence of consent through negotia-tions between hegemonic blocs.[13] I agree with the main thrust of Herman and Chomsky's argument, but qualify the true/false dichotomies implicit in their stance on propaganda. Admittedly, state discussions about nuclear power have a propagandist tone, but this does not mean that simply peeling back the layers exposes the "real truths" underneath them. Moreover, Herman and Chomsky's argument cannot account for the belief that a phantasmal and compelling secret lies at the heart of the nuclear state.

Developing Foucauldian ideas that power resides in the nexus of knowledge and the visible, Michael Taussig (1999) argues that power also thrives on the unknown, the invisible, and the censored, the hidden heart of the nuclear state. However, rather than focusing on what Taussig calls the "public secret"—"that which is generally known, but cannot be articulated" (1999, 5; cf. Lakier's chap-ter in this volume)—I would like to invert this dynamic to focus less on what is withheld and more on what is revealed, albeit in a sanitized or fetishized man-ner. In this exercise, I am greatly inspired by the Hegelian notion of the "labor of the negative" (the interstices, the unspoken) and the Nietzschean "breath of empty space" (Taussig 1999, 1). But here my focus is on what might, for want of a better phrase, be called "the labor of the positive."

I explore the nexus of pageantry and secrecy in the wake of India's 1998 nuclear tests, seeing them as foundational principles that facilitate the manufac-ture both of consent and of desire for the nuclear prerogative of nation-states. A variety of information and imagery appears in the performative space of the nation through media reportage, documentaries, national parades, nuclear tests, documents and leaflets, parades, ceremonies, public meetings, party politics, and festival displays. The "labor" of such "positives"—ranging from informational disclosures to spectacular affirmations—is what interests me here. Some of these sites have direct links with governmental authorities. Others have more indirect ones, but nevertheless, the majority of these sites concur with the hegemonic state in "the performative-affective suturing of a nationalist fantasy."[14] This concordance is due to a number of complementary factors. After President George W. Bush visited India in March 2006 and he and Prime Minister Manmohan Singh confirmed a civil nuclear partnership, the press became even more celebratory of India's nuclear prowess and aspirations to the status of regional superpower.[15] The nuclear discourse in India is of course influenced by the changing status of nuclear power at the global level, particularly in the context of the predicted scarcity of fuel and the "war on terror." India's growing middle class and modern lifestyles bring an increasing appetite for energy, whatever its source. Nuclear power is often touted as a clean source of energy, compared to oil and gas—a view which takes little heed of the vast amount of fuel and resources required to construct plants and their limited lifespan, as well as the long half-life of radioactive materials. The fact that the nuclear is deeply imbricated in the national—as neatly summed up by Praful Bidwai and Achin Vanaik's (1999) phrase "nuclear nationalism"—makes it even more difficult to target the former without the protective mantle of the latter. The laborious detail imparted by government reports and sympathetic news reports—which nevertheless do not reveal much—provide little to inform an open and critical debate on nuclear power.[16]

To Censor or Not to Censor

The word "censorship" is used in both broad and specific ways.[17] Several kinds of censorship have been identified, including political, invoked by a local or national government to keep itself in power; military, invoked to protect the nation in the face of an enemy; religious, invoked to prevent anything from undermining the faith of the flock as adjudged by authorities; and cultural, invoked to prevent anything in printed texts, movies, plays, art, or radio or television broadcasts from undermining public morals. There is also the phenomenon of self-censorship. The looseness of the term has led some critics to argue that it has little value (see Burt 1994, xii). As William Mazzarella and I argue in chapter 1 of this volume, "cultural regulation" offers a broader purview, but we should not overlook the statist aspects of censorship. Addressing the nuclear topic highlights the point that the understanding of cultural regulation varies according to not just spatial and temporal contexts, but also the kind of material in question. Essentially, I will be taking a top-down perspective on cultural regulation—that is, moving from considering state structures that deploy a fairly distinct policy of censorship and revelation to considering the availability of images and information in the wider society.

From a more theoretical viewpoint, however, censorship can never be total, because of the inherent limits of regulation. As Judith Butler observes, censorship is characterized by "(a) the failure to institute a complete or total subjectification through legal means and (b) the failure to circumscribe effectively the social domain of speakable discourse" (1997, 132). Furthermore, state censorship is only ever partial, for in a supposedly democratic state, legitimacy or a public consensus has to be (or at least appear to be) actively sought. Thus there is a measured revelation of certain issues, debates, and imagery for public consumption, enough to claim that the dictates of democracy are followed, at least on paper.[18]

By considering censorship in relation to nuclear weapons, we uncover specific dynamics quite distinct from those of censorship as it pertains to media and public culture in general. Fears for India's national security are periodically fueled by the twin threats of Pakistan and terrorism. But citizens of a democratic nation have to be "brought into the bargain"—that is, mainstream society must grant legitimacy, and the government must provide at least the appearance of transparency. National security (fear of espionage, uranium smuggling, and other inimical acts) drives a demand for total censorship, withholding all information from the public; the need for legitimacy drives the dissemination of information and the staging of campaigns, demonstrations, parades, and other spectacles in an effort to favorably influence public opinion and appear to promote a free society or a culture of "openness." The spectacles of nuclear tests, Republic Day parades, and informational films distributed by the government, for instance, contribute to the fetishization of the nuclear discourse and the measured revelation of nuclear agendas. Abraham notes that the state as fetish hides "political reality" from the public gaze:

> If following Michael Taussig, the state as fetish seeks to mask the gaze of the public from political reality, the state fetish equally seeks to conceal the conditions of its creation, to marginalise questions of its origins, to naturalize the displacements of its production, to fulfil simultaneously all the multiple economies in which it circulates. (1998, 156)

However, this understanding of the state fetish is limited. As Mazzarella (2006) argues, it is equally true that the state fetish conceals the fact that there is nothing behind it except our own collective investment in there being something—that is to say, we meet not "the state" but rather our own desire.

Measured revelation is propelled by the increasing power of images in a consumerist society (Debord 1973).[19] John Cherian states,

> Nuclear weapons have always been viewed as a "currency of power" and the "ultimate weapon" by the BJP and a group of hawks on strategic issues whose contributions to the nuclear debate in India have had more than their fair share of play in the media. (Cherian 1998)

If the Ayodhya movement to construct the Ramjamnabhumi *mandir* on the site of the Babri *masjid* redefined Ram as an all-India deity and warrior-prince,[20] the Pokhran nuclear test explosions altered the meanings of Buddha and "peace" or *ahimsa*. The tests were deliberately scheduled on Buddha Purnima, the full moon in the month of Vaisakh (April–May) on which the Buddha was born, attained enlightenment, and attained nirvana when he died. They were nick-named "Buddha Smiles Again" and Gandhian ideas of *ahimsa*—in that the tests were "peaceful" and that the weapons are intended to maintain "peace"—were co-opted and promoted (Bharucha 1998). A show of Indian might and inde-pendence in decision making has enabled Hindu nationalists to pick up the mantle of anti-imperialism, resisting the nuclear powers in the glorified tradition of the anticolonial freedom movement. In the words of the BJP's manifesto for the 1991 election, they harbored ambitions to give India's armed forces "nuclear teeth." Images and metaphors of bravado became instrumental to broadening consent and maximizing national honor and strength. After the 1998 tests, Prime Minister Atal Behari Vajpayee, a member of the BJP, declared,

> India is now a nuclear weapons state. . . . the decision to carry out these tests was guided by the paramount importance we attach to national security. . . . the tests . . . have given India shakti, they have given strength, they have given India self-confidence. (Vajpayee 1998)

Now that the nuclear genii are out of the bottle, other parties have also adopted this tone. Scientists too rhapsodized about how India's strength had been rec-ognized. The Chairman of the Atomic Energy Commission, R. Chidambaram, stated (1998), "India must become strong. The greatest advantage of recog-nised strength is that you don't have to use it," demonstrating parallels with the power of the secret which is not disclosed. And A. P. J. Abdul Kalam (the former President of India) emphasized a similar point after successful tests of the Agni, Prithvi, and Trishul missiles: "India must stand up to the world. . . . In this world fear has no place. Only strength respects strength," he declared (Jayaraman 2002).

Not all of these statements were endorsed by the state. A substantial number are arranged by other interested communities for a range of private, political, commercial, and religious purposes. Thus, regulation takes manifold forms—it can be directly coordinated by state authorities, or it can be indi-rectly managed by controlling the availability of information about and imag-ery of nuclear power in Indian public culture. Regulation could be overt or it could manifest internalized assumptions about the necessity of nuclear power to national strength and security. Despite these complex capillary flows, the source of nuclear news is clear: it is the state which, in its patronage of nuclear power, has supreme access to knowledge about it, and it is the state from which information about the nuclear industry flows—sometimes freely, sometimes only in a slow trickle—to the public.

Abraham notes that the practice of releasing only certain types of information has led to the formation of "a sanitised official narrative on scientific and peaceful progress,"

> a narrative produced through glossy publications like *Nuclear India*, published by the Indian department of atomic energy, through memoirs which bear heavily on a selective recall of events and causes, and, most important, through the creation of an official myth around the figure of Homi Jehangir Bhabha, the first leader of India's nuclear establishment. (Abraham 1998, 4)

Such is the tenacity of this official narrative that subsequent recollections by individuals working in the nuclear industry have also been shaped by it:

> Owing to the weight of the official state narrative and the centralisation of decision making being in the hands of so few people, most individuals one would have expected to be in a position to know something had replaced their own recollections with the official version of what happened, had never been in a position to know what had transpired at key moments, or just would not talk on the record for various reasons, including fear. (Abraham 1998, 4)

These official narratives pervade public culture, impairing the efficacy of critical debate. Ramana notes that even though the Nuclear Power Corporation of India Limited (NPCIL, a public sector enterprise of the DAE) offers many details about nuclear projects on its website, it also withholds information that is "critical to making informed assessments of the economics, the environmental and public health impacts, or the potential for serious accidents at nuclear facilities" (forthcoming, 5). Thus, while certain kinds of information and displays are made available, others remain obscured. But even here, one cannot fathom the exact nature of what is censored: something deemed a security risk in one department may be available through contacts in another. At other times, anything with "nuclear" in its title could be tucked away as secret. As Joseph Masco has observed about U.S. activism against the nuclear complex, the boundary between "what is secret and what is not secret is also secret" (Masco 2006, 225).

Even though a focus on the labor of the positive discloses what is known and revealed about nuclear issues, we cannot assume that this material is as consistent as nuclear states would wish. The line between secrecy and openness is not only nebulous; it is also inconsistently deployed by individuals variously stationed within the nuclear complex. The inconsistency of censorship strategies is aptly illustrated by the following anecdote. A conservationist in Kanyakumari District once told me how he tried to get information from the Indian Rare Earths Limited plant (IREL, a Government of India undertaking) in Manavalakuruchi about its sand mining and thorium processing. Thorium emits alpha radiation and is present in the monazite in the sand. IREL management would not give him any data, claiming that it was confidential. But he

Figure 6.1
Signboard of Indian Rare Earths Limited and trucks transporting sand
based in Manavalakuruchi in Kanyakumari district. Photo by author.

later found the information he needed printed in the 1995 *Gazetteers of India, Tamil Nadu State, Kanyakumari District*, a Government of India publication!

States are represented by their officials, so censorship strategies, no matter how stringent, can diverge as officials in different departments work to differing agendas. Individuals may assess and enact them idiosyncratically. One retired senior army officer, when giving a presentation on India's nuclear capability in a conference at New Delhi's Habitat Centre in April 2006, said that he gave only information that was already available in public documents and books. However, not all of this literature was available to the public. In personal conversation afterward, he told me that he maintained a mental filing system, with anything highly confidential at the back of his head, material that was not so confidential further forward, and information available to the public right at the front. The process of releasing information and making it available is not always systematic, but this officer's mind certainly appeared to be.

The Labor of the Positive

Idiosyncrasies notwithstanding, the modalities of state-backed revelations range from the straightforward presentation of information to extravagant spectacle. They include government or government-related educational programs, broadcasts on the state-run television channel (Doordarshan), the print media,

Figure 6.2

International Conference: "Current Developments in Atomic, Molecular & Optical Physics with Applications." University of Delhi, March 2006. Photo by author.

exhibitions, conferences, parades, seminars, conferences, and websites such as those of the Department of Atomic Energy (http://www.dae.gov.in) and the Nuclear Power Corporation of India Limited (http://www.npcil.nic.in). Each of these examples warrants attention, but only a brief summary of each can be provided in this overview.[21]

While we can only speculate on, and indeed be fascinated by, what lurks behind particular representations, we can at least examine nuclear revelations in public culture. It is noteworthy that in all such revelations, the facts delivered are manicured, stripped of their messiness, so as to appear less complex than sociopolitical realities might dictate. This is as true of words as it is of images. Revelations of nuclear information are not standardized, but the information is banalized and embellished, made into a rosy and often entertaining presentation to increase its audience appeal. The image of the nuclear missile, for instance, has become a fetish, taken away from its messier modes of production and commodified as an image-icon that works according to its own logics.[22] These logics shift the focus away from the costs of building and maintaining such missiles, the risks of contamination in the nuclear industries, and so forth, to the missiles' function as spectacle in a world where countries wielding nuclear weapons can claim global might. It is as if the missile is extracted from its use-value (referring to the missile's mode of production, but also, at a stretch, to its destructive potential) to become an icon of a formidable exchange-value—that is, its use-value has become its spectacular exchange-value.[23] Nuclear weapons become "political weapons," which are implicit, if not explicit, in international negotiations and national parades but not intended ever to be used. Rough edges are smoothed, as the icon is packaged for consumption and paraded as a sexy, sleek symbol of the hypermodern era.

The dominant rhetoric of indigenous technology also helps to valorize the nuclear industry as essentially Indian, in the service of the nation, and therefore worthy. Religious discourse aids the processes of fetishization, attributing a supposedly unique Indian character to them. For instance, the idea that atomic power stations and missiles resemble Shiv *lingam,* which have equally stupendous (albeit spiritually derived) powers, has become widespread (Abraham 1998, 10). Other examples are explicit in the naming of events, sites, and weapons: the 1998 nuclear tests and their site were named Shakti (much as American nuclear tests were called Trinity, a term from Christian theology), missiles are called Agni and Trishul, and cosmic and mystical images are used to describe nuclear detonations (the phrase "brighter than a thousand suns" is taken from the Bhagavad Gita [Ramana 2000]).

Other parts of the nuclear hegemony concentrate on the privileged status of discourses of science and technology, in which scientists are venerated as quasi-deities and their work seen as sacred, especially if it is intended to benefit the nation. Science's privileged association with colonial government—a fruit denied to the general native populace—was reproduced by the elitist alliance between Indian scientists and government after Independence. The sacralization of science goes back at least to colonial times, as do revisionist accounts of signs of nuclear power in the Vedas and other ancient texts (Prakash 1999).[24] Such accounts figure atomic power as *shakti,* and the force of the *brahmastra,* a fearfully powerful weapon used by Ashvatthaman in the Mahabharata, is likened to a nuclear bomb (Kaur 2005).

Official documents, many of which are steeped in obscurantist jargon, are also key outlets for regulated information on the nuclear state. For example, according to the Bombay *Indian Express* (September 1, 1998), a report on behalf of the Formations of a Strategic Nuclear Command discussing nuclear options, prepared by the Planning Directorate and approved by the army, navy, and air force, declared that "the National Strategic Nuclear Command (NSNC) should have cost-effective redundancy to cater for primary system neutralisation due to first strike." Such reports obscure as much as they purport to reveal. Often they are reproduced without critique by mainstream national newspapers. National media coverage, particularly since Indo-U.S. agreement on a civil nuclear partnership in 2006, is largely supportive of the nuclear establishment, and journalists often base their articles entirely on press releases from the Department of Atomic Energy. This is largely because specialized knowledge is required to understand nuclear technology, which not only creates an elite out of those who have that knowledge but also veils the exact purpose and implications of the technology. Those not privy to this elitist discourse can either wonder at or, alternatively, bask in its aura of superiority, marveling at India's technological and military might.

Other kinds of literature issued by state-backed authorities are bombastic and celebratory. The Nuclear India Archive on the DAE's website contains material suitable for a hagiography of the nuclear nation. It proclaims the nuclear industry a panacea for India's development and power needs. Similarly, one pro-nuclear journalist waxed lyrical:

> The word "nuclear" is not a nightmare, quite to the contrary; from radioactive isotopes for cancer diagnostics and therapy, to preservation of grain and *dal* seeds, to desalination, to nuclear reactors, to accelerators, it is a grand panorama. Every section of this, once used and channelled properly, would make "nuclear" the inevitable solution for Asia, and India in particular. (*Telegraph*, Calcutta, November 25, 1999)

Community welfare is another mantra of the nuclear state. A souvenir booklet available from the Kudankulam Nuclear Power Project (KKNPP), whose construction began in 2002, is keen to promote the benefits the project will provide, not just to the nuclear industry and the nation, but also to the local community. In it, the Project Director, S. K. Agrawal, proudly announces,

> It has indeed been a very satisfying journey of bringing up the Kudankulam Nuclear Power Project from barren land to this stage of construction. A beautiful Township with all amenities & facilities was constructed at war footing and practically ready by mid 2003. . . . On the 3rd anniversary of "FIRST POUR OF CONCRETE," I want to give the assurance on behalf of committed team of KKNPP that we shall complete the Project ahead of schedule and in cost less than sanctioned cost of the Project. (*A Journey towards Excellence* 2005)

Agrawal presents himself as a patron of the masses, conducting work in everyone's interests. In an ironic twist, he salvages terms from a Marxist vocabulary and portrays those who are not pro-nuclear as spreading "negative propaganda," with the implication that he is disseminating "positive propaganda":

> Our very transparent, fair and open approach in reaching out to the masses made the difference and the villagers understood the real situation. The journalists workshop organised by KNPP was well attended and it was quite successful because all the questions about the safety of the plant were answered with facts and figures. Regular interaction and site visit for media persons were arranged and thereafter they provided good support to the Project. (*A Journey towards Excellence* 2005)

The idea that much of the public is misinformed about nuclear power is endemic amongst the nuclear authorities. Their mission then becomes to enlighten the populace as to the true benefits of nuclear power. An announcement of the 2007 Annual Conference of the Indian Nuclear Society in Hyderabad, with the theme "Exploration, Mining and Processing of Atomic and Rare Minerals," stated that the main challenges in doing so are

Figure 6.3
Road sign for the Kudankulam Nuclear Power Project. Photo by author.

minimizing the environmental, radiological and ecological impacts of these activities and even a bigger challenge is addressing the public concerns and managing the perceptions and misconceptions prevalent in the society regarding the perceived health impacts of uranium mining and processing. ("Annual Conference of the Indian Nuclear Society" 2007)

The idea of educating and managing public opinion is a constant refrain amongst the nuclear elite. Their discourse posits a dichotomous world in which the open and transparent scientific bureaucracy is contrasted with the dark and ignorant masses, with the rationality of facts and figures held aloft over the irrationality of popular fears. The bureaucrats and scientists have recourse to the supposed neutrality of science, with its facts and figures, while emotions are identified with the masses and with deluded activists who lead the people into erroneous forms of thinking.

The rest of the KKNPP souvenir booklet details the costs and progress of the construction of the atomic power plant, which is being built with the help of the Russian team, Atomstroyexport. In addition, it lists a number of welfare programs carried out by the project, such as drilling wells and providing computers to villages, constructing medical camps and classrooms for local schools, funding roads in the area, and assisting orphans, women's self-help groups, and tsunami-affected villagers.[25] Community welfare has become a latter-day mainstay of the Nuclear Power Corporation of India Limited. The KKNPP worked to ingratiate itself with local communities through public relations

Figure 6.4

A journey towards excellence . . ., souvenir booklet for the
Kudankulam Nuclear Power Project. Photo by author.

efforts, acting as if it was a patron of their interests even though many of the welfare projects to do with water, roads, and gas stations were planned primarily for the benefit of power plant construction workers and staff.

Exhibitions, conferences, and seminars have been instrumental to the nuclear state's strategy to reach out to local communities in order to lecture wary villagers on how people-friendly, safe and important nuclear power is. "The effort is to dispel doubts and fears about nuclear power," says the Koodankulam project engineer from NPC [the Nuclear Power Corporation of India, Limited], C R Prabhakaran. . . . the NPC, so far known for its ivory-tower aloofness, decided to woo Koodankulam. Two batches of villagers have already been brought on junkets to Kalpakkam and Chennai to learn some basic nuclear lessons.[26] . . . Most villagers today say they do not mind risks and discomforts for the greater glory of the country. . . . Villagers were told the visit would show them how much less polluting nuclear power would be. . . . As for safety, Koodankulam has been assured a leak-proof set-up. "They told us the project will not harm people like in Russia (Chernobyl). We thought we were all going to be killed. But yesterday they told us there will be double-sealing," says panchayat leader Anbazhagan, echoing NPC's promise of double containment, with a steel-lined inner layer. . . . "They told us we will have good roads, even hospitals." . . . the group returns cheerily to pack its bags at Kalpakkam. "Let it come, let all the 2,000 MW of it come to our village. We will be on the international map," shouts out a farmer. (*Telegraph*, Calcutta, August 31, 1998)

Descriptions such as "people-friendly," "safe," and "important," phrases like "the greater glory of the country" and "being on the international map," even unexplained yet apparently reassuring steps such as "double-sealing" the reactors form part of Agrawal's positive propaganda. Clearly the nuclear authorities only reveal those details which will allay people's fears, emphasizing the benefits rather than the drawbacks of nuclear power stations. Not all of the article is to be believed wholeheartedly, for the media only present a selection of views in their weaving of a story. Plenty of village residents in the Kudankulam region may have prospered from the development, but they also point out the KKNPP's hollow promises of jobs for local people, and fishing communities in particular worry about how their livelihoods will be affected once the power plant is up and running and nuclear waste has to be managed. There is thus much public debate at the local level (Kaur n.d.). The main problem is that critics cannot independently evaluate the veracity of state revelations. They can only work with state disclosures, basing their critique on humanitarian ethics, economics (if the figures issued by nuclear agencies are to be taken as accurate), and past nuclear mishaps and atrocities around the world.

Television programs show state representatives aspiring to domesticate nuclear weapons, making their possession out to be not only in the national interest, but also in the interest of the individual. These efforts are aimed less at the "common man" than at the "modern man"—middle-class, educated, articulate, and aware of India's global status.[27] Entrenching politics in the person and in everyday discourse has the effect of normalizing nuclear weapons. For instance, T. Jayaraman notes that

Television discussion panel participants, talk show hosts, members of studio audiences, scientists in talk shows of various kinds (with some honourable exceptions) sustain the discussion in the bland language of strategic analysis. "Nuclear weapons are not weapons of war," intones an analyst on a BBC discussion panel, "they are political weapons." (Jayaraman n.d.)

Nuclear weapons are not imagined as potential instruments of destruction; rather, they are seen as essential pawns in a political game, for without them you cannot be king (or queen, for that matter). Similarly, disjointing nuclear weapons from the horrors that they are capable of and associating them instead with banalized political strategy or the scientific credit of the nation is the rule among documentaries on this topic archived at the National Films Division. The titles are self-explanatory: *Hidden Treasure* (1957, dir. Biren Das), *Atomic Energy and India* (1972, dir. Vijay Chandra), *Atom—Man's Most Powerful Servant* (1975, dir. P. B. Pendharkar), *In the Service of Mankind* (1980, dir. Murzban Sepoy), and *Nuclear Power: A National Achievement* (1980, dir. Dilip Gupta). The programs index independent India's modernity, and the sacred status of the nuclear industry developed along with the nation. The nuclear industry's regulation is unquestioned, for to disturb this status quo would be to unravel the very fabric of the nation.

Even television documentaries shown on the independent cable station, NDTV, are not immune to state influence. Although professing to be a liberal channel not hemmed in by state strictures, it still favors an uncritical pronuclear agenda. In April 2006, NDTV broadcast an exclusive documentary entitled *Inside India's Fast Breeder*, in which a reporter, Royden d'Souza, went inside the plutonium fast breeder reactor under construction in Kalpakkam. D'Souza called the reactor "India's big secret" and proclaimed, "Indian scientists have proved that they are far ahead of the world. . . . We are the first journalists ever to be allowed to enter the fast breeder reactor complex and these are the first pictures of the enigmatic project that till now no camera has ever recorded." This bombastic report trumpeted the idea that India is becoming a superpower and the claim that it pioneered the use of thorium in reactors (a claim which has not yet been substantiated). Here the program not only presents a curtain which the crusader journalist is supposed to have pierced, but in the process creates an even greater desire for what is not yet revealed, what is yet to come.

Disturbingly, the program was broadcast in the same month as the twentieth anniversary of the Chernobyl disaster in the former USSR, yet its reference point was not the former USSR but the United States, which it saw as the world's superpower. Its mood was aspirational, not commemorative. More critical documentaries, such as Anand Patwardhan's *Jang aur Aman* (War and Peace, 2002), have to struggle first with the Censor Board and then with problems of distribution, and even then they can fall through the crevices of mainstream discourse, since they very rarely get the same kind of coverage as pro-nuclear offerings.

Even the popular film industry stands to gain from producing movies which are pro-national and, by implication, pro-nuclear. Films that are declared in the national interest need not pay tax on their box office returns. Although few films make the nuclear industry an integral part of their plot, nuclear missiles and bombs have appeared in several. In such films, nuclear weapons are legitimately part of the state machinery, necessary for India's safety and security as the hero fights it out with his unscrupulous enemies, who want to use the technology for themselves. *The Hero: Love Story of a Spy* (dir. Anil Sharma, 2003) shows an army intelligence officer named Arun (Sonny Deol) who, in one big burly mass, is an Indian amalgam of James Bond and Rambo. His mission is to overturn plans by a renegade Pakistani team of politicians, priests, and scientists to build a nuclear bomb by acquiring nuclear isotopes in association with a Pakistani-Canadian firm. The sore point, as ever, is Kashmir, a disputed region between the two countries since Independence. A Pakistani renegade says to his cronies, "Just once, just get us the nuclear bomb and Kashmir will be ours. If Pakistan cannot openly give you the Islamic bomb, then we can steal it." Indian intelligence officers have secretly filmed this meeting, and one of them concludes about Pakistan, "On the one hand it tries to create terrorism in our country. On the other it tries to give a good image of itself to the world." The film implies that only India, the good guy, is capable of handling such powerful weapons for the benefit of the nation. Others want them only out of megalomaniacal greed and power.

Images of nuclear-capable missile launches and nuclear tests (the latter approved and released by the government) invite the public to celebrate and participate in the might of a strong and modern nation. The only cameras allowed at the 1998 blast site were under the control of the government, and vivid images of the one fusion and four fission bombs were released after the event (*Business Standard*, Calcutta, September 7, 1998).[28] Similar tentative public relations practices were adopted by Indira Gandhi's government after the 1974 Pokhran tests, which it declared a "peaceful nuclear experiment." R. N. Rao, the founder of India's foreign intelligence agency, RAW (Research and Analysis Wing), recalled in the Calcutta *Business Standard* (June 18, 1997), "It was a secret known to hundreds. But no outside power came to know of it in time. Not even the Americans." His remark highlights how revelation is contingent on the projected audience: the Indian masses, the scientific community, the intelligentsia, or the world at large, in which the U.S. holds a position of alluring supremacy. Such spectacles have unleashed a phenomenal wave of appreciation. A year after the 1998 tests, Anil Kakodkar, Director of the Bhabha Atomic Research Centre, recalled that for the first time in his life he had been treated almost like a film or cricket star when he went to the Indian Institute of Technology in Madras to deliver a convocation address; hordes of graduates wanted his autograph (Kanavi 1999).

Parades, especially on Republic Day (January 26) in New Delhi, are key events instituted in the post-Independence years to help produce a patriotic Indian citizen. The Republic Day parade has now become a showcase for the country's military might, featuring regional floats in a performative spectacle of "unity in diversity" (see S. Roy 2007). The latest missiles—Agni, Prithvi, and Trishul—take pride of place in regimented processions by the military. The parade's annual recurrence seeks to reinforce a feeling of national camaraderie and to encourage a celebration of both conventional and nuclear arsenals.

Museum exhibits of nuclear technology, although paltry in comparison, imbue the subject with an educational mission. Displays may be historical, illustrating the development of Indian science and its pioneers, such as Homi Jehangir Bhabha, who is heralded as the architect of India's nuclear program and one of the men responsible for leading India into the atomic age. Often representations of Bhabha will be placed alongside those of pioneers in related disciplines, such as Chandrasekar Venkata Raman, a renowned physicist in the field of spectroscopy, and Vikram Sarabhai, a pioneer of space research.

The displays dramatize the "ethical" use of nuclear science, as was demonstrated by an exhibition at the Nehru Planetarium in Mumbai entitled "Atoms for Peace." Here ethics was invoked in a triple sense: nuclear power for civilian use, according to the post-1953 global trend in which industrialized nations began to preach the peaceful use of nuclear energy; a no-first-use policy, according to which nuclear weapons serve as a deterrent and are thereby deemed to promote peace in the region; and an aura of peaceful resistance created by appropriating Mahatma Gandhi's concept of *ahimsa*.

The displays may also be "culturalist," invoking ancient texts that appear to presage nuclear science and technology. The Pragati Maidan Science and Technology Museum in New Delhi had displays outlining 2,500 years of the atom, describing the system of Nyaya—"Valsesika atomism"—and comparing models of atoms from the fourth century BC to Rutherford's model of 1911.

Exhibitions may celebrate both nuclear achievements and related ones, such as satellite and rocket launches. Such exhibitions have been mounted at the Kerala State Science and Technology Museum in Thiruvananthapuram and at the Nehru Planetarium in New Delhi. The latter exhibition claimed that the world's first rocket was developed during Tipu Sultan's rule in southern India in the eighteenth century. In the Pragati Maidan Science and Technology Museum, nuclear power stations were placed next to other ways of generating electricity, such as solar panels, thermal power plants, and hydroelectric plants. Despite this seeming equivalence between different sources of energy, nuclear power is, the display proclaimed, still "the most powerful and logical safe alternative to use of fossil fuels for electricity production."

In spite of such exhibitions by national institutions, and state claims to openness and transparency, key institutions such as the Bhabha Atomic Research Centre and the Department of Atomic Energy remain closed to the public (even though they have a public relations office). They operate from the

Figure 6.5

Display of a rocket. Kerala State Science and Technology Museum,
Thiruvananthapuram. Photo by author.

belief that they, not the public, should define the relations between them. The same is true of nuclear power stations unless you have special permits or are a postgraduate science student from a government-accredited college—that is, a prospective member of the next generation of nuclear scientists and engineers, the next nuclear in-crowd.

Finally, there is the arena of vernacular media (Ramaswamy 2003; Brosius 2005; Jain 2007), or festival displays and celebrations, many of which are encouraged and sponsored by Hindu nationalist parties and sympathizers (Kaur 2005). Not all of them can be said to be state-regulated, but because of the tenacity of hegemonic ideas of the nation, they tend indirectly to reinforce

Figure 6.6

Board displaying sources of electricity and other scientific innovations,
including nuclear power stations. Pragati Maidan Science and Technology
Museum, New Delhi. Photo by author.

the impression that nuclear weapons protect and strengthen the nation, that they are necessary for national security and for peace in the region, that India's growing energy needs require atomic power stations, and that nuclear research is needed to generate ever more discoveries, especially in the fields of medicine, radiology, and agro-food processing.

Each of these modalities works in different ways and to different ends, and a further study might investigate particular arenas of reception. Here I have attempted an overview of the contours of measured revelation underpinned by theories of concealment and the numinous. Such revelations variously inform, educate (with the goal of creating a morally upright national citizen), entertain, and fascinate the populace and celebrate India's nuclear prowess vis-à-vis other nations while radiating the allure of a treasured secret. Whereas some revelations are made by the nuclear state itself (such as those of the Department of Atomic Energy), others (such as festival displays of nuclear prowess) are part of the capillaries of public culture. Media reports act as bridges between the state and its publics, in the spaces where the need to both reveal and withhold is manifested most fervently. This contradictory pressure results in measured coverage of nuclear issues. What appears is either sanitized and summarized, like the information presented in Department of Atomic Energy leaflets, or commodified and spectacularized, as are reports on the plutonium fast breeder

Figure 6.7

Postcard of Bharatmata (Mother India) with a representation of nuclear tests in Pokhran, Rajasthan. Image courtesy of Surya Sinha.

reactor on NDTV and Republic Day parades in which missiles act as shining emblems of India's management of modernity. Both processes, of sanitization and commodification, resist the fluidity of critical debate. They result in trenchant truths whose affective resonance makes them difficult to dislodge.

× × ×

In this chapter, I have discussed the tangle of censorship and transparency/publicity in their plaited collusion. I have noted how the nuclear topic enables us to examine state-linked strategies of both withholding and disclosure. These strategies enable nuclear authorities to deflect accusations of being undemocratic while also availing themselves of the power of publicity and spectacle and the persuasive force of information and image dissemination amongst the public.

Figure 6.8

Deepavali (Divali) greeting card with representations of a nuclear missile and radioactive glare being emitted by the *diya*. Image courtesy of Surya Sinha.

After all, the nuclear authorities are, in their own words, on a mission to promulgate positive propaganda on a war footing, while at the same time retaining an aura of mystique as representatives of a privileged and powerful nuclear state.

These modalities of concealment and revelation have led to a nuclear culture which is continuously being molded by the state, yet also shaped and reshaped by the unceasing efforts of conscientious objectors against nuclear power to gain more information, and compensation or protection for people displaced by nuclear projects or whose health and safety are at risk. This is the focus of current agitations against uranium mining in eastern India and against planned nuclear power stations in Kudankulam in Tamil Nadu and in the Sunderbans in West Bengal.[29] In Kudankulam, even though the nuclear authorities have withheld the environmental impact assessment (EIA), the site evaluation study, and the safety analysis report that were apparently completed back in 1988, campaigners managed, by hook and crook, to circulate the EIA report in 2006. Still, the NPCIL claimed that the report was out of date and denied its statement that the project would use water from the Pechiparai reservoir, on which the people of Kanyakumari District depend. Another publicity campaign was swiftly launched by the nuclear state to refute the campaigners' accusations (Kaur n.d.).

The shifting mechanics of measured revelation were visible at a mandatory public hearing regarding nuclear reactors 3–6 at the Kudankulam Nuclear Power Plant in 2006. According to the 1994 Notification of the Environmental Protection Act, a public hearing and an environmental impact assessment are required for large-scale development projects. No public hearing was held for reactors 1 and 2; the NPCIL argued that the decision to construct them was first made in 1988, six years before the Act went into effect. In fact, that decision had been shelved and the question reopened in 1998 under different heads of state, with modified plans for what was to be done with the radioactive waste, and with higher interest rates on a Russian loan. Despite its rhetorical juggling, the NPCIL could not forestall a public hearing on additional reactors in 2006. But it could still manage the event so as to make sure decisions went in its favor. With minimal fuss, it advertised the hearing in August in the New Delhi edition of the *Economic Times,* a newspaper which is not read in Kanyakumari, Tirunelveli, and Tuticorin Districts in Tamil Nadu, the districts most likely to be affected by the plant. Another advertisement was published a day before the hearing in a Tirunelveli edition of a Tamil daily, *Dinakaran,* leaving little time for local communities to gather their thoughts, make an appearance, and register their opinion. Despite the state's control over publicity for the event, local activists quickly rose to the occasion and, to the NPCIL's surprise, managed to get six to seven hundred people to attend the hearing (Udayakumar 2006). The afternoon ended with a declaration by the NPCIL and the Tirunelveli District Collector that another hearing would be held with adequate publicity in all three districts. Instead, three months later, they tried to hold a "public hearing" in the closed and high-security precincts of the nuclear plant township, Anuvijay. Realizing that this too would be controversial, they held another one, chaired by the Tamil Nadu Electricity Minister, Arcot Veerasami, on March 31, 2007. The people responded with widespread criticism, rallies, road blockades, and a hunger strike, and organized their own, more accountable public hearing (Udayakumar 2007). The first point to note here is that the nuclear state has constantly had to modify its strategies. Legally, it cannot ride roughshod over people who will be displaced or affected by a large-scale development project (even though, together with the police, intelligence bureaus, security forces, and the military, it may well use strong-arm tactics to control protests). On paper, at least, the nuclear state has to appear fair and democratic. The second point is that its public strategies are constantly being shaped by peoples' responses to its revelations.

Figure 6.9

Public hearing on nuclear reactors 3–6 of the Kudankulam Nuclear Power Plant, held at the Tirunelveli district collector's office, October 2006. Photo by author.

But such protests by local populaces against nuclear projects hardly make a mark on mainstream media—the overwhelming consensus is that nuclear power provides clean fuel to develop a strong India and that it is a key factor in stemming global warming. On a national scale, the publicity drives conducted by the nuclear state are much more powerful and seductive: many people in other parts of the country have not even heard of the issues debated in Kudankulam, let alone been informed of contention about the nuclear industries. With the power of the state and the national media ranged against that of community organizers, it appears to be a case of a nuclear Goliath against an ordinary David. But as this biblical analogy reminds us, the giant is not invincible.

Notes

The research for this essay was enabled by a British Academy Small Research Grant (SG-35512) and an Economic and Social Research Council Research Award (RES-000-23-1312). Thanks to William Mazzarella for his insightful comments and to the anonymous reviewers of this volume.

   1. On public culture, see Appadurai and Breckenridge 1988 and Pinney 2001.

   2. For a discussion of the sacred and profane levels of the state, see Hansen 2001.

3. Similarly, Joseph Masco, reporting on the U.S. case, notes that secrecy "cordons off workers, keeps them under control, it keeps out the public, it creates a priesthood, it protects against inquiry, and can hide lousy work" (2006, 225).

4. Ramana notes that these acts have been rarely invoked, and when they are, the Indian judiciary has tended to interpret them "in favour of secrecy rather than the people's right to know" (forthcoming, 9).

5 Restricted information concerns the location, quality, and quantity of nuclear substances; the processing, extraction, or production of fissile materials; the theory, design, construction, and operation of plants and nuclear reactors; and research and technological work on nuclear-related materials.

6. Itty Abraham argues, "In short 'national security' expresses the paranoias of the modern state; it remains a major contradiction within democratic states" (1998, 13).

7. This is true of other countries as well. Writing on Britain in the 1980s, Patrick Birkinshaw observes that "the arguments of those who advocate maximum secrecy for security and intelligence, viz. the unqualified claims of the operatives can be weighed against those who claim that the power wielded by such officials is too important to avoid any form of democratic accountability. To accept the debate in these latter terms and to give official sanction to such a debate would be to change the very nature of existing power configurations. The boundaries determining who is on the inside, and who the outside, of secrecy would be shifted irretrievably. For the British democrat, the image of so many East Europeans raiding the headquarters of security forces and rifling their files ranks with any moment in the tumultuous events of 1989 for its dramatic power" (1990, 34–35).

8. The Prime Minister, A. B. Vajpayee, is reported to have sent identical letters to the heads of government of the five nuclear powers after India's 1998 nuclear tests. The letter sent to Bill Clinton was leaked to the *New York Times* and later published in the Indian media. Although all earlier official briefings had scrupulously avoided identifying the external threat which compelled India to advance its state of nuclear preparedness, Vajpayee seemed to suffer no such compunction: "We have an overt nuclear weapon state on our borders, a state which committed armed aggression against India in 1962. Although our relations with that country have improved in the last decade or so, an atmosphere of distrust persists mainly due to the unresolved border problem." Suspicions had been heightened by the material help this state had rendered "another neighbour of ours to become a covert nuclear weapon state." Relations with this latter neighbor were especially embittered by "three aggressions in the last fifty years," and by the "unremitting terrorism and militancy sponsored by it in several parts of our country." The letter is available on the website of the Indian embassy to the U.S., http://www.indianembassy.org/indusrel/pmletter.htm (accessed October 1, 2008).

9. It was followed a year later by the International Conference on the Peaceful Uses of Atomic Energy in Geneva, intended to share scientific and technical know-how about nuclear energy with the world.

10. The cases of the former USSR and China present another series of questions, which I do not have space for here.

11. For example, Praful Bidwai argues that "worshippers of the state, of raw power, and supplicants to militarism dominate our scientific community" (1998). Similarly, he comments, "Indian nuclear scientists are very conformist and there is still no culture of activist science as there is on medical ethics" (Ghose 1998).

12. Ramana (forthcoming) recounts how, even though nuclear reactors are surrounded by an exclusion zone with a radius of 1.6 km, enterprising goatherders had made a hole in the fence surrounding one plant to allow their herd to graze in the exclusion zone. Lapses in secrecy are also frequent. Whereas Ramana's paper focuses on the culture of secrecy surrounding nuclear issues, this chapter pays more attention to the culture of disclosure of nuclear information.

13. Elsewhere, Herman and Chomsky argue,

> The special importance of propaganda in what Walter Lippmann referred to as the "manufacture of consent" has long been recognized by writers on public opinion, propaganda, and the political requirements of social order. Lippmann himself, writing in the early 1920s, claimed that propaganda had already become "a regular organ of popular government," and was steadily increasing in sophistication and importance. We do not contend that this is all the mass media do, but we believe the propaganda function to be a very important aspect of their overall service. (Herman and Chomsky 1994, xi)

However, my analysis of censorship and nuclear power does not follow the "propaganda model," in which the state hides information and which, as Herman and Chomsky maintain, "describes the forces that cause the mass media to play a propaganda role, the processes whereby they mobilize bias, and the patterns of news choices that ensue" (1988, xi–xii). I am critical of the idea that lies or screens or indeed fetishes simply hide fundamental truths, or that, masked by the available information, there is a truth at the core of the nuclear project that can be disclosed to the public. This idea of a truth may in fact be created by state disclosures.

14. My thanks to William Mazzarella for this evocative phrase.

15. The Indo-U.S. agreement was discussed in 2005, signed by the President and Prime Minister in 2006, and passed by the U.S. in 2006 and by India in 2008. The agreement promises nuclear, economic, and research collaboration between the two countries so long as certain conditions are met. In particular, India's nuclear power plants must be divided into those for civilian and those for military use, and civilian plants will be inspected by the International Atomic Energy Association.

16. I do not mean to dismiss existing debates; I simply want to state that the available information strongly affects the kinds of debates that can occur on the nuclear issue. Much of the nuclear debate in India is concerned with the need for more transparency in the nuclear industry (as noted above); the separation of civil uses of nuclear power from its weaponization, with more autonomy and transparency granted to the civil sector; the dismantling of all nuclear weapons; or the expense, safety risks, failures, and environmental effects of nuclear power stations.

17. The word "censorship" comes from the Latin *censere*, to tax, value, or judge, and the concept is based on the Roman idea of social and legal justice. Today, the meaning of the word

> varies from the very specific to the very broad. Psychoanalytically speaking, the censor is the psychic agency that represses unacceptable notions before they reach consciousness. In the wider social sense, however, censorship generally refers to official prohibition or restriction of any type of expression believed to threaten the established order. (Hoyt and Hoyt 1979, 9)

18. Leaks are another intriguing subject for which I do not have space here.

19. For example, shortly after the May 1998 nuclear tests, Shiv Visvanathan observed,

> There is a tremendous sense of euphoria, of achievement. Of competence. Of David against the Goliaths. Every—almost every—Indian stands proud at being nuclear, of becoming Goliaths. . . . Our tryst with destiny is complete. Everyone feels nationalistic. . . . It could be a hockey match. A Tendulkar century. A riot or a nuclear blast. . . . Our scientific Tendulkars have struck effortlessly five times in a row. The crowd is berserk with joy. Yet there is a sadness when everything is a spectacle. A match. A riot. A blast. When there is little difference between these events. Worse. People forget that the worst kind of consumerism is the unquestioning consumption of science. (Visvanathan 1998)

20. For earlier instances of this phenomenon, see Christopher Pinney's chapter in this volume.

21. See my forthcoming work, "Outside the Atom," for more details.

22. See also Masco 2006, 20–23.

23. Interestingly, the only time the Indian state emphasizes "use-value" is when it criticizes the imperialism and hypocrisy of the United States, a nation that is constantly referred to as a superpower but also vilified for its lack of ethics in that it is the "only country to have ever utilised nuclear weapons" (Muralidharan and Cherian 1998).

24. However, as Itty Abraham notes (1998), the colonial government did not have a very close relationship with the science and technology establishment. Scientists in post-Independence India had to argue forcefully for full recognition and patronage by the Nehruvian state. Since the 1990s in particular (the 1974 tests notwithstanding), scientific discourse has been enhanced by the supposed magical potential of nuclear power. The Nehruvian and the contemporary era have different valences. Earlier, in the post-Independence Nehruvian period, scientists like Homi J. Bhabha, as well as later ones such as Vikram Sarabhai, saw science as an integral tool in the task of development. As is well known, Jawaharlal Nehru saw scientific and technological projects as "the modern temples of independent India." Now, as Dr. T. Jayaraman (a theoretical physicist at the Institute of Mathematical Sciences, Chennai) argues, science and technology are being incorporated into a siege mentality associated with an

> insecure nationalism that sees nuclear explosions as the only means to secure "respect" for India in the community of nations. . . . The current scene seems to have room only for unrelieved hawkishness, cloaked occasionally in the language of strategic analysis that sees scientific achievement purely in terms of the power advantages that it brings. (Jayaraman n.d.)

25. The KKNPP is located on the southernmost coastline of Tamil Nadu in the district of Tirunelveli. While the plant was saved from the worst ravages of the tsunami of December 26, 2004, by the Sri Lankan landmass, surrounding villages, particularly in Kanyakumari District, were not so lucky.

26. Kalpakkam houses the Indira Gandhi Centre for Atomic Research. It is situated 80 km south of the state capital, Chennai.

27. The "modern man" may be seen as the contemporary neo-liberal version of Sanjay Srivastava's "Five Year Plan hero" (2004)—that is, the urban, metropolitan, secular, and rational person who would live happily in Nehru's vision of India.

28. The restriction on independent photography and the release of these gripping images were primarily intended to ward off protests before the tests took place, but they are also part of a consistent strategy to reveal certain kinds of information at certain times.

29. For more information on these campaigns, see the website of South Asians against Nukes (http://www.s-asians-against-nukes.org/) and the articles on India at the website of MAC: Mines and Communities (http://www.minesandcommunities.org/).

References

Abraham, Itty. 1997. "Science and Secrecy in Making of Postcolonial State." *Economic and Political Weekly.* August 16–23: 2136–46.

———. 1998. *The Making of the Indian Atomic Bomb: Science, Secrecy and the Postcolonial State.* London: Zed Books.

"Annual Conference of the Indian Nuclear Society." 2007. Announcement in *Nuclear India* 41 (July–August): 28. http://www.dae.gov.in/ni/nijul07/ni.pdf, accessed September 2, 2008.

Appadurai, Arjun, and Carol A. Breckenridge. 1988. "Why Public Culture?" *Public Culture* 1(1): 5–10.

BCAS Foundation. 2005. *Right to Know: Citizen's Guide.* Mumbai: Bombay Chartered Accountants' Society Foundation.

Bharucha, Rustom. 1998. "Politicians' Grin, Not the Buddha's Smile." *Economic and Political Weekly.* May 30:1295–98.

Bidwai, Praful. 1998. "India Defiled, Indians Diminished." *Frontline: India's National Magazine* 15(11) (May 23–June 5). http://www.frontlineonnet.com/fl1511/15110240.htm, accessed October 1, 2008.

Bidwai, Praful, and Achin Vanaik. 1999. *South Asia on a Short Fuse: Nuclear Politics and the Future of Global Disarmament.* New Delhi: Oxford University Press.

Birkinshaw, Patrick. 1990. *Reforming the Secret State.* Milton Keynes: Open University Press.

Brosius, Christiane. 2005. *Empowering Visions: The Politics of Representations in Hindu Nationalism.* London: Anthem.

Burt, Richard. 1994. "Introduction: The 'New' Censorship." In Richard Burt, ed., *The Administration of Aesthetics: Censorship, Political Criticism and the Public Sphere.* Minneapolis: University of Minnesota Press.

Butler, Judith. 1997. *Excitable Speech: A Politics of the Performative.* New York: Routledge.

Cherian, John. 1998. "The BJP and the Bomb," *Frontline: India's National Magazine* 15(8) (April 11–24). http://www.frontlineonnet.com/fl1508/15080040.htm, accessed October 1, 2008.

Chidambaram, R. 1998. "India Must Become Strong." Interview by T. S. Subramanian. *Frontline: India's National Magazine* 15(11) (May 23–June 5). http://www.frontlineonnet.com/fl1511/15110110.htm, accessed October 1, 2008.

Debord, Guy. 1973. *The Society of the Spectacle.* Translated and with a foreword by Kenn Knabb. London: Rebel Press/Aims Publications.

Frontline. 1999. "Issues of Nuclear Safety." Editorial. *Frontline: India's National Magazine* 16(6) (March 13–26). http://www.hinduonnet.com/fline/fl1606/16060820.htm, accessed October 1, 2008.

Ghose, Sagarika. 1998. "Muted Voices." *Outlook,* May 25. http://www.outlookindia.com/archivecontents.asp?fnt=19980525, accessed October 1, 2008.

Hansen, Thomas Blom. 2001. *Wages of Violence: Naming and Identity in Postcolonial Bombay.* Princeton, N.J.: Princeton University Press.

Herman, Edward S., and Noam Chomsky. 1988. *Manufacturing Consent: The Political Economy of the Mass Media.* New York: Pantheon.

Hoyt, Olga G., and Edwin P. Hoyt. 1979. *Censorship in America.* New York: Seabury.

Jain, Kajri. 2007. *Gods in the Bazaar: The Economies of Indian Calendar Art.* Durham, N.C.: Duke University Press.

Jayaraman, T. 2002. "Kalam's World-View: A Critique." *Frontline: India's National Magazine* 19(13) (June 22–July 5). http://www.hinduonnet.com/fline/fl1913/19130140.htm, accessed October 1, 2008.

———. N.d. "Of Science and Nuclear Weapons: A Scientist's Perspective." In *Nuclear Politics in South Asia,* a website maintained by Progressive South Asians (proXsa). http://www.proxsa.org/politics/nonuke/jayaraman.html, accessed October 1, 2008.

A journey towards excellence. . . 2005. Souvenir booklet produced by the Kudankulam Nuclear Power Project. Sivakasi: Sunfire.

Jungk, Robert. 1979. *The Nuclear State.* London: Calder.

Kanavi, Shivanand. 1999. "Thorium Is the Word." *Business India,* September 6–19: 58–63.

Kaur, Raminder. 2005. *Performative Politics and the Cultures of Hinduism: Public Uses of Religion in Western India.* London: Anthem.

———. N.d. "Outside the Atom: Public Representations and Perceptions of Nuclear Issues in India." Unpublished ms.

Krishnakumar, B. 2000. "Nuclear Tests Served Their Purpose." *The Week.* September 24.

Masco, Joseph. 2006. *The Nuclear Borderlands: The Manhattan Project in Post–Cold War New Mexico.* Princeton, N.J.: Princeton University Press.

Mazzarella, William. 2006. "Internet X-Ray: E-Governance, Transparency and the Politics of Immediation in India." *Public Culture* 18(3): 473–505.

Muralidharan, Sukumar, and John Cherian. 1998. "The BJP's Bombs." *Frontline: India's National Magazine* 15(11) (May 23–June 5). http://www.frontlineonnet.com/fl1511/15110040.htm, accessed October 1, 2008.

Nuclear India: A Dream Gone Sour. 1992. Yorkshire Television. Produced by James Cutler.

Pinney, Christopher. 2001. "Introduction: Public, Popular, and Other Cultures." In Rachel Dwyer and Christopher Pinney, eds., *Pleasure and the Nation: The History, Politics and Consumption of Public Culture in India.* New Delhi: Oxford University Press.

Prakash, Gyan. 1999. *Another Reason: Science and the Imagination of Modern India.* Princeton, N.J.: Princeton University Press.

Raj, N. Gopal. 1989. "Issues Nuclear: The Safety Concerns." *Frontline: India's National Magazine* 6(5) (March 4–17): 89–95.

Rajagopal, Arvind. 2001. *Politics after Television: Religious Nationalism and the Reshaping of the Indian Public.* Cambridge: Cambridge University Press.

Ramana, M. V. 2000. "The Bomb of the Blue God." *South Asian Magazine for Action and Reflection* 13 (winter–spring). http://www.samarmagazine.org/archive/article.php?id=36, accessed May 21, 2008.

———. Forthcoming, 2009. "India's Nuclear Enclave and the Practice of Secrecy." In Itty Abraham, ed., *South Asian Cultures of the Bomb: Atomic Publics and the State in India and Pakistan.* Bloomington: Indiana University Press.

Ramaswamy, Sumathi, ed. 2003. *Beyond Appearances: Visual Practices and Ideologies in Modern India.* New Delhi: Sage.

Roy, Arundhati. 1998. "The End of Imagination." *The Guardian.* August 2.

Roy, Srirupa. 2007. *Beyond Belief: India and the Politics of Postcolonial Nationalism.* Durham, N.C.: Duke University Press.

Salwi, Dilip M. 2004. *Homi J. Bhabha: Architect of Nuclear India.* New Delhi: Rupa.

Shapiro, Jerome F. 2002. *Atomic Bomb Cinema: The Apocalyptic Imagination on Film.* New York: Routledge.

Srivastava, Sanjay. 2004. "Voice, Gender and Space in the Time of Five-Year Plans: The Idea of Lata Mangeshkar." *Economic and Political Weekly.* February 17:2019–28.

Taussig, Michael. 1999. *Defacement: Public Secrecy and the Labor of the Negative.* Stanford, Calif.: Stanford University Press.

Udayakumar, S. P. 2006. "A Fiasco for a Public Hearing." *South Asian.* October 8. http://www.thesouthasian.org/archives/2006/a_fiasco_for_a_public_hearing.html, accessed January 10, 2008.

———. 2007. "Aborted Public Meeting and Protests in Koodankulam." *South Asian.* February 16. http://www.thesouthasian.org/archives/2007/aborted_public_meeting_ii.html, accessed May 21, 2008.

Vajpayee, Atal Bihari. 1998. "We Have Shown Then That We Mean Business." Interview by Prabhu Chawla. *India Today,* May 25. http://www.india-today.com/itoday/25051998/vajint.html, accessed October 1, 2008.

Visvanathan, Shiv. 1998. "The Patriot Games." *Himal Southasian,* July. http://www.himalmag.com/The-Patriot-Games_nw1312.html, accessed September 2, 2008.

SEVEN

Specters of Macaulay
Blasphemy, the Indian Penal Code, and Pakistan's Postcolonial Predicament

Asad Ali Ahmed

The publication of cartoons ridiculing the Prophet Muhammed by a Danish newspaper, *Jyllands-Posten*, in 2005 and the ensuing outrage of Muslims, who protested and demonstrated around the world against what they perceived as the vilest blasphemy, revived a history in which blasphemy accusations are understood as an irruption of medieval irrationality and religiosity that threatens political modernity.[1] This perception had acquired force in the wake of the Salman Rushdie affair, that seminal moment when "blasphemy" and "Islam" were conjoined in the global liberal imaginary. Copies of *The Satanic Verses* were burned in Bradford in January 1989, and the book burnings were followed by Muslim protests in Pakistan and India, which in turn prompted Ayatollah Khomeini's *fatwa* calling upon Muslims to execute Rushdie and his publishers (Appignanesi and Maitland 1989). The recent protests have reignited the perennial discourse of the Muslim threat to Europe. Muslims, whether immigrants or safely insulated within their own nation-states, have been characterized as unthinking repositories of religion and culture, the constitutive outside of liberal societies. From the Rushdie affair to the recent cartoons, blasphemy, as a trope, enlists a tested set of binaries to reductively make sense of the world: secular/religious, liberal/fundamentalist, rational/irrational, and, by simple deduction, "the West" and "Islam"—as if all these categories were internally coherent, consistent, and informative about the imagined orders they describe (Chatterjee 1986; Chakrabarty 2007). Yet the debate over blasphemy constantly reinscribes these frames (Vishwanathan 1995).

Juxtapose, if you will, an impassioned defense of secular reason in the wake of the cartoon affair by the editor of *Harper's Magazine*, Lewis Lapham (2006), with a group of demonstrators outside the Norwegian and Danish embassies in Islamabad vowing to sacrifice their lives in defense of the Prophet's honor.[2] Passion is permissible in the defense of secular reason, but the demonstrations of agitated emotions and hurt sensibilities on the part of religious subjects are

considered intimidating and terrorizing.[3] Despite his own emotive intervention, Lapham seeks to subordinate passion to reason and reestablish the disjuncture between sense and sensibility so critical to the narrative of modernity. No doubt, as he inadvertently demonstrates, the history of the relations
between reason, affect, and public discourse in the West is more complex than
its dominant political imaginary allows. In postcolonial South Asia, the relationship between religious dispositions and political discourse is more evident,
but one cannot subscribe to simplifying reductionisms that posit instances of
religio-politics as indicating the failure or incompleteness of modernity.[4]

A consideration of blasphemy and blasphemy laws in South Asia disrupts
these comforting essentializations and reveals a history of imperial connections,
displacements, and elaborations of discourses of cultural difference. It was in
colonial South Asia that a discourse of blasphemy emerged as one aspect of
the constitution and consolidation of the binary between a secular "West" and
"Islam." There is a peculiarly South Asian history to the Salman Rushdie affair
that has been erased—indeed, that has to be erased if the discourse of blasphemy is to continue to perform its cultural work of essentializing difference
and perpetuating seemingly immutable oppositions.

During the course of the campaign to ban *The Satanic Verses*, the Indian
Muslim parliamentarian Syed Shahabuddin alluded to the existence of laws
in the Indian Penal Code under which, he said, Rushdie could be prosecuted.
These laws, he explained, criminalized insulting religious beliefs and wounding
religious feelings (Appignanesi and Maitland 1989, 45–49). But these were
not recently enacted laws. On the contrary, the laws and the Code date from
the colonial period. These laws, as I will explicate, enabled the colonial state
to assume the role of the rational and neutral arbiter of supposedly endemic
and inevitable religious conflicts between what it presumed were its religiously
and emotionally excitable subjects. The subsequent utilization of these laws
was then understood to be the natural result of especially sensitive religious
sensibilities. However, rather than reflecting primordial religious attachments,
the cases before the colonial courts were not only enabled by the law but largely
constituted by it. That is, the laws required the plaintiffs to prove that their
sensibilities had been wounded. In other words, the laws demanded both the
demonstration of emotionality and its containment and regulation through
judicial process.

In the late nineteenth and early twentieth centuries some of these court
cases, particularly those in which the defendant accused of wounding religious
feelings was acquitted, became *causes celèbres* for emerging religious movements. This was especially so when they were picked up by a developing and
burgeoning vernacular press. The decision by the Allahabad High Court that
denied sacred status to cows was instrumental in the escalation and expansion of the Cow Protection Movement (Freitag 1989, 150; Pandey 1999, 164).
The acquittal of a Hindu accused of publishing a scurrilous tract against the

Prophet Muhammed was an important moment in the emergence of a new affective urban Muslim public community, one centered on the public display of emotion in defense of the Prophet (Gilmartin 1991).[5] Thus these laws, and the cases they engendered, were important factors (though not the only ones) in the constitution of publics oriented around highly symbolic issues such as the defense of the cow or the protection of the Prophet.

Through a focus on postcolonial Pakistan, where blasphemy accusations and trials have come to symbolize ongoing struggles between religious parties and postcolonial liberal regimes, I attempt to complicate the simple oppositions that the trope of blasphemy enables by attending to its colonial genesis. The antagonism of religious and secular-liberal groups over Pakistan's blasphemy laws occludes the complex history and genealogy of these laws. Therefore I track their colonial genealogy and attempt to show how colonial ideas about Indian religiosity and difference coalesced with linguistic and legal theories of codification. As a result, a capacious legal arena developed where insulting language became subject to criminal law. I then move to Pakistan's additions to and expansions of this body of law. Although based on the original chapter of the Indian Penal Code, they nonetheless differ significantly. Finally, I consider an intra-Muslim blasphemy allegation that occurred during my fieldwork and describe the sectarian and religious differences that led to the filing of the case. Here I track the complex constitution and interplay of religious attachments, excitation, and incitement occasioned by these laws and the demands for the performance of state sovereignty they impel. However, the specter of sectarian violence led state officials to encourage extra-legal means of resolving the dispute. Indeed, the example illustrates how non-state discourses on Muslim law are regarded as more legitimate than state laws ostensibly designed to protect the most revered persons and texts in the Islamic firmament.

Law, Sovereignty, and Society

In 1991 the Federal Shariat Court (FSC) ordered the government to remove the option of life imprisonment as a sentence for violation of section 295-C of the Pakistan Penal Code (henceforth PPC), the law that criminalizes "defiling the sacred name of the Holy Prophet." The court accepted the petitioner's argument that, according to Islamic law, the only punishment for such an offense was death.[6] This change was the culmination of efforts by an umbrella religious organization, the Tehrik-i-Khatm-i-Nabuwwat (Finality of Prophethood Movement), to protect the Holy Quran, the Holy Prophet, and his family and companions from insult and abuse. Nor would the Tehrik or the religious parties allow such laws to be relaxed, despite widespread international criticism and domestic secular-liberal opposition. This law continues to be a source of much embarrassment to Pakistani governments that have proclaimed themselves liberal, such as Benazir Bhutto's and General Musharraf's. Both attempted to modify it so as to make it more difficult to lay charges.[7] These attempts to circumscribe the laws have met with stiff opposition, including street demonstrations. As the protests against Musharraf's most recent attempt to make procedural changes made evident, these laws have created powerful affective attachments. Only weeks after announcing his proposed changes, Musharraf backed down, (*Dawn*, May 17, 2000).[8]

The laws, which demonstrators expressed their willingness to die for, had all been added to Chapter 15, "Of Offences against Religion," of the PPC between 1980 and 1986, during General Zia's regime (1977–88). These additions are popularly called the "blasphemy laws." Although the laws were ad hoc responses by General Zia's regime to moral panics, religious agitation, and fears of sectarianism, they are now considered part of his policy of "Islamization." This appellation refers to a wide range of state initiatives of varying effect, duration, and significance.[9] Zia's program included institutional innovations such as the Federal Shariat Court, a variety of administrative regulations encouraging public servants to perform their Muslim-ness, and, most dramatically, transformations of criminal law that introduced a variety of purportedly Islamic laws into a system of adversarial justice. This codification of Islamic law ignored the methodological procedures and epistemological assumptions of classical Islamic jurisprudence.[10]

Despite the provision of capital punishment, no one has yet been executed.[11] The paradox of nonenforcement is regarded by those critical of the state's inaction as indicative of state corruption and failure. However, this assessment is based upon a conception of the state as omniscient, omnipotent, and transcendent. I draw upon recent political and anthropological literature to show that these formal and juridical understandings of the state and sovereignty have always been principally a matter of idealization (Abrams 1988; Das and Poole 2004; Hansen and Stepputat 2001, 2005; Mitchell 1991).

The idea of the state, Abrams argues (1988), attributes a unity and independence to disorganized and diverse political practices and enables it to be thought of as an autonomous, agentive, and volitional actor. As the "state's emissary," to appropriate Guha's phrase (1987, 142), the law is one of the paradigmatic institutions sustaining this conception of state coherence and its corollary of sovereignty. Political theorists who conceive of power juristically have been central to the representation of the state in the form of an exterior sovereign that stands above and outside society. Such statist theories have enabled a hard and fast distinction to be drawn between state and society (Mitchell 1991, 1999). In colonial India this representation of the state has been particularly dominant. Not only did it allow the rule of law to be distinguished from "Asian despotism," but it also epitomized the rational, enlightened, civilizing imperative—one consolidated and centered in the state (Cohn 1989; T. Metcalf 1995). The distinction between state and society was particularly realized and made visible in colonial rule, in which it was marked by cultural, linguistic, and racial differences between the governors and the governed (Chatterjee 1993). Both the political theory of sovereignty—one based on monarchical political orders—and the practical administrative order of colonial regimes lend themselves to demarcating the state as the site of transcendent order and sovereign power radically separate from social life. Thus political and legal theories of sovereignty have understood it as a formal *de jure* property that the state exercises over its territory. Indeed, nineteenth-century legal positivists and colonists elaborated a symbolic imaginary of state law as pervasive, prohibitory, and omniscient. This sovereign fantasy was both informed and sustained by plans for the rational administration of justice. Territories, populations, and practices would be made subject to a system of jurisdictions and a universe of law that mapped the social body.[12] As Eric Stokes has argued (1959), this vision was most compellingly articulated by Jeremy Bentham and his utilitarian disciples in India.

In contrast to these historically elaborated formations of distinction and difference, anthropological studies of law have shown that law is a social practice through which sovereign power and its limitations are constituted as well as contested (Starr and Collier 1989; Lazarus-Black and Hirsch 1994). Further, the law is not concerned only with ending or resolving conflicts but can also be the means of their expansion and perpetuation (Cohn 1987, 569). Building on the insights of political and legal anthropology, with their attention to how power is discursively constituted, institutionally negotiated, and contested in everyday practice and social life, Hansen and Stepputat have recently argued that sovereignty should no longer be thought of as a formal *de jure* property that the state exercises over its territory, but as a performative practice of power exercised upon bodies and populations. This enables sovereign power to be understood as tentative and unstable, something that states aspire to in the face of "internally fragmented, unevenly distributed and unprecedented configurations of political authority" (Hansen and Stepputat 2005, 3).

Although a complex and extensive system of sovereign power was envisaged, articulated, and after 1857, with the enactment of criminal and procedural codes, increasingly realized, the Indian colonial state was characterized not by the extent and reach of sovereign power, but by its limitations (Baxi 1992; Guha 1997; Kaviraj 1994). Through policies of indirect rule, colonial states delegated aspects of sovereignty to a variety of affiliated actors and institutions, be they chiefs, princes, or communities, giving rise to fragmented sovereignty and multiple legalities (Hansen 2005, 170–71).

What emerges from a consideration of the history of the blasphemy laws is how power and sovereignty remain fragmented and dispersed. When considering the intersection of the state, society, and the law, then, it can be illuminating to examine how legal instruments allow sovereignty to be performed. General Zia's additions to and expansion of the blasphemy laws were an attempt to constitute state authority and sovereignty in the face of social and religious agitation. Blasphemy laws, in short, have enabled particular stagings of state sovereignty and legitimacy in both the colonial and postcolonial periods.

The colonial state in India partly justified its imperial mission as impartially regulating and administering a multiplicity of particularistic communities through the rule of law. In this imperial legal rhetoric, the colonizers had brought peace to, and secured order in, primordial, fractious, and antagonistic religious communities (Pandey 1999; Ludden 1993, 267). One means through which this co-constitution of a secular state and an affective religious public was demonstrated and exemplified was the adjudication of religious disputes. In postcolonial Pakistan, on the contrary, the state has attempted to justify its authority, legitimacy, and sovereignty by imagining a unity of state and society achieved through prosecutions of blasphemers. It could be considered an irony of history that this postcolonial sacralization and constitution of state sovereignty has been built on the basis of colonial laws that sought to do the reverse, that is, to effectively secularize sovereign authority. But this irony, I suggest, is misplaced, for while revealing difference it conceals similarities between colonial legacies and logics and their postcolonial elaborations and entanglements.

Underlying the original laws and their postcolonial additions is an unstable dynamic of incitement and containment (see Mazzarella and Kaur, this volume; Butler 1997)—that is, the laws' attempt to regulate wounded attachments and religious passions can conversely constitute them. They have in actuality enabled social groups to organize in order to ensure the state takes cognizance of blasphemous events and practices. These groups can, on occasion, challenge the state's ability to legally regulate and adjudicate these instances, and a number of alleged blasphemers have been murdered during or after their trials. Before turning to how blasphemy accusations are a source of both power and anxiety for the postcolonial state, it is first necessary to examine the colonial rationale behind Chapter 15 of the Indian Penal Code.

Macaulay, Blasphemy, and the Indian Penal Code

In an 1833 parliamentary address supporting the renewal of the East India Company's charter, Macaulay comments on the anomalous nature of the Company, which he says is both a "trader" and a "sovereign" (Macaulay 1898a: 543–86). This anomaly, he argues, was mitigated by the practical improvements the Company had made in governance. Admitting the perfidy and depredations of its early years, he nonetheless goes on to defend it by contrasting it with the dissolution of Indian society in the last century of Mughal rule, when the evils of despotism, he says, were compounded by the evils of anarchy. The latter evil had been extinguished when the Company reunited the country, consolidating its own power along the way. At this point Macaulay exhibits a common fantasy about sovereign power. He says, "The power of the new sovereigns penetrates their dominions more completely, and is far more implicitly obeyed, than was that of the proudest princes of the Mogul dynasty" (1898a, 564–65).

For Macaulay it was not the functional anomalies and potential contradictions of the Company as trader and sovereign that impaired its ability to provide good governance, but the division of power in India between the Supreme Court and the Government. The Charter Act would rectify this by conferring supreme legislative power on the Government, and Macaulay proposed a law commission to codify the laws of India and further reduce the scope of judicial activism. However, he recognized that, although the aim was to achieve a uniform and certain law, "feelings generated by differences of religions, of nation, and of caste" would have to be taken into account (1898a, 581). The principle on which the codes ought to be framed, he succinctly stated, would be "uniformity where you can have it; diversity where you must have it; but in all cases certainty" (1898a, 582).

Macaulay was appointed as Law Member to the Governor-General's Council, established the first Indian Law Commission, and undertook the task of writing a comprehensive series of legal codes (E. Stokes 1959, 213–14). The drafting of this code was, as Stokes has argued, part of an attempt to reorganize the entire judicial administration and law of India on the basis of Benthamite ideas.[13] Despite this grand vision, the draft Indian Penal Code of 1837 was Macaulay's only concrete realization of this scheme.[14] After revisions, it was eventually enacted by Act 45 of 1860, and remains in force in India, Pakistan, and Bangladesh today.[15] It was Macaulay's inclusion of a blasphemy law in the code that made possible Pakistan's contemporary predicament vis-à-vis the blasphemy laws.

Despite his many differences with the utilitarians, Macaulay espoused Benthamite jurisprudence, which he felt had immediate practical benefits in improving legislation and the administration of justice. Similarly, he shared James Mill's scathing assessment of Indian civilization as despotic, hierarchical, stultifying, and mired in superstition.[16] Macaulay's code reflects Bentham's advocacy of a scientific jurisprudence that could rationalize the law, make it reflect legislative will, and express this to laymen in clear and precise terms. The legal subject posited by the code is an autonomous liberal subject tempered by Indian prejudices, sensitivities, and particularities. Indeed, Macaulay considered the code a means by which Indians could become agentive subjects. This attitude is evident in his discussion of whether he has given too much latitude to the right of self-defense:

> And we are ourselves of opinion that if we had been framing laws for a bold and high-spirited people, accustomed to take the law into their own hand, and to go beyond the line of moderation in repelling injury, it would have been fit to provide additional restrictions. In this country the danger is on the other side; the people are too little disposed to help themselves; the patience with which they submit to the cruel depredations of gang-robbers and to

trespass and mischief committed in the most outrageous manner by bands of ruffians, is one of the most remarkable, and at the same time one of the most discouraging symptoms which the state of society in India presents to us. Under these circumstances we are desirous rather to rouse and encourage a manly spirit among the people than to multiply restrictions on the exercise of the right of self-defense. (Macaulay 1898d, 55–56)

Along with this putative lack of agency, Macaulay detects a peculiar Indian vulnerability to mental anguish in response to insulting language, especially if caste, religion, or women are involved. This vulnerability is recognized in the chapters on defamation, homicide, and offenses against religion. Indeed, the final chapter of the code, entitled, "Of Criminal Intimidation, Insult and Annoyance," is entirely devoted to forms of offensive language not previously criminalized.

This sensitivity to the affective aspects of language indicates that Macaulay was not fully persuaded by the emerging instrumentalist theory of language espoused by Bentham in his attempt to construct a scientific jurisprudence. For Bentham, language had to be stable, although not entirely fixed, for the law to be certain and communicable. Bentham and other legal codifiers understood and required language to be a neutral communicative tool (Bentham 1843b, 298).[17] Offenses such as blasphemy and obscenity posed a problem for Bentham, because utilitarian theory was based on a somatics of pain and pleasure and he recognized that loaded words could cause "simple mental injuries" (Bentham 1970, 224–25).[18] Despite this recognition of speech acts, Bentham associated such sensitivity with the realm of unreason, the passions, which are indicative of a "rude," uncivil state (1843b, 301–302). In another essay, "On the Influence of Time and Place in Matters of Legislation," which clearly influenced Macaulay, Bentham identified a site of such religious passion: Bengal.[19] He argued, on pragmatic grounds, that the legislator would have to take these sensitivities and prejudices into account (1843a, 173–76).

Macaulay had famously expressed his disagreement with the utilitarian *a priori* assumption of a universal human nature from which a science of politics could be logically deduced (Macaulay 1978). His privileging of historical experience, the diversity of human life, and the complexity of tastes, desires, and imagination in the motivation of human actions, and his rhetorical skills and eloquence, are testimony to his attentiveness to the performative aspects of language and sociality—that is, apart from the pragmatic considerations, Macaulay was not convinced that language could be understood simply as a communicative mechanism. On the contrary, he recognized that speech could be a form of conduct, and therefore a hard and fast distinction between speech and acts could not be made. Consequently, he disagreed with Livingston's Louisiana Code, which sought to exclude speech acts as a mitigating factor for homicide.[20] He argued that offensive and insulting language should be considered a speech act and ought to be subject to criminal jurisprudence

(Note M, "On Offences against the Body," Macaulay 1898b, 121–23).[21] In other words, Macaulay understood the performative dimension of speech to be a general feature of language. This understanding is also indicated in the changes he proposed to the laws of defamation. In English criminal law, he acknowledged, the pain arising from defamation is only actionable if the defamation is written and causes a breach of the peace.[22] He proposed, however, that defamatory spoken words should be considered an offense irrespective of whether they caused a breach of the peace, on the grounds that the mental pain they inflict is a sufficient basis for an action.[23] India, on Macaulay's assessment, is characterized by a predisposition toward mental agitation and hurt sentiments in response to loaded words, offensive gestures, and transgressions of hierarchical order:

> There is perhaps no country in which more cruel suffering is inflicted, and more deadly resentment called forth, by injuries which affect only the mental feelings.
>
> A person who should offer a gross insult to the Mahomedan religion in the presence of a zealous professor of that religion; who should deprive some high-born Rajpoot of his caste; who should rudely thrust his head into the covered palanquin of a woman of rank, would probably move those whom he insulted to more violent anger than if he had caused them some severe bodily hurt. (1898b, 123)

It is perhaps not surprising that Macaulay's understanding of language, attention to Indian difference as manifest in mental sensitivity, and encouragement of Indian agency coalesce in the chapter that seeks to incorporate the inaugural site of Indian difference—religion—within the criminal law. "There is," he said, "perhaps, no country in which the government has so much to apprehend from religious excitement among the people" (1898b, 106).

Macaulay's interest in rationalizing the law of offenses against religion, however, long preceded his departure for India. As a secular Whig, he advocated the separation of church and state but defended Christian values, virtues, and mores (Macaulay 1841). He was especially averse to religious fanaticism, which he thought disallowed the possibility of a conciliatory politics that could engender stable and progressive reform. His father, Zachary Macaulay, was a key member of the evangelical Society for Suppression of Vice, together with William Wilberforce (Hamburger 1976, 18; Nash 1999, 75–78). This organization was involved in bringing a number of blasphemy prosecutions in England—a course of action at which Macaulay evinced some unease (Macaulay 1974, 43–44). In a parliamentary speech supporting the removal of civil disabilities against the Jews, he registered his disapproval of England's existing blasphemy laws and specified the principle on which he would frame such a law: that everyone should be at liberty to discuss religion, but not so as to cause pain, disgust, or outrage and thereby infringe on the rights of others (Macaulay 1898c, 534–35). He recalled this principle four years later in Note J to Chapter 15:

The principle on which this chapter has been framed is a principle on which it would be desirable that all Governments should act, but from which the British Government in India cannot depart without risking the dissolution of society; it is this, that every man should be suffered to profess his own religion, and that no man should be suffered to insult the religion of another. (1898d, 105)

Invoking the specter of religiously tumultuous, excitable, and violent peoples, he argued for a policy of strict state neutrality and toleration with respect to religion.[24]

The original sections in Chapter 15 protected places of worship from damage and defilement (section 295), religious assemblies from disturbance (section 296), funeral remains and burial sites from malicious trespass (section 297), and finally the religious feelings of any person from deliberate insult (section 298).[25] In addition, Macaulay made it a criminal offense to deprive Hindus of their caste. Missionaries, in particular, objected to this provision (which was not included in the version enacted in 1860) and to the section protecting "religious feelings," which they argued curtailed their ability to proselytize (Clive 1973, 462–66). There was also considerable disquiet amongst administrators and judges, who argued that making wounded sentiments a cause of action was a recipe for disaster (Macaulay et al. 1888, 409–17; Mayne 1862, 179). Even friendly critics such as Sir Lawrence Peel, chief justice of the Supreme Court in 1848, argued that the "wounding" of religious feelings should not be subject to sanction unless it led to public disorder (Peel 1848, 17). Subsequent advocates of codification such as Fitzjames Stephen, who otherwise thought the code "a remarkable success" and appreciated the attempt to rationalize offenses against religion, nonetheless balked at this section.[26] He agreed with earlier critics that it was too easy to make accusations, and further that the section could criminalize religious debate. This danger, he concluded, would be averted as long as English magistrates continued to interpret it restrictively, but, he warned, it "might lead to horrible cruelty and persecution if the government of the country ever got into Hindoo or Mohammedan hands" (Stephen 1996, 312).

A second critique centered on the code's "vagueness and generality of language," a vagueness particularly evident in Chapter 15 (Peel 1848, 18). This criticism was ironic, considering that one of the aims of codification had been linguistic precision and simplicity: the laws were to be certain, consistent, communicable, and transparent to the average citizen (Mack 1963). In his "Introductory Report upon the Indian Penal Code," Macaulay espoused the goal of linguistic clarity, consistency, and systematicity, but recognized that human languages "furnish but a very imperfect machinery to the legislator" (1898b, 4).[27] Unlike the utilitarians, he was aware of the polyvalence, malleability, and affective qualities of language. Ever the Whig, he eschewed the possibility of deriving perfect models from first principles. Instead, he advocated gradual improvement whenever the code was found to be inconsistent, imprecise, or unclear. However, he advised that any future amendments or additions should "be framed in such a manner as to fit into the code. Their language ought to be that of the code" (1898b, 19).

Postcolonial Revisions: General Zia and Protecting Islam

Subsequent amendments and additions to the code, both by colonial authorities and by General Zia's regime, have adhered to Macaulay's advice, deploying similar phrasing and expressions. To do otherwise would be to invite contradictions and complications into the code. With respect to the blasphemy laws, however, this has only further exaggerated the code's original propensities. Many of the criticisms directed at Macaulay's sections are also directed at General Zia's additions. The ease with which the law can be used by those with tender religious feelings, the vagueness about what specifically constitutes an offense, and the error of allowing "wounded feelings" to be a cause of action have all been compounded in the postcolonial blasphemy laws (Rehman 1998; D. Patel 2000; Amnesty International 1994). This is not to argue that Zia's additions, and the contemporary disquiet concerning the current laws, is reducible to a colonial legacy; it would be fallacious to collapse two distinct historical moments into a single legal logic. However, the colonial genealogy of these laws is important, for it illuminates the conditions of possibility that frame postcolonial elaborations.

Between 1860 and 1980 only one additional law was enacted, 295-A, which was added in 1927 by the colonial authorities. It followed a series of cases against Punjab-based Arya Samaj polemicists who had written sacrilegious tracts, distributed by a burgeoning vernacular press, against the Prophet Muhammed. The state, unable to prosecute under section 298 (which criminalized only spoken blasphemy, not written), had therefore prosecuted the offenders under other sections.[28] However, considerable difficulties were encountered in these prosecutions. In particular, the attempt to prosecute the author and publisher of a scurrilous tract titled *Rangila Rasul* (The Colorful Prophet) failed when the defendant was acquitted by the Lahore High Court (Thursby 1975, 40–47).[29] The trials and the attendant media interest in these cases heightened community antagonisms, and the colonial state, fearing a glut of scurrilous publications and religious agitations, moved quickly to introduce a new law. The new section retained the capaciousness of the earlier laws, and especially of section 298, in that it criminalized visible representations as well as spoken and written words that "insult or attempt to insult [the] religion or religious beliefs" of any class of subjects. However, unlike section 298, under which charges could be brought as a private prosecution, action under 295-A could only be initiated by the state.

General Zia's additions and amendments were even more expansive in their scope and severe in their sentencing provisions. Five new sections were introduced over a six-year period. Section 298-A, introduced in 1980, criminalized derogatory remarks against the early caliphs, as well as the family and companions of the Prophet. The *ulema* had demanded such a law at the Ulema Conference that Zia's government had organized in an attempt to garner support for his Islamization program. The enactment of this law, however, was one of the few demands of the conference that he fulfilled (Amin 1989, 128). The demand had arisen as a result of increasing sectarian tensions between Shias and Sunnis. These long-standing tensions had been stoked by other aspects of the Islamization program that led to increases in both Shia and Sunni organization and militancy (Abou Zahab 2002a, 2002b; Ali 2000; Nasr 2000; Zaman 1998).

Section 295-B, which criminalized the desecration of the Quran, was enacted in response to a media-induced moral panic over the alleged defilement of some copies of the Quran (Christian Study Centre 1985, 111). In 1984, sections 298-B and C, the anti-Ahmadi ordinance, were introduced in response to threats of direct action by the Tehrik-i-Khatm-i-Nabuwwat (Finality of Prophethood Movement). This ordinance criminalized the use of "Muslim terminology" by members of the Ahmadiyya sect, a late-nineteenth-century Muslim reform and revival movement that was declared non-Muslim by Pakistan's National Assembly in 1974.[30]

The last new section, 295-C, was introduced when it was realized that, despite all these additions, no law explicitly protected the Prophet Muhammed from insulting language. Unlike the other sections, it was introduced by an act of Parliament. These laws were haphazardly introduced because they were contingent responses to a series of religious agitations, moral panics, and sectarian tensions. Indeed, the laws can be seen as attempts by the postcolonial state to co-opt social violence and to rationalize and legalize it.

Unlike Macaulay's laws, which protected all religions, Zia's only protect Islam. They have also been criticized, correctly, for not specifying intention—a critical constituent in determining criminal liability—and for being even less specific in their phrasing than Macaulay's sections. These omissions, and a corresponding slackness in ensuring procedural safeguards to the registration of cases, have made these laws even easier to use. Their vagueness about what constitutes a blasphemous or insulting utterance, like that of Macaulay's language, enables a case to be easily registered and the alleged culprit to be arrested.[31] It is then up to the legal administration to assess whether the utterance constitutes a punishable offense. Thus, the capaciousness of the original law is continued in its more pernicious postcolonial formulations.

A more fundamental similarity between the original laws drafted by Macaulay and Zia's postcolonial additions is that both constitute a structure of incitement and regulation. The colonial laws required demonstrably outraged

sentiments and wounded feelings in order for charges to be laid—a potentially dangerous requirement, as commentators repeatedly noted. However, as
Fitzjames Stephen remarked above, as long as the British governed, this danger
could be managed. Here, then, we see the colonial logic: these laws bolstered
the already articulated ideological justification of imperial rule in a multire-
ligious society. In the colonial moment, these laws reflected the assumption
of an essentially religious and affective populace and a rational administrative
state. More emphatically, they enabled the two to be juxtaposed.[32] In adjudicat-
ing these cases, the administration displayed its dispassionate, objective, and
impartial neutrality. By contrast, the plaintiffs had to prove that their religious
sentiments had been outraged and thus on occasion had to exaggerate this
aspect of the case in their legal submissions. But the danger of these cases was
that these emotions, once incited, could not be regulated or dissipated by legal
process and judgment.

In General Zia's specifically postcolonial moment, the laws carried on
this structure of incitement and regulation. Now, however, the ideological
framework of these laws is more complicated. They are no longer intended to
demonstrate state neutrality, but are an explicit defense of sacred Muslim persons and texts. In this they have enabled an affective connection to be forged
between the state-led policy of Islamization and the public. Indeed, the greater
and most visible aspect of Zia's Islamization policy was concerned with the
introduction of purportedly Islamic criminal law. In particular, the Hudood
Ordinances had complex and adverse consequences for the status of women
(Shaheed and Mumtaz 1987; Weiss 1986).[33]

In espousing Islamic penal laws, state officials consolidated a tentative and
contested relationship between sacred and temporal sources of power in the
constitution of postcolonial sovereignty.[34] Zia's emphasis on penal reform was
an attempt to extend sovereign power by means of Muslim values.[35] It is in
interdiction, prohibition, and punishment that sovereign power is manifested,
through the law's violence and regulations. By prescribing *hadd* punishments,
such as amputation and stoning, this reconstituted sovereign power was to be
inflicted and inscribed on the bodies of transgressors. These bodily inscrip-
tions were ameliorated, however, when the judiciary, balking at *hadd* punishments, instituted whipping as an alternative.[36] During the first few years of
Zia's regime, whippings were often carried out in public.[37]

The conjugation of divine and temporal in the reconstitution of sovereign
power has been strengthened by the postcolonial blasphemy laws. These have
translated the commitment to uniting divine and republican sources of sovereignty into criminal sanctions. They were based on the assumption that Muslims were minimally united in their determination to protect the Prophet and
revelation. In cases of alleged blasphemy, the state, conceptualized as a sovereign
and unitary actor, is expected to manifest its exemplary sovereign power in the
form of criminal law, by apprehending, trying, and, if convicted, executing the

blasphemer. But this expectation that power will be seamlessly wielded has often been disappointed. On many occasions, state officials have displayed considerable reluctance to arrest blasphemers, and even more to execute them. Although the Pakistani state does not provide figures, there have not been, as yet, any judicial executions. This paradox of nonenforcement is, to many who support these laws, all the more extraordinary given that they protect the Prophet and his divine revelations—the constitutive sources of Islam. State officials have been particularly reluctant to intervene in disputes between Muslims, for fear that trials will further sectarian conflict. The attempt to forge a bond between the state and the nation founders on the numerical preponderance of intra-Muslim cases.[38]

To sum up, the capaciousness of the original laws in constituting a field of criminalizable words, gestures, and representations that require only wounded sentiments to authorize criminal charges has been compounded by the procedural laxity of the postcolonial laws. The latter have furthered individual agency in initiating such cases, in effect democratizing accusatory practices. This has aggravated the already unstable structural dynamic of incitement and regulation, encouraging the filing of blasphemy allegations and demands for state-sanctioned punishments. I will now describe an intra-Muslim dispute that occurred during fieldwork, in whose course state officials managed to circumvent their own laws by resorting to alternative sources of legal authority.

Invoking the Sovereign

On Rabbi-ul-Awwal 12, AH 1421 (June 16, 2000), the Ahl-i-Sunnat (Barelwi) *ulema* of the town of Kamonke celebrated *eid-i-milad-un-nabi*, the Prophet's birthday, with their usual fervor.[39] Streamers, banners, and flags bedecked mosques, homes, and public buildings. Favorite animals such as donkeys and goats were decked out with colorful ornamentation. *Naat khwani* (devotional poetry) and *qawwali* (Sufi devotional songs) celebrated people's happiness at the Prophet's birth and expressed their love (*ishq*) for the Prophet and his continuing presence in the world. The majority of the town celebrated with them. According to the Ahl-i-Sunnat *ulema*, everyone but Iblis (Satan) was celebrating this auspicious day.

One sect conspicuous by its refusal to celebrate, however, was the Ahl-i-Hadith (AIH). On the following day, the latter's *ulema* and local community leaders, as was their custom, held a Seerat-un-Nabi (Character and Conduct of the Prophet)[40] conference, which was lavishly advertised by large multicolored posters all over town. The posters urged those who "love the Prophet" to attend, and promised "special prayers for forgiveness"—this was directed at their antagonists, the Ahl-i-Sunnat (Barelwis), who understand man as inescapably mired in sin and thus in need of prophetic intercession with God in order to secure forgiveness. The posters prominently displayed the names of community leaders and "special guest" *ulema*, and promised "special appearances" by visiting *ulema*. According to the AIH, this was the twenty-seventh annual Seerat-un-Nabi conference in Kamonke.

One of the visiting religious scholars was Abdur Rauf Yazdani. He was well aware of the criticism that the Ahl-i-Sunnat had directed toward his sect over the previous twelve days and chose to respond. Satan did not have to celebrate, he said, "for he can take a rest as he has entrusted that task to the Ahl-i-Sunnat." Having reversed the satanic association, he continued by averring that Satan's time was short, "for this is an age of enlightenment and people are literate and reading and understanding our sect's books." He then proceeded to critique Ahl-i-Sunnat (Barelwi) devotional and celebratory practices, in particular their use of music and song. Warming to this theme, he further criticized the mannerisms and habits of the Barelwi *ulema*, contrasting them to the exemplary model and practice of the Prophet—and by implication the comportment and discipline of the Ahl-i-Hadith, who emphasize strict imitation of prophetic practice. Throughout his speech, he stressed that imitating, enacting, and iterating the Prophet's *sunna* (exemplary practice)—and the example of his companions (*sahaba*)—was the only way to become a true and authentic Muslim subject. It was not the Ahl-i-Hadith, he said, who had insulted the Prophet, but those others whose disregard for prophetic example had led them to depart from the true path. This willful refusal in an age when one can use reason (*aql*), he suggested, was why sectarian difference and violent conflict plagued the country. He closed his oration by calling on the sovereign to pay attention to the words that were being used about the Prophet:

> Oh Sovereign! Look what is happening in your country. Pay attention to the kinds of words that are being said about the Prophet; if you do not, then you will also suffer the curse of God.

Rauf Yazdani's words would come back to haunt him. The sovereign did pay attention, albeit, as I shall describe, with some reluctance. Along with some colleagues from the Seerat conference, Yazdani was charged, under section 295-C, with defiling the Prophet. In fact, the AIH had first registered a case against the Barelwi *ulema* under sections 295-A and 298, charging them with wounding and outraging religious feelings. The Barelwis then returned the charge with interest, filing a return complaint under sections 295-A, 298-A, and 295-C; that is, outraging religious feelings, making derogatory remarks about holy persons, and blaspheming against the Prophet, respectively.[41] The speeches of the AIH leaders were, by the standards of sectarian polemical exchange in contemporary Pakistan, not particularly extreme. Nonetheless, on this occasion they initiated a series of events that culminated in both sects accusing each other. Yet it was not until forty days or so after the alleged blasphemy that the authorities filed a formal charge.

Many of my Lahore-based interlocutors expressed surprise at the very possibility of such a case. How, they asked, could any Muslim conceive of insulting the Prophet? They considered it a crime so unimaginable that, as some of Yazdani's codefendants said, "it could not be forgiven." In addition, my Lahori interlocutors asked, what explained this anomaly of an intra-Muslim dispute? But it was not as anomalous as they assumed. The popular conception is that blasphemy charges are almost exclusively laid against religious minorities. From the liberal-secular perspective, such charges are explained as examples of the alliance between a fundamentalist polity and discriminatory laws targeting minorities. Defenders of the laws and of blasphemy prosecutions, on the other hand, argue that Muslims cannot insult their own religion, and point to a long history of Christian and Hindu polemics against the Prophet. Without discounting the importance of these polemics, I argue that the current accusatory discourse of blasphemy can only be fully grasped if it is located within a wider intra-Muslim debate that emerged in nineteenth-century India.

The law protecting the Prophet has garnered widespread support. All major religious parties and organizations have repeatedly insisted that it is necessary to protect the Prophet from insult. Despite this unanimity, they nonetheless have different ideas as to what constitutes both respect for and dishonor to the Prophet. Although all sects agree that the Prophet Muhammed is the perfect man (*insan-i-kamil*) whose exemplary practice is the ideal model of human conduct, they have significantly different ideas of how to realize his virtues and manifest his qualities in everyday practice. These differences, as I will outline below, have led to accusations of *bidat* (innovation), *shirk* (polytheism), and *kufr* (infidelity). However, apart from accusations against the Ahmadis, they do not usually lead to accusations of *irtidad* (apostasy) or disrespect verging on abuse (*gustakhi*).[42] Nonetheless, Barelwis have developed grievances with both Deobandi and Ahl-i-Hadith critiques and depictions of their prophetology. There is a long-standing sectarian literature in which the Barelwis accuse both Deobandis and AIH *ulema* of beliefs that in their view amount to disrespecting the Prophet, and at times border on insulting (*tawhin*) the Prophet. These differences emerged in the late nineteenth and early twentieth centuries and some disputes were adjudicated in the colonial courts.[43] However, the postcolonial blasphemy laws have made it easier for these social and sectarian conflicts to enter the field of law.

Like the Deobandis and the Ahl-i-Hadith, the Barelwis emerged as a nineteenth-century reform movement. They too sought to reform Muslim practice by emphasizing the Prophet as a model for personal reform. However, unlike the AIH, who were extremely critical of Sufi and devotional practices associated with shrines, the Barelwis, who emerged from Sufi orders based in North India, sought to curb these excesses rather than dismiss them.[44] Unlike more ecstatic Sufis, these orders acknowledged the centrality of the *sharia* and emphasized conformity to the ritual obligations, ethical prescriptions, and injunctions and prohibitions of Islamic law. Nonetheless, they emphasized an intense, inward devotional faith centered on the heart. It was in this milieu, which sought to bring mosque and shrine together, that the founder of the movement, Ahmed Riza Khan, developed a full-fledged theological position that eventually became institutionalized as the Ahl-i-Sunnat wa'al-Jamaat. As Sanyal argues, their theology, self-understanding, and community identity emerged from debate and disputation with a wide range of contemporary Muslim reformists, including Sayyid Ahmed Khan, Ghulam Mirza Ahmed, the *ulema* of Deoband, and the AIH (Sanyal 1996, 166–267). The latter two groups, influenced by Delhi-based *ulema*, were considered by the Ahl-i-Sunnat to be directly inspired by the earlier Wahhabi movement, the Tariqa-i-Muhammadiya, of Sayyid Ahmed Barelwi and Muhammed Ismail Dehlawi.[45]

By the 1890s the differences between these reformist movements were clear, and the debates between them had become standardized. Central to Barelwi differences with the AIH were their oppositional understandings of the Prophet and the beliefs, rituals, and practices that flowed from them. This difference can be best summed up by what is referred to as the *nur/bashr* (light/human) dispute. The AIH argue that the Prophet Muhammed, as *insan-i-kamil* (the perfect man), was exactly that—human. His exemplary practice (*sunna*) was to be imitated and emulated. Reform, therefore, involved dispensing with all the accretions that had accumulated through history, custom, and culture. They prioritized the revival of original prophetic practice through independent study of the *sunna* via the *hadith* (the authoritative record of the Prophet's exemplary conduct).

Ahmed Riza Khan, however, emerged from a context in which veneration of the Prophet had a long history in Sufi and popular devotionalism. In Sufi conceptions, the Prophet is suprahuman in that he is made of the original substance, light (*nur*). He existed from before the creation of the world, was called into being at a particular historical moment, and his earthly death did not mean that he ceased to exist. As Ahmed Riza Khan argued, and Barelwis continue to assert, the Prophet is alive in his grave, remains attentive to the prayers of his community, and, when invoked, can intercede with Allah on their behalf. That is, the Prophet can be in one's presence and can observe one (*hazir-o-nazir*). This intercessionary role is critical to Barelwi thought and practice. To the Ahl-i-Hadith, however, this exaltation of the Prophet to a quasi-divine status is nothing less than *shirk* (polytheism); they consider it a denial of the fundamental unity of Allah (*tauhid*), which is absolutely central to the Prophet's message and enshrined in the confession of Muslim faith.[46] For Ahmed Riza Khan, by contrast, the Prophet's extraordinary attributes and qualities were derived from his closeness to God.

To achieve proximity to the divine, to the ultimate reality, was only possible by approaching pious figures imbued with *barkat* (God's grace), such as *pirs* (spiritual guides) and *shaykhs*. Love for the Prophet (*ishq-e-rasul*) was so central to Riza Khan, Sanyal argues, because it was the best way of showing love for God (Sanyal 1996, 151–65). The annual *milad-un-nabi* celebrations are the focal point of this intense devotion, which is expressed through devotional poetry, songs, and the recitation of *durud*, verses preceding the primary prayers. Some of these directly address the Prophet, as if he is present in the world. (The AIH, on the other hand, refuse to say *durud* invoking the Prophet, and Barelwis find their arguments against doing so equivalent to abuse of the Prophet [Malik 1990, 43–44].) Many Ahl-i-Sunnat expect the Prophet to be present at these celebrations. Popular practice at times elevates the Prophet to quasi-divine status; devotion to him, critics argue, seems to replace worship of God. Thus, the AIH have accused those influenced by Sufism of polytheism. They also regard them as *mubtabis* (reprehensible innovators) for celebrating festivities associated with the death anniversaries of saints (*urs*) and devotional verse (*qawwali*). In defense of the Prophet's suprahuman status, Ahmed Riza Khan tended to regard all those who saw the Prophet as merely human at best as disrespectful, and at worst as unbelievers (Sanyal 1996, 244–64). He considered the AIH's excoriation of intercessors and their reliance on individual reason to be a manifestation of their arrogance.[47] By contrast, he emphasized the overwhelming presence of the Prophet as a source of grace and an intercessor with God. From the Barelwi perspective, one becomes a Muslim through mediated oral and aural techniques that excite affection and allow love for the Prophet to develop in one's heart. Any disrespect for the Prophet, on the other hand, can constitute grounds for allegations of infidelity (*kufr*).

The escalation of these sectarian polemics into legal cases has been enabled by the expansion of the blasphemy laws. The law's facility has effectively given state sanction to these historically developed accusatory practices. I return to the case in Kamonke to describe how the laws' existence incited, furthered, and escalated religious conflict. Unlike the vast majority of blasphemy cases, this one included in the available evidence a tape recording of the allegedly blasphemous words.[48] These cassette tapes proved crucial in the police's resolution of the case. They also reveal the rhetorical techniques through which the speakers constituted their own authority and denigrated their opponents: mimicry, parody, burlesque, and invective.

Mutual Accusations in Kamonke

Kamonke is just over an hour outside of Lahore, some forty-two kilometers on the way to Gujranwala. Prior to Partition it was a village, but by 2001 it had grown into a small town with a population estimated at 150,000. It began as a rice market and developed into a major rice-trading center with ancillary industries such as rice husking and milling, particularly in the 1960s and '70s. The majority of employment is connected with either the rice trade or farming. Local landowners and successful traders own the larger houses in the older and more established part of town. The majority of the population are Barelwis, but there is also a significant Ahl-i-Hadith presence and a few Shias. According to the police, as of 1999 there were 110 Barelwi mosques (including three seminaries), about ten Ahl-i-Hadith mosques, and one Shia *imambara*. No one could recall any prior blasphemy incidents in the town, although locals indicated that the *milad-un-nabi* celebrations had become the focal point of increasing sectarian tension over the past few years.

Among Abdur Rauf Yazdani's audience that day were some young men from one of the Barelwi organizations in the city. They attended because they were keen to see how their Wahhabi opponents responded to the criticism that had been leveled against them. Others were intrigued by the posters advertising the gathering, which urged "those who love the Prophet" to attend, a phrase that echoed Barelwi devotionalism. Indeed, it had been chosen to assert that the Ahl-i-Hadith were not lacking in such love, and to attract rural Barelwis into the audience. It was the dismay and anger of these young men at the Ahl-i-Hadith's sermons that initiated the process that would culminate in the two sects' mutual accusations.

Among the speakers at the AIH's gathering, two in particular became the focus of the young Barelwis' anger and accusations: Abdur Rauf Yazdani and a local, Nawaz Cheema. In their subsequent complaint to the police, the Barelwis stated that these two had implied that the Barelwis were like "dance girls" and "prostitutes" in their celebrations of the Prophet's birthday, had made fun of the mannerisms, habits, and bodies of Barelwi *maulvis* (clerics) and *pirs*, and, most egregiously, ridiculed their insistence on the Prophet's intercessory role and presence. Nawaz Cheema, they alleged, had satirized the *durud*, saying, "With every breath you say the *durud* and the Prophet is present! Sisters show me, is he [the Prophet] sitting under your chair? Is he here? Or is he there? *Hazir-o-nazir*? [That is, is the Prophet present and observant?] Can you not see him?"

The AIH speakers were unsparing in their criticism of both the Barelwi *ulema* and the devotions centered on *pirs* and shrines. Their argument was intended to convince the audience to use their own reason rather than relying on religious intermediaries. Neither clerics, nor *pirs*, nor saints, nor the Prophet, they insisted, could intercede on behalf of the individual. The Prophet was the perfect man, but he was human—and it was this humanness that made his imitation possible. Replicating his prophetic practices and prayer would bring people closer to God and allow them to receive his beneficence. This emphasis on rational reform of the self in accordance with the message of the Quran and the *hadith* led them to criticize Barelwi celebration of the Prophet on a number of terms.

First, they insisted that, as a man, the Prophet had died. Clerics and Sufis who proclaimed to the contrary and utilized mediatory practices to incite strong emotional love for the Prophet were, they said, in fact engaging in satanic practices that the Prophet had disapproved of. Second, they associated the festive practices and rituals of shrine worship with women. Unlike mosques, from which Punjabi women are by and large prohibited, shrines are accessible to them. By gendering shrines as feminine, and furthermore as

Hindu, they emphasized their irredeemable heterogeneity. Third, they expostulated on their own steadfastness, their ethic of commitment in following the *sharia*. This was the exemplary ethical posture, they argued, through which real love of the Prophet was demonstrated. Further, this absolute insistence on imitation of the Prophet was reflected, they suggested, in their bodily comportment and disposition. In contrast, they ridiculed the Barelwi *ulema* for taking too much interest in the tactile pleasures of this world, in particular food, and, conversely, the ascetic *pirs* for disavowing them. Avoiding the excesses of both indulgence and denial, and espousing moderation and self-control, they repeated *hadith* from the Prophet's life to emphasize their fidelity. They saw themselves as modern, urban, literate, and disciplined as compared to the rusticity, affective dispositions, and undisciplined bodies and minds of their Barelwi opponents.

In order to expose the hierarchical structure of intercessionary authority and to show that *pirs'* and Sufis' claims to privileged access to the Prophet and thereby to the divine were fraudulent, the AIH speakers insisted on the Prophet's humanity. Since he was a man who died, they foreclosed the possibility of suprahuman intervention. They stressed that neither the Prophet nor any of the saints were present, and that the entire responsibility for salvation rested upon the individual. Nawaz Cheema's comment, in particular, became the object of the Barelwis' ire, for he encapsulated the AIH's rationalist critique when he mocked the Barelwi claim that the performance of *durud* prayer could elicit the presence of the Prophet—a presence, he said with mock incredulity, that no one but the Barelwi *ulema* had as yet been able to ascertain.

This comment was regarded as especially insulting. However, the Barelwis did not originally intend to involve the administration or the police. They had been upset by the speeches that ridiculed their beliefs, and wanted to give a full and fitting answer (*jawab*) to their opponents' criticisms. To this end, they approached one of their clerics, Mufti Naeem Akhter Naqshbandi, who agreed to write a pamphlet in response. In this pamphlet, he followed a familiar polemical literature in which specific texts are quoted to prove the error of one's opponents and their disrespect for the Prophet. In addition, the Barelwis decided to organize a gathering of their own and invited speakers who could answer the Wahhabis in kind. This gathering was held on June 29, some twelve days after the AIH's conference. The principal speaker recruited to respond was one Maulana Sialvhi from Faislabad.

Sialvhi started his oration by explicitly saying he would answer the Wahhabis point by point. He also promised not to abuse them. Nonetheless, in responding to each insult directed against his sect, he turned each back against his opponents. In doing this, he was consistent with the cultural ethos of proportionality that first prompted the demands for an answer. The majority of his two-hour speech, however, was concerned with expounding the Barelwis' conception of the Prophet in contrast to that of the AIH. Disparaging the AIH stress on literacy and rationality as inadequate, he said to an imagined AIH interlocutor, "It is easy to read the *kalyma* [the Muslim statement of faith], you without faith, but it is difficult to sustain it. That only comes from love." Throughout, he emphasized that the cultivation of the heart and of love was the means through which one becomes close to the Prophet. Outward conformity to the practices and signs of Islam, he said, may make one look like a Muslim, but if one's heart is small, then one cannot know what being a real Muslim is.

The speech operated in two registers. On the one hand, Sialvhi utilized dense poetical forms when he recounted stories from the Prophet's life through which he sought to instruct his audience—"lovers of the Prophet"—and incite the appropriate affective responses among them. On the other hand, he often complemented these moments with a prosaic conversational register, using parody, burlesque, and ironic humor against his opponents. However, his ribald witticisms, characteristic of peasant Punjabi humor, often slid into outright insults and abuse. As far as the Barelwis were concerned, Sialvhi's response was a great success. They had given a fitting riposte, and the matter was therefore settled. However, it was now the AIH's turn to be offended by what they considered to be the crassness and vulgarity of the Barelwis' response.

The leading members of the AIH informed me that they, like the Barelwis, had not originally intended to file charges. However, they wanted to bring the inflammatory aspects of Sialvhi's speech, which they said incited sectarian hatred, to the administration's attention, hoping that action would be taken against Sialvhi. The administration, they said, tried to discourage them, but conceded that they could make a complaint to the police if they insisted upon pursuing the matter. The police too were reluctant to pursue the matter. As they later explained, they thought it was a frivolous case that would not only waste their time, but also lead to sectarian tension. Administrative and police reluctance discouraged and delayed the AIH, but they eventually made a formal complaint under sections 295-A and 298 of the PPC, accusing the Barelwis of outraging and wounding their religious feelings.

The police began formally investigating the complaint. Before it was registered as a criminal charge, the police and administration, in alliance with leaders of both sides, attempted to secure a compromise. To this end, they established a peace committee. Initially, attempts by the mediators looked as if they would be successful, but they foundered when Mufti Naeem and his associates consulted a local lawyer, who advised them that Nawaz Cheema's words constituted disrespect to the Prophet under section 295-C. Insulting the Prophet, as Mufti Naeem repeatedly informed me, could be neither tolerated nor forgiven. As he wrote in one of his pamphlets addressed to the AIH and justifying why he was pursuing the case,

> Have you ever read the law? The government of Pakistan did not make 295-C an offense just for non-Muslims, but rather, in fact, it was made for insulters of the Prophet like you. That's why you have been charged with the offense.

Accordingly, he refused to compromise and filed a formal complaint with the police accusing the AIH under sections 295-A, 298-A, and 295-C: outraging religious feelings, making derogatory remarks about holy persons, and blaspheming against the Prophet, respectively. In one of their own pamphlets, the AIH directed their ire at the lawyer, who in their view sabotaged the compromise and made false and instrumental allegations:

> But lawyer sahib Allah does not like those who break the limits imposed by Allah. People may like you a lot. But you have committed a blasphemy by writing the application. You've accused innocent people and registered a case against them, but tell us this: in the eyes of God, how will you hide this great calumny? You have exceeded the limits of God to get false fame in this world. What benefit will you get from this if God does not favor you? Allah does not like those who cause disputes. The two parties had compromised. Through your intervention and bad advice you have started a civil war in Kamonke. How will you bear the burden of making this false accusation on Judgment Day? Get as much false fame as you wish but ultimately you will have to account for it. May God destroy those who have insulted the Prophet! May God destroy those who have falsely accused innocent people!

The AIH complaint was, after investigation, accepted by the police's legal officer, who determined that the accused could be formally charged under sections 295-A and 298. Two days later, Mufti Naeem responded by announcing over the mosque loudspeakers that the AIH had insulted the Prophet and calling for financial and physical support. After Friday prayers, a Barelwi procession went to the police station and pressurized the police into filing a first information report (FIR) against the Ahl-i-Hadith. On this occasion, however, the police did not formally investigate the complaint but registered the FIR immediately. One police officer admitted to me that this was the only way of defusing the situation. He thought that since the case involved reciprocal accusations, it would be easier to reach a compromise. But, as he later realized, he was mistaken. The inclusion of 295-C in the Barelwis' complaint had created a serious imbalance in the severity of the alleged offenses on the two sides: violation of 295 C is a capital offense, and an accusation of such a crime cannot be withdrawn or "compromised" by the complainant.

Once the 295-C charge had been registered, the Barelwis argued that they could not compromise. Thereafter, Mufti Naeem mobilized networks, wrote pamphlets, organized protests, raised funds from the neighborhood, demanded the arrests of those accused, and resisted the administration's attempts to resolve the case. Administrators, however, were able to delay the bringing of formal charges by prolonging the police investigation, still hoping to effect a compromise. They first clamped down on public protests and subsequently banned them. They tried to persuade Mufti Naeem to be reasonable and cited instances in the Prophet's life when he had forgiven those who had abused and insulted him. They indicated that the Barelwi case was weak and that the allegations against Nawaz Cheema in particular were not backed up by the tapes of his speech. Throughout they impressed upon the Barelwis that, for the greater good of the Muslim community, they should withdraw their charges (and the authorities would overlook the inclusion of 295-C). However, Mufti Naeem refused to withdraw. He argued that the AIH speakers had insulted the Prophet and could not be forgiven; indeed, that such an act placed them outside the boundaries of Islam.

While refusing to admit that they had committed blasphemy, the AIH were, given the seriousness of the charge against them, more amenable to administrative efforts to find a compromise. While disparaging of both groups, administrative officials were slightly more sympathetic to the AIH. This was a result partly of their shared interest in dropping the case and partly of the fact that the Kamonke officials I spoke with had an affinity with the AIH. They too considered themselves literate, temperate, and rational, and regarded the Barelwi *ulema* as unreasonable and antimodern. As one police official said to me, "We could not make these mullahs see reason." He was particularly aggravated by the fact that the major allegation of a violation of 295-C in the Barelwis' complaint against Nawaz Cheema did not square with the audio record. In the FIR, the Barelwis alleged that Nawaz Cheema had said,

> With every breath you say the *durud* and the Prophet is present! Sisters show me, is he [the Prophet] sitting under your chair? Is he here? Or is he there? *Hazir-o-nazir?* Can you not see him?

On the audio tape he was in fact determined to have said,

> My brothers, the decision is up to you. . . . It is a matter of regret that those who say that the Prophet has come, is present, or is coming, that "he is here, he has taken a seat,"[49] oh, there he is." If the *maulvi*s can see him, then, brother, don't you have eyes too?

These differences enabled the police to argue that there was in fact no insult offered to the Prophet. They called the leading antagonists to a closed meeting and made them listen to the tape. I was not allowed to attend this meeting, but Mufti Naeem later informed me that he had tried to explain that Nawaz Cheema had pointed to an empty chair on stage and waved his handkerchief in its direction. The Barelwi had translated these paralinguistic gestures into words in order to convey the full extent of the insult. When they registered the FIR they had not yet procured the tape, and therefore based their accusations on the reports of audience members. This, he explained, accounted for the discrepancy between what they had earlier reported and the tape. The police, however, argued that Nawaz Cheema was only mimicking and mocking Barelwi belief in the Prophet's presence. As far as the latter were concerned, however, this amounted to mocking the Prophet. The police, however, insisted that the discrepancy between the tape and their allegations would scupper any chances of the case's being upheld in court and urged them to reconcile. In the end, the Barelwis, realizing that their antagonists would not be arrested and under pressure from the administration, which had asked both groups to write *tauba nama*s (deeds of repentance), sought a way out of the impasse. However, they refused to write a *tauba nama*, which would mean admitting a similarity between the two parties. Nor were they willing to admit any fault. Further, they were concerned that if they dropped the case, they could be considered criminals in God's eyes. Consequently, they decided to consult higher juristic authorities within their sect. In these consultations, they were informed that their principal duty had been to bring this crime to the attention of the sovereign. It was, however, up to the latter to then make a decision. That is, under Islamic law, only the sovereign had the right to forgive. The police also asked the AIH to write a *tauba nama* apologizing to the Barelwis. Without admitting to having committed blasphemy or any offense that might be punishable, they informally expressed their contrition if anything that they had said was considered insulting to Barelwi beliefs.

This resort by state actors to nonlegal forms of contrition, repentance, and forgiveness, indeed, to non-state Islamic law, to extricate themselves from state-based laws protecting Islam speaks to the manifold complexities, conjunctures, and disjunctures in the application and understanding of Islamic law in contemporary Pakistan. In the end, Mufti Naeem accepted the juristic opinion of a senior figure within his denomination, allowing the legal proceedings to end. However, he was less than satisfied with this outcome. The government, he said, had failed to fulfill its duty, in that it had not arrested the blasphemers. As far as he was concerned, ridiculing the *durud* and mocking Barelwi assertions of the Prophet's suprahuman status was equivalent to disrespecting the Prophet, and therefore blasphemous. He had not been able to prevail upon the administration, but he had fulfilled his obligations in bringing the matter to the attention of the authorities. Nor could he forgive the AIH for their crime, as this right, under Islamic law, belonged only to the sovereign. That is, his agency under state law to initiate a prosecution and receive a resolution had been disappointed. He had been able to justify his withdrawal under non-state Islamic jurisprudence.

Locals whom I interviewed for their reactions to the settlement understood the compromise as a defeat for the Barelwis. The Wahhabis, they felt, were institutionally stronger and had more influence in the state. It is this gap between the filing of the case and their inability to prosecute, between their expectation that the government would perform its sovereign duty and its refusal to do so, between the law's incitement to action and the administration's tenuous regulatory capability that has led the blasphemy laws to become a site of a passionate attachment and mobilization, and in this case, at least among the local Barelwis, a site of disaffection and betrayal by the state.

×   ×   ×

Both the colonial and postcolonial blasphemy laws have enabled particular stagings of sovereign power and state ideologies. In the colonial era, they enabled the state to represent itself as secular and rational, as the impartial umpire between antagonistic religious communities. In Zia's postcolony they enabled the authorities to invest themselves with sacredness and claim to be establishing an Islamic state. As we have seen, in both periods the state criminalizes blasphemous utterances and texts. The laws with which it does so incite religious affect and attempt to regulate the resulting social disorder. In both periods it was not ecclesiastical or *sharia* courts, but secular criminal courts, that adjudicated questions of blasphemy. But there are also important differences between the periods. Whereas the colonial laws were designed to arbitrate difference, the postcolonial laws have been premised on the assumption of Muslim unity—at least with respect to the Quran and the Prophet. As the constitutive foundations of Muslim existence, they are considered indisputable and transcendent. At the same time, they are interpreted, appropriated, routinized, and ritualized in diverse ways among sectarian groups and in everyday life.

For both the Ahl-i-Hadith and the Barelwis, the Prophet, considered as the representative, archetypal perfect man, is the very ground of Muslim ontology. The AIH constantly invoke him for moral reference and instruction. His exemplary practice (*sunna*) is routinized and embodied as they attempt to imitate his perfect example. Whether deciding on an appropriate tone of voice, bodily comportment, mealtime etiquette, or ethical stance in a particular situation, it is to the Prophet's example they turn. He is referenced in instruction, in admonishment, and in argument.

Barelwis, however, emphasize that *ishq* (love) for the Prophet is the necessary first step toward existing as a Muslim. Imitation and emulation through pedagogical techniques, and the emphasis on individual reason, are secondary to love. Only after love has opened the heart can one use reason. Human reason is fallible and by itself dangerous, as it could lead one to all kinds of errors, paradoxes, and confusions. Satan's fall, one cleric informed me, resulted from his resort to reason. Love for the Prophet is the inaugural act of becoming a true Muslim, and reason should be exercised within the boundaries of religion, or, as another cleric said, "When one loves the Holy Prophet then the mind will follow the right direction." The AIH's emphasis on individual reason, they argued, led them into errors. As Mufti Naeem of Kamonke said (and other Barelwi clerics I interviewed concurred), "One cannot speak of the Prophet in ordinary language. The key difference between us and the AIH is that when they speak of the Prophet they speak of him as an ordinary human being."

These historically constituted differences and arguments among South Asian Muslims became, as we have seen, potentially criminal in the colonial period. Macaulay's attentiveness to religious dispositions, assumption of Indians' religious sensitivity, and drafting of blasphemy laws that emphasized emotional hurt as the basis of a criminal offense have played a significant role in the constitution of religious sentiment in public life. Zia's attempt to co-opt this religious sentiment and contain it within legal structures has been undermined by the intense emotions that blasphemy accusations can produce, the procedural defects of the laws, and the interest of sections of the media in publicizing such cases. Further, the Muslim unity that the laws assume and invoke has been undercut by the social reality of difference. Faced with having to decide whether a sect's beliefs or practices are un-Islamic, a decision that could lead to violence however it is made, the administration has resorted to extra-legal means of resolution. In failing to fulfill its own prosecutorial requirements, the law, as far as domestic religious proponents of prosecution are concerned, allows satanic presences and practices to persist. Internationally, the laws and the cases and sentiments they provoke continue to position Muslims, in secular discourse, as the West's irrational and disavowed other.

Notes

1. The cartoons were published on September 30, 2005. The protests were at their height in February 2006.

2. A small Norwegian Christian newspaper, *Magazinet,* was one of the first publications to reproduce the cartoons. Hence, there were demonstrations against both the Danish and Norwegian embassies in Islamabad.

3. Lapham demonstrates an almost complete ignorance of the Prophet's life and, astonishingly, refers to William Bolitho's *Twelve against the Gods* (1929) and H. G. Wells's *The Outline of History* (1920) as key sources on it. Not surprisingly, he peddles medieval and orientalist calumnies against the Prophet. Note that *Harper's Magazine* reprinted the scurrilous cartoons that June. For a better argued, but nonetheless absolutist, defense of free speech that also fails to understand the importance of emotions and sensibilities in political life and ignores the colonial genealogy of blasphemy laws in South Asia, see Post 2007.

4. Although "modernity" may be neither a verifiable object nor a useful analytical concept, it remains, as Asad notes, a political project that captures the imagination and sustains various political and theoretical interventions (Asad 2003, 12–16). For critiques of the concept, see Kelly 2002 and Cooper 2005.

5. Gilmartin argues that a rhetoric of the heart, of expressing feelings, developed from the conjunction of a vernacular Urdu press that relied upon idioms and motifs of Urdu poetry and the emergence of individuals rooted in an urban marketplace which emphasized not just autonomy but desires and emotions. Occasions such as the *Rangila Rasul* (Colorful Prophet) case, which I detail later, provided an issue around which this emerging public coalesced to define the meaning of the Muslim community in radically new ways (Gilmartin 1991).

6. The Federal Shariat Court directed the government to amend the law by April 30, 1991. See *Muhammed Ismail Qureshi v. Pakistan* (PLD 1991, FSC10). The government, however, has not complied, thus implicitly leaving open the option of life imprisonment. For a detailed analysis of the FSC's decision, see Mangi 2000, 70–105.

7. Musharraf's government sought to make it more difficult to lay blasphemy charges by stipulating that the District Commissioner, rather than the police, must undertake the initial inquiry into the charge.

8. Eager to assert his liberal secular credentials, Musharraf had made the announcement at the government-sponsored Pakistan Convention on Human Rights and Human Dignity within six months of his coup.

9. For accounts of Islamization, see Mehdi 1994, Amin 1989, Kennedy 1996, and R. Patel 1986.

10. For accounts of appropriation of classical Muslim law by modern states, see Christelow 1988; Asad 2003, 205–56; Messick 1993, 54–72; and Buskens 1993, 65–100. For histories of the colonial transformation of Muslim law in South Asia, see Fisch 1983, Anderson 1993, Strawson 1999, and Kugle 2001.

11. There have, however, been a number of extra-judicial murders.

12. Bentham coined the term "pannomium" to describe his endeavor to create a "complete body of law." See E. Stokes 1959, part 3, chapter 4, and Lieberman 1989, 257–76. Compare Foucault's discussion of panopticism (1995, 195–230).

13. For an excellent account of how Macaulay's speech encapsulated the utilitarian reform program, which aimed at legislative consolidation, state centralization, a complete overhaul of the judicial administration, and the drafting of a complete code of laws, see E. Stokes 1959, and particularly pp. 51–75 for Bentham's ambition to be an Indian Solon. On the historical background of the codification movement in England, see Lieberman 1989.

14. On the Indian Penal Code, see E. Stokes 1959, 219–33; Rankin 1946, 197–217; Clive 1973, 427–78; W. Stokes 1887, 1–72; and Stephen 1996, 283–346.

15. Although enacted in 1860, it did not come into effect until January 1, 1862. It has subsequently been amended and revised in each of these countries.

16. Macaulay's view of Indians is most clearly expressed in the "Minute on Indian Education" (Macaulay 1972) and Mill's view in his seminal *History of British India* (1820).

17. "In general, language is seldom considered in any other point of view than that of an instrument of communication—an instrument employed by one mind in making communication of its contents to another mind" (Bentham 1843b, 298). More generally, see Bentham 1988 and Mack 1963, 151–203.

18. See Bentham 1970, 224–25, especially the footnotes. The editors of this volume remark that Bentham had considerable doubts as to whether offenses against religion should be included within his model penal code (1970, 202n1).

19. Here Bengal is metonymically standing for India.

20. This and the penal code of Napoleon were considered to be the first attempts to realize Bentham's codification project in practice.

21. Macaulay does not use the term "speech act," and his discussion is not always that sophisticated, but he clearly refuses to reduce language to the communication of information alone.

22. Spoken defamation was only grounds for civil action.

23. He does not, however, argue that all prejudicial imputations are a basis for criminal action or conviction. The most important exception is where the defamatory libel is ascertained to be true. This consideration of truth, he acknowledges, differs

radically from the English law of the time, in which the truth of the allegation seems to have been irrelevant to successful prosecution.

24. In addition, he was also keen to counter Christian missionaries.

25. In the draft 1837 code these were sections 275, 276, 280, and 282. The code that was enacted in 1860 revised them slightly. Technically only section 298 was a blasphemy law, and unlike the other sections it was procedurally a private action. All the other sections defined offenses against the state. See Hanif 1999 for current laws and Macaulay et al. 2002 for the draft chapter.

26. He said of the provisions of Chapter 15, "They present an extraordinary contrast to the English law on that subject as it stood in early times, though they reflect precisely the tone of modern English sentiment" (Stephen 1996, 312). Fitzjames Stephen was Law Member from 1869 to 1872. See Hostettler 1992, 165–91.

27. Nonetheless, compared to the abstruse technical language of English law, Macaulay's code was hailed as a model of precision and simplicity. See J. S. Mill 1990, 19–30; Stephen 1996, 303; and Rankin 1946, 203–204.

28. The defendants were charged under section 153-A, which criminalizes the incitement of hatred of other religions, races, or caste, community, or linguistic groups. For a detailed account of the case that provides the historical and legal context, see Thursby 1975, 19–71.

29. The presiding judge, Justice Dalip Singh, decided that section 153-A was intended to prevent attacks on contemporary communities and did not cover attacks on deceased religious leaders. The defendant was later murdered by a Muslim, Ilm-ud-Din, who was subsequently prosecuted. He was defended by M. A. Jinnah, but he confessed and was executed. His grave in Lahore is still visited and he has been memorialized in popular discourse as a *ghazi* (warrior) and *shaheed* (martyr) of Islam.

30. The Ahmadiyya have always been regarded as controversial by the majority of the *ulema*, because their founder claimed to be the recipient of divine communication and revelation, and thus a prophet. The orthodox Muslim position, however, is that revelation ceased with the Prophet Muhammed. For the theological background to this controversy, see Friedmann 1989. For a history of the Ahmadiyya, see Lavan 1974.

31. See sections 113 concerning sedition, 469 concerning defamation, and 485 concerning criminal insult in the 1837 code. The postcolonial sections also borrow from subsequent criminal amendments introduced by the colonial authorities, such as section 153-A concerning public order.

32. Considering Macaulay's anxieties over blasphemy cases and religious fanaticism in England, this could be yet another example of the displacement of metropolitan anxieties.

33. Introduced in 1979, they comprised four separate ordinances: the Offences against Property Ordinance, the Offence of Zina (Unlawful Intercourse) Ordinance, the Offence of Qazf (False Allegations) Ordinance, and the Prohibition Order. The Property Ordinance introduced Islamic punishments for theft and robbery but has brought major change neither to the law of theft nor to the punishments prescribed. The Zina Ordinance made adultery and fornication criminal offenses. The Qazf Ordinance made false allegations of fornication or adultery offenses. The Prohibition Order criminalized the selling and drinking of wine by Muslims (Mehdi 1994, 109–56). The other major act of Islamization was the replacement of the 1872 Law of Evidence by

the Qanun-e-Shahadat (Law of Evidence) Order of 1984. Some scholars have argued that this was little more than a cosmetic translation of the 1872 law into Muslim terminology, and that few specifically Islamic provisions were added (Kennedy 1990, 67–69). Others, while agreeing that there were few changes, note that one significant change was the reduction of women's ability to witness financial instruments (R. Patel 1986; Mehdi 1994).

34. Muslim criminal law had been initially applied by the colonial authorities but was progressively transformed and eventually completely dispensed with. See Fisch 1983 and Singha 1998.

35. It is significant that Zia did not make any changes to personal law, despite intense *ulema* and Islamist pressure to amend the Muslim Family Law Ordinance of 1961. Insofar as changes have been made in Anglo-Muhammadan personal law, they have been driven by judicial appropriation and interpretation of the *sharia*.

36. *Hadd* is the technical term for acts that have been forbidden or for which punishments have been laid out in the Quran. *Tazir* is the discretionary punishment administered by the state for crimes it defines itself, and for which no *hadd* punishment exists.

37. Along with the Hudood Ordinances, Zia instituted the Execution of Whipping Ordinance, which made slight changes to the colonial Whipping Act of 1909. However, most whippings seem to have been ordered by martial law courts.

38. The *Dawn* (January 21, 2001) reported that figures it managed to acquire from the Interior Ministry showed that 90 of 122 registered blasphemy cases were laid against Muslims. Nonetheless, the number of cases against minorities is disproportionate to their representation in the population.

39. I will use the terms "Ahl-i-Sunnat" and "Barelwi" interchangeably.

40. *Seerat* means quality, nature, character, or conduct.

41. The fact that the Barelwis charged their opponents under 298-A, which criminalizes derogatory language against the Prophet's family, reflects the fact that they consider Sufi saints to be his genealogical successors.

42. I confine myself here to intra-Sunni disputation. I do not deal with the variety of Sunni responses to Shias in South Asia.

43. See *Ata-Ullah v. Azim-Ullah* (1890) ILR 12, Allahabad 494; *Jangu v. Ahmad Ullah* (1891) ILR 13, Allahabad 419; *Queen Empress v. Ramzan* (1885) ILR 7, Allahabad 461; *Fazl Karim v. Maula Baksh* (1891) 21 IA 59; and *Abdus Subhan v. Korban Ali* (1908) ILR 35, Calcutta 294. On Ahl-i-Hadith, see B. Metcalf 1982, 269–96; Brown 1996, 21–26; and Ahmed 1966.

44. The following account of reformist movements is mainly drawn from Sanyal 1996 and B. Metcalf 1982, and that of Sufis from Schimmel 1975, Chittick 2000, and Ernst 1997.

45. On the Tariqa-i-Muhammadiya see, for example, Pearson 1979. This movement was categorized as Wahhabi by the colonial authorities, and the term continues to be used by the Barelwis as a derogatory label for Deobandis and the Ahl-i-Hadith.

46. For Sufi interpretations of the *kalyma-shahada*, which are considerably more complex than the Ahl-i-Hadith's literalist reading, see Chittick 2000, 3–17; and Ernst 1997, 45–58.

47. The Ahl-i-Hadith's refusal to be bound by a particular *fiqh* and their denial of gnostic knowledge reflect their methodological as well as theological differences

from the Barelwis. They are methodologically suspicious of interpretive knowledge, whether of the legal scholars or of Sufi orders, considering it prone to deviating from the truth as embodied in the Quran and Sunna. For more on their differences, see Sanyal 1996, 257–61,

48. Some cases center on printed texts, but the vast majority of allegations are based on speech.

49. Barelwis often expect the Prophet to be present at celebrations performed in his honor and sometimes reserve a special seat for him.

References

Abou Zahab, Mariam. 2002a. "The Regional Dimension of Sectarian Conflicts in Pakistan." In Christophe Jaffrelot, ed., *Pakistan: Nationalism without a Nation?* New Delhi: Zed Books.

———. 2002b. "The Sunni-Shia Conflict in Jhang Pakistan." In Imtiaz Ahmed, ed., *Lived Islam in South Asia.* New Delhi: Social Sciences Press.

Abrams, Philip. 1988. "Notes on the Difficulty of Studying the State." *Journal of Historical Sociology* 1:58–89.

Ahmed, Qeyamuddin. 1966. *The Wahhabi Movement in India.* Calcutta: Mukhopadhyay.

Ali, Mukhtar Ahmad. 2000. *Sectarian Conflict in Pakistan: A Case Study of Jhang.* Colombo: Regional Center for Strategic Studies.

Amin, Mohammed. 1989. *Islamization of Laws in Pakistan.* Lahore: Sang-e-Meel.

Amnesty International. 1994. *Pakistan: Use and Abuse of the Blasphemy Laws.* AI Index ASA 33/09/94. New York: Amnesty International.

Anderson, Michael R. 1993. "Islamic Law and the Colonial Encounter in British India." In David Arnold and Peter Robb, eds., *Institutions and Ideologies.* London: Curzon.

Appignanesi, Lisa, and Sara Maitland, eds. 1989. *The Rushdie File.* London: Fourth Estate.

Asad, Talal. 2003. *Formations of the Secular.* Stanford, Calif.: Stanford University Press.

Baxi, Upendra. 1992. "The States Emissary: Law in Subaltern Studies." In Partha Chatterjee and Gyanendra Pandey, eds., *Subaltern Studies: Writings on South Asian History and Society,* vol. 7. New Delhi: Oxford University Press.

Bentham, Jeremy. 1843a. "Essay on the Influence of Time and Place in Matters of Legislation." In John Bowring, ed., *The Works of Jeremy Bentham,* vol. 1. Edinburgh: William Tait.

———. 1843b. "Essay on Language." In John Bowring, ed., *The Works of Jeremy Bentham,* vol. 8. Edinburgh: William Tait.

———. 1970. *Introduction to the Principles of Morals and Legislation.* Ed. J. H. Burns and H. L. A. Hart. London: Athlone.

———. 1988. *A Fragment on Government.* Cambridge: Cambridge University Press.

Brown, Daniel. 1996. *Rethinking Tradition in Modern Islamic Thought.* Cambridge: Cambridge University Press.

Buskens, Leon. 1993. "Islamic Commentaries and French Codes." In Henk Driessen, ed., *The Politics of Ethnographic Reading and Writing: Confrontation of Western and Indigenous Views.* Fort Lauderdale, Fla.: Plantation.

Butler, Judith. 1997. *Excitable Speech: A Politics of the Performative*. London: Routledge.

Chakrabarty, Dipesh. 2007. *Provincializing Europe: Postcolonial Thought and Historical Difference*. New ed. Princeton, N.J.: Princeton University Press.

Chatterjee, Partha. 1986. *Nationalist Thought and the Colonial World*. Minneapolis: University of Minnesota Press.

_____. 1993. *The Nation and Its Fragments: Colonial and Postcolonial Histories*. Princeton, N.J.: Princeton University Press.

Chittick, William C. 2000. *Sufism: A Short Introduction*. Oxford: Oneworld Publications.

Christelow, Allan. 1988. "The Transformation of the Muslim Court System in Colonial Algeria." In Aziz Al-Azmeh, ed., *Islamic Law: Social and Historical Contexts*. New York: Routledge.

Christian Study Centre. 1985. *News from the Country, Pakistan, 1980–84*. Rawalpindi, Pakistan: The Centre.

Clive, John. 1973. *Macaulay: The Shaping of the Historian*. New York: Vintage.

Cohn, Bernard. 1987 (1959). "Some Notes on Law and Change in North India." In *An Anthropologist amongst the Historians and Other Essays*. New Delhi: Oxford University Press.

_____. 1989. "Law and the Colonial State in India." In June Starr and Jane F. Collier, eds., *History and Power in the Study of Law: New Directions in Legal Anthropology*. Ithaca, N.Y.: Cornell University Press.

Cooper, Frederick. 2005. *Colonialism in Question: Theory, Knowledge, History*. Berkeley: University of California Press.

Das, Veena, and Deborah Poole, eds. 2004. *Anthropology in the Margins of the State*. Santa Fe: School of American Research Press.

Ernst, Carl. 1997. *The Shambhala Guide to Sufism*. Boston: Shambhala.

Fisch, Jorge. 1983. *Cheap Lives and Dear Limbs: The British Transformation of the Bengal Criminal Law, 1769–1817*. Wiesbaden: Steiner.

Foucault, Michel. 1995 (1977). *Discipline and Punish: The Birth of the Prison*. New York: Random House.

Freitag, Sandra. 1989. *Collective Action and Community: Public Arenas and the Emergence of Communalism in North India*. Berkeley: University of California Press.

Friedmann, Yohanan. 1989. *Prophecy Continuous: Aspects of Ahmadi Religious Thought and Its Medieval Background*. Berkeley: University of California Press.

Gilmartin, David. 1991. "Democracy, Nationalism and the Public: A Speculation on Colonial Muslim Politics." *South Asia* 14(1): 123–40.

Guha, Ranajit. 1987. "Chandra's Death." In *Subaltern Studies: Writings on South Asian History and Society*, vol. 5, ed. Ranajit Guha. New Delhi: Oxford University Press.

_____. 1997. *Dominance without Hegemony: History and Power in Colonial India*. Cambridge, Mass.: Harvard University Press.

Hamburger, Joseph. 1976. *Macaulay and the Whig Tradition*. Chicago: University of Chicago Press.

Hanif, C. M. 1999. *The Pakistan Penal Code*. Lahore: Lahore Law Times Publications.

Hansen, Thomas Blom. 2005. "Sovereigns beyond the State: On Legality and Authority in Urban India." In Thomas Blom Hansen and Finn Stepputat, eds., *Sovereign Bodies: Citizens, Migrants and State in the Postcolonial World*. Princeton, N.J.: Princeton University Press.

Hansen, Thomas Blom, and Finn Stepputat, eds. 2001. *States of Imagination: Ethnographic Explorations of the Postcolonial State.* Durham, N.C.: Duke University Press.

———. 2005. Introduction to *Sovereign Bodies: Citizens, Migrants and States in the Postcolonial World,* ed. Thomas Blom Hansen and Finn Stepputat. Princeton, N.J.: Princeton University Press.

Hostettler, John. 1992. *The Politics of Criminal Law Reform in the Nineteenth Century.* Chichester: Barry Rose.

Kaviraj, Sudipta. 1994. "On the Construction of Colonial Power: Structure, Discourse, Hegemony." In Dagmar Engels and Shula Marks, eds., *Contesting Colonial Hegemony: State and Society in Africa and India.* London: I. B. Tauris.

Kelly, John Dunham. 2002. "Alternative Modernities or an Alternative to 'Modernity': Getting Out of the Modernist Sublime." In Bruce Knauft, ed., *Critically Modern: Alternatives, Alterities, Anthropologies.* Bloomington: Indiana University Press.

Kennedy, Charles. 1990. "Islamization and Legal Reform in Pakistan, 1979–89." *Pacific Affairs* 63(1): 62–77.

———. 1996. *Islamization of Laws and Economy: Case Studies on Pakistan.* Islamabad: Institute of Policy Studies.

Kugle, Scott. 2001. "Framed, Blamed and Re-named: The Recasting of Islamic Jurisprudence in Colonial South Asia." *Modern Asian Studies* 35(2): 257–313.

Lapham, Lewis. 2006. "Mute Button." *Harper's Magazine* 312(1871) (April): 9–11.

Lavan, Spencer. 1974. *The Ahmadiyah Movement.* New Delhi: Manohar.

Lazarus-Black, Mindie, and Susan F. Hirsch, eds. 1994. *Contested States: Law, Hegemony, and Resistance.* New York: Routledge.

Lieberman, David. 1989. *The Province of Legislation Determined: Legal Theory in Eighteenth-Century Britain.* Cambridge: Cambridge University Press.

Ludden, David. 1993. "Orientalist Empiricism." In Carol A. Breckenridge and Peter Van der Veer, eds., *Orientalism and the Postcolonial Predicament.* Philadelphia: University of Pennsylvania Press.

Macaulay, Thomas Babington. 1841. "Church and State." In *Critical and Miscellaneous Essays,* vol. 3. Philadelphia: Casey and Hart.

———. 1898a (1833). "Government of India Speech." In *The Complete Works of Lord Macaulay,* vol. 11. New York: Longman Green.

———. 1898b (1837). "Introductory Report upon the Indian Penal Code." In *The Complete Works of Lord Macaulay,* vol. 11. New York: Longman Green.

———. 1898c (1833). "Jewish Disabilities." In *The Complete Works of Lord Macaulay,* vol. 11. New York: Longman Green.

———. 1898d (1837). "Notes Upon the Penal Code." In *The Complete Works of Lord Macaulay,* vol. 11. New York: Longman Green.

———. 1972 (1835). "Minute on Indian Education." In J. Clive and T. Pinney, eds., *Thomas Babington Macaulay: Selected Writings.* Chicago: University of Chicago Press.

———. 1974. *The Letters of Thomas Babington Macaulay.* Ed. Thomas Pinney. 6 vols. Cambridge: Cambridge University Press.

———. 1978 (1829). "Mill's Essay on Government: Utilitarian Logic and Politics." In Jack Lively and John Rees, eds., *Utilitarian Logic and Politics.* Oxford: Oxford University Press.

Macaulay, Thomas Babington, et al. 1888. *The Indian Penal Code, as Originally Framed in 1837, with Notes by T. B. Macaulay . . . [and others] and the First and Second Reports There-on . . . by C. Cameron and D. Eliott*. Madras: Higginbotham.

———. 2002 (1838). *A Penal Code Prepared by the Indian Law Commissioners, and Published by Command of the Governor General of India in Council*. Union, N.J.: Lawbook Exchange.

Mack, Mary Peter. 1963. *Jeremy Bentham: An Odyssey of Ideas*. New York: Columbia University Press.

Malik, Jamal. 1990. "The Luminous Nurani: Charisma and Political Mobilization among the Barelwis of Pakistan." *Social Analysis* 28 (July): 38–50.

Mangi, Aziz. 2000. "Blasphemy in Pakistan: The Pakistani Experience." J.D. thesis, Harvard Law School.

Mayne, John Dawson. 1862. *Commentaries on Indian Penal Code*. Madras: J. Higgenbotham.

Mehdi, Rubya. 1994. *The Islamization of the Law in Pakistan*. Richmond: Curzon.

Messick, Brinkley. 1993. *The Calligraphic State*. Berkeley: University of California Press.

Metcalf, Barbara. 1982. *Islamic Revival in British India: Deoband, 1860–1900*. Princeton, N.J.: Princeton University Press.

Metcalf, Thomas R. 1995. *Ideologies of the Raj*. Berkeley: University of California Press.

Mill, James. 1972 (1820). *The History of British India*. New Delhi: Associated Publishing House.

Mill, John Stuart. 1990 (1838). "Penal Code for India." In John M. Robson, Martin Moir, and Zawahir Moir, eds., *Writings on India*. Collected Works of John Stuart Mill 30. Toronto: University of Toronto Press.

Mitchell, Timothy. 1991. "The Limits of the State: Beyond Statist Approaches and Their Critics." *American Political Science Review* 85(1): 77–96.

———. 1999. "Society, Economy and the State Effect." In George Steinmetz, ed., *State/Culture: State Formation after the Cultural Turn*. Ithaca, N.Y.: Cornell University Press.

Nash, David. 1999. *Blasphemy in Modern Britain: 1789 to the Present*. Aldershot, UK: Ashgate.

Nasr, Seyyed Vali Reza. 2000. "The Rise of Sunni Militancy in Pakistan: The Changing Role of Islamism and the Ulema in Society and Politics." *Modern Asian Studies* 34(1): 139–80.

Pandey, Gyanendra. 1999 (1990). *The Construction of Communalism in Colonial North India*. New Delhi: Oxford University Press.

Patel, Dorab. 2000. *Testament of a Liberal*. Karachi: Oxford University Press.

Patel, Rashida. 1986. *Islamization of Laws in Pakistan?* Karachi: Faiza.

Pearson, Otto. 1979. "Islamic Reform and Revival in Nineteenth-Century India: The Tariqa-i-Muhammadiyah." Ph.D. diss., Duke University.

Peel, Lawrence. 1848. *Observations on the Indian Penal Code*. Calcutta: Military Orphan Press.

Post, Robert. 2007. "Religion and Freedom of Speech: Portraits of Muhammed." *Constellations* 14(1): 72–90.

Rankin, George Claus. 1946. *Background to Indian Law*. Cambridge: Cambridge University Press.

Rehman, I. A. 1998. "The Flaw of the Law." *Newsline* (July): 73–76. Karachi.

Sanyal, Usha. 1996. *Devotional Islam and Politics in British India: Ahmed Riza Khan Barelvi and His Movement, 1870–1920.* New Delhi: Oxford University Press.

Schimmel, Annemarie. 1975. *Mystical Dimensions of Islam.* Chapel Hill: University of North Carolina Press.

Shaheed, Farida, and Khawar Mumtaz, eds. 1987. *Women of Pakistan: Two Steps Forward, One Step Back.* London: Zed Books.

Singha, Radhika. 1998. *A Despotism of Law: Crime and Justice in Early Colonial India.* New Delhi: Oxford University Press.

Starr, June, and Jane F. Collier, eds. 1989. *History and Power in the Study of Law: New Directions in Legal Anthropology.* Ithaca, N.Y.: Cornell University Press.

Stephen, James Fitzjames. 1996 (1883). *History of the Criminal Law of England.* Vol. 3. London: Routledge.

Stokes, Eric. 1959. *The English Utilitarians and India.* Oxford: Clarendon.

Stokes, Whitley, ed. 1887. *The Anglo-Indian Codes.* 2 vols. Oxford: Clarendon.

Strawson, John. 1999. "Islamic Law and English Texts." In Eve Darian-Smith and Peter Fitzpatrick, eds., *Laws of the Postcolonial.* Ann Arbor: University of Michigan Press.

Thursby, Gene R. 1975. *Hindu-Muslim Relations in British India.* Leiden: E. J. Brill.

Vishwanathan, Gauri. 1995. "Blasphemy and Heresy: The Modernist Challenge." *Comparative Studies in Society and History* 37(2): 399–412.

Weiss, Anita, ed. 1986. *Islamic Reassertion in Pakistan.* Syracuse, N.Y.: Syracuse University Press.

Zaman, Muhammed Qasim. 1998. "Sectarianism in Pakistan: The Radicalization of Shia and Sunni Identities." *Modern Asian Studies* 32(3): 689–716.

Cases Cited

Abdus Subhan v. Korban Ali (1908) Indian Law Reporter 35, Calcutta 294.

Ata-Ullah v. Azim-Ullah (1890) Indian Law Reporter 12, Allahabad 494.

Fazl Karim v. Maula Baksh (1891) 21 Indian Appeals 59.

Jangu v. Ahmad Ullah (1891) Indian Law Reporter 13, Allahabad 419.

Muhammed Ismail Qureshi v. Pakistan (1991) Palestinian Legal Decisions, Federal Shariat Court 10.

Queen Empress v. Ramzan (1885) Indian Law Reporter 7, Allahabad 461.

After the Massacre
Secrecy, Disbelief, and the
Public Sphere in Nepal

Genevieve Lakier

Public life is the realm of truth, but it must be a truth concealed in its intention.

—Richard Burghart, "The Political Culture of Panchayat Democracy"

On the evening of Friday, June 1, 2001, the deadliest royal massacre in modern history took place in the Narayanhiti Palace in Kathmandu when the king of Nepal, Bir Birendra Bikram Shah Dev, and almost his entire family were gunned down at point-blank range during a private family gathering. The perpetrator of the murders was allegedly none other than the crown prince himself, Dipendra, who supposedly shot and killed his parents and seven other members of his family in a dispute over his choice of bride, before turning a pistol on himself. Dipendra lingered in a coma for almost two days after the shootings and was officially designated the eleventh Shah king of Nepal. He was the last of his line, however. After he died, his father's younger brother, Gyanendra, was crowned king and his son, Paras, became the new crown prince.

But did Dipendra do it? In the aftermath of the massacre, large segments of Nepal's population refused to believe that the prince could have committed the murders of which he was accused. That a son could shoot and kill his father and mother, brother and sister, and five other members of his family was shocking enough. It was doubly hard to accept these murders given the blackout not only of government radio and television, but also of the private press and eventually the foreign satellite television that had been the only reliable sources of news. Rumor ran rampant. Many suspected that the new king had orchestrated the affair, either for his own benefit or at the behest of a foreign power, most commonly thought to be India but also perhaps Pakistan or the United States. The facts that details of the murders were not forthcoming, that the culprit was not named for almost two days, and that palace security seemed to have been nowhere in the vicinity when the shootings took place became mixed with wilder stories. Among these were rumors that the British ambassador had heard the sounds of a forty-five-minute firefight in the palace the night of the shootings, that army trucks drove away from the palace full of dead soldiers, and that the surgeon who had worked on the injured royals had subsequently been murdered (Harder 2002).

Public pressure led King Gyanendra, immediately after his coronation, to announce the formation of a high-level investigative committee to review the facts of the case, although this committee too faced its share of scandal when Madhav Kumar Nepal, leader of the Communist Party of Nepal (United Marxist-Leninist), resigned from his post on it, announcing that it had been organized unconstitutionally by the palace, rather than by Parliament, and hence was outside the law.[1] The 220-page report that the committee ultimately produced only confirmed the palace account and contained little new analysis (*Narayanhiti Rajdarbarko 2058 Jet 19 ko Ghatna* 2001). Post mortems were not performed on the dead royals before their cremations, and a forensic examination of the crime scene was not within the committee's mandate, so essentially the only evidence provided to it was the personal testimony of eyewitnesses and the doctors who had treated the wounded or dying royals. In the absence of definitive information, the pervasive suspicion that Gyanendra was somehow responsible for the murders continued to undercut the new king's popularity in the years after the shootings. Suspicion only intensified after he dismissed the sitting Prime Minister and dissolved Parliament in October of 2002, ultimately taking power himself.[2] The gaps in the public record allowed conspiracy theories to continue circulating in private, and to surface at moments of political turmoil and protest even years after the shootings.[3]

Foreign observers were quick to interpret the extensive public disbelief and anger visible in the wake of the murders as an expression of the Nepali people's ancient faith in the divinity of their king. An article written by Jeff Greenwald in the American online magazine *Salon*, for example, argued that Nepalis were refusing to believe because belief itself was too horrible. "The massacre of Nepal's royal family is more than a blow to the country's ethnic stability," Greenwald wrote.

> It shakes the foundations of every Nepali citizen's worldview in a way that most Americans, inured to savage and random crimes, can barely comprehend. . . . For Prince Dipendra to slaughter his family in cold blood is an act so astonishing, so profoundly taboo in the culture, that the majority of Nepalese simply refuse to accept it—no matter the evidence or the eyewitness accounts. (Greenwald 2001)

Political history belies this simple account, however. Only a decade before the murders, participants in the 1990 Movement for the Restoration of Democracy, which eventually brought down the king's government, shouted slogans defaming both Birendra and his queen, Aishwarya. Protesters placed images of the royal couple on dogs (Kondos 1992, 274), they burned a picture of Prithvi

Narayan Shah, founder of the Shah dynasty (Ogura 2001, 112–13), and they shouted disrespectful slogans about the king in defiance of police repression (Adams 1998, 62). Fifty years before that, as Erica Leuchtag recounts in her memoir of life in Kathmandu in the 1940s, few Nepalis were familiar with the image of their king, and he was dismissed and mostly forgotten not only within Nepal but by the Indian and British governments as well (Leuchtag 1958, 58). The shifting importance of the monarchy over the course of the twentieth century testifies more to its contested political function than to its simple and unequivocal sacredness.

In this chapter I argue that the public disbelief that followed the news of Dipendra's guilt indexes a series of complex changes in the conception and function of the monarchy since the end of Rana rule. These transformations are tied in crucial ways to the emergence of a mass media in Nepal. Indeed, the rejection of the official narrative of events, and of the foreign press that reported it uncritically, enunciated a defense of modern press freedom and democratic transparency that rejected the power and privilege of the palace as archaic and undemocratic. The circulation of rumors and the widespread popular anger evident immediately after the murders can thus be understood not as a kind of culturally overdetermined misrecognition, a turning away from the horribleness of the truth "no matter the evidence or the eyewitness accounts," but instead as an ironic consequence of the pervasive exclusions of Nepal's modern public sphere.

In what follows, I will use the aftermath of the Narayanhiti murders to explore the constitutive function of disbelief in the construction of the national public. Public disbelief, paranoia, and the production and circulation of conspiracy theories are phenomena by no means restricted to Nepal. They appear in fact to be intrinsic to the social practices of mass mediation itself.[4] Nonetheless, in the aftermath of the murders at Narayanhiti, the social fact of disbelief came into marked and widespread visibility for a variety of reasons, not least of which was the role of the Nepali press in fanning the flames of doubt. The conspiracy theories and doubt that circulated in the wake of the murders, I will argue, were attempts to resolve the contradictions of a modern national public organized around a king. By displacing blame onto foreign aggressors, conspiracy theories occluded not only the complicity of the Nepali press in the immediate blackout of information; they occluded as well the inevitable conflict between the king's older sacred authority and his new national publicity.

Ultimately these occlusions allowed the authority of the monarchy to be reimagined on terms more congenial to an era of publicity, and the local press to emerge as the authentic agents of the modern national public. But this was a national public defined by its secrets. The Narayanhiti incident thus suggests the power of secrets to mediate contradictions and redeem a sacred king for a secular age. But it also suggests the extent to which Nepali national identity continued, ten years into democracy, to be organized around a collective exclusion from the truth.

The Narayanhiti Incident

The murders that took place at the Narayanhiti Palace on the night of June 1, 2001, have by now been rendered sensible by the overdeterminations of myth and prophecy.[5] After the fact, people remembered the old myth of the curse of Goraknath, the tutelary deity of the Shah lineage, that there would be only ten generations of the Shah dynasty and no more. After the fact, it seemed clear that the chariot which broke during the New Year's Rato Machindranath festival was an inauspicious sign of an impending fracture in the body politic itself, and the evil fate predicted by the court astrologer at Crown Prince Dipendra's birth was recalled (Harder 2002).

But news of the murders broke upon the capital as a rupture, rather than a fulfillment. This was an unprecedented trauma for a political institution whose stability had been assured over the last decade in part because it was no longer explicitly political. Since the democratic uprising of 1990, the king had assumed a primarily symbolic role in Nepal's governance, although the powers accorded to him in the new democratic constitution were in several important respects a great deal more than most constitutional monarchs enjoy.[6] Yet Birendra had chosen to stay out of parliamentary politics. Now the news of royal murders shook the still fragile balance of power between palace and Parliament, and the immediate reaction of the palace authorities was to clamp down on any and all information until more details were known. Government radio and television stopped broadcasting. Nepal Television switched from regular programming to shots of the Vishnu temple, Pashupatinath, closely associated with the king, who was himself considered an incarnation of Vishnu. The private radio and newspapers based in Kathmandu also held back once news began circulating of what had happened. International news channels broke the story early Saturday morning, and by the time Nepal awoke, the outside world was beginning to hear about it. Inside the country, however, there was little information to be had. In the print press, only two of ten national dailies published anything about the murders the morning after, and the two that did published short articles which mentioned neither the culprit nor the cause of the deaths.[7] The other dailies did not come out all; the leading Nepali daily, *Kantipur*, finally issued a special edition that night. To combat the spread of undesirable information within Nepal, the palace also ordered satellite television transmissions be blocked, thereby cutting off access to international news sources (except the Internet, which was entirely, and importantly, overlooked).[8]

Most Nepalis learned that something terrible had happened at the palace through private channels, often via phone calls from relatives in the diaspora. The news spread quickly thereafter through word of mouth. With the press silent, increasing numbers of people gathered outside the palace the morning after the shootings to protest the silence, to mourn the dead, to see what was happening. The mood was tense. Ann-Marie Harder describes that time:

Walking the streets in front of the Royal Palace that morning, I along with everyone there knew the king was dead, and the state knew the people knew, and yet in their silence, continued to deny. As a counterfeit reality, the populace must live under the delusion that history does not unfold unless authorized by the state. (Harder 2002)

The metaphor of a counterfeit reality had been used earlier by the anthropologist Richard Burghart to describe the condition of life under Nepal's Panchayat regime (1994, 11), which held power from 1962 to 1990 and whose final king was Birendra. The Panchayat, as Burghart described it, was a period of strict state control of media and public life—a control so strict it eventually undermined its own credibility. The reemergence of attempts to control national news, ten years after the demise of the monarchical regime and in such terrifying circumstances, served only to inflame popular suspicion that foul play was afoot and the progress of the last decade about to be turned back. Aditya Man Shrestha reports that politicians in Kathmandu, fearing a political coup, went into hiding (Shrestha 2001, 14), and ordinary Nepalis rushed to buy essential commodities—kerosene, cooking gas, sugar.

They did not, it turned out, need to do so. This was a news blackout orchestrated by the palace, rather than by the government or by any unitary agent called "the state," and its cause and effects were far more ambiguous than political strategy alone could explain. Indeed, the palace—which since the establishment of democracy was supposed to be entirely separate from formal government—kept the political bureaucracy almost entirely sidelined; the army, which remained under the king's command, handled all arrangements. The extent to which even the sitting Prime Minister, Girija Prasad Koirala, was kept in the dark in the immediate wake of the murders came out in his testimony before the investigation commission some weeks later.[9] Koirala recalled being informed, almost two hours after the shootings took place, that the king had suffered a heart attack, and his confusion when it became clear that this was not the case:

It was ten minutes to eleven that night when Chairman of the Royal Council Dr. Rayamajhi called me to say that His Majesty had been hospitalized after suffering from a serious heart attack . . . As I went to change my clothes, I received a call from Pashupati Bhakta Maharjan, the principal secretary at the palace . . . When he came to my place, he didn't say much. He just said that His Majesty received gunshot wounds. [At the hospital] there was nobody I could ask . . . I just stood there. I couldn't figure out what was going on. (quoted in Harder 2002)

It was precisely the lack of any clear political significance to developing events that made the Narayanhiti shootings so troubling and made it so difficult to figure out what was going on. This distinguished what came to be known as the Narayanhiti *(Hatya)khanda* from the Kot Massacre of 1846 to which it was frequently compared. In both cases, mass killings took place in a royal palace in Nepal. But the 1846 massacre by Jang Bahadur Rana of all potential rivals to power inaugurated a new regime—that of the Rana Prime Ministers, who would control political power in Nepal for over a hundred years. The Narayanhiti *khanda*, however, had no larger political consequence, as far as could be determined. The murder of the king, no matter how shocking, was no longer supposed to be able to affect the democratic order. It was in this context that the clampdown on information by the palace appeared so mysterious—and, after the fact, significant.

But the canceling of all regular programming on government TV in the immediate aftermath of the shootings, in favor of shots of the temple of Pashupatinath, the site of the royal *ghat*, seemed designed not to hide but to call attention to a tragedy that could not be easily named. Indeed, the palace's silence can be seen to emerge from the crisis of representation posed by royal authority in an age of publicity.[10] Despite the reorganization of Nepal into a bureaucratic and formally democratic state, the monarch remained above and outside the public domain. Not only was the royal family immune from prosecution and from taxation, it was also among the very few subjects about which the democratic press could not freely write. The Press and Publication Act, passed in 1992, prohibits "causing hatred or disrespect or ignominy or inciting malice against His Majesty or Royal Family or causing harm to the dignity of his Royal Majesty." To write of the king's death at the hands of his son, therefore, might have been considered a punishable offense, not only "inciting malice against His Majesty or Royal Family" but also "adversely affecting the ethics, morals and social mores of the public"—another of the Act's several prohibitions. While the Palace Press Secretariat was responsible for most communication with the media, only the Raj Parishad, or Royal Council, could announce the death or succession of a king. Until the Parishad met, on Saturday afternoon the day after the murders, the palace bureaucracy had literally nothing it was authorized to say. The fact that the new king was the major culprit in the death of the old made this all even more complicated. As Jonathan Gregson argues, "So long as Dipendra was King of Nepal there could not be any investigation of what he had allegedly perpetrated inside the Royal Palace. No one had the authority to order such an investigation apart from the King himself" (2002, 183). The crisis of Narayanhiti thus exposed the conflict between the principles of equality, publicity, and legality that were supposed to characterize the democratic period, and the enduring, legally enforced, construction of the king's authority as not only above the law but also immune to public oversight.

This was not simply a question of the legal order. The blocking of even international television transmissions within Nepal points to a concern with the sanctity and preservation of national borders during a time of crisis that was not strictly litigable but which instead hearkened back to Rana-era constructions of the country as a sacred, and hence vulnerable, territory. Until the end of their regime, the Ranas allowed very few foreigners into Nepal, and strictly

controlled the importation of foreign media and commodities, in order to protect, so they claimed, the last *asal Hindustan*, or pure Hindu land, from the
pollution of the outside world—including India, defiled as it was first by Muslim and then by British rule (Liechty 1997, 10–11). By establishing the sacred
exceptionalism of the country, the Rana Prime Ministers justified their absolute political control over migration and the economy in Nepal, and guarded
against the political upheaval sweeping the subcontinent to the south.

But the Rana regime fell in 1951, with the active intervention of now-
independent India. The Shah kings returned to power at the head of a formally
democratic government, although elections were only held once; King Mahendra
then founded and led the partyless Panchayat raj. Along with the return of
the king came the international project of development, and Nepal suddenly
opened up to the outside world—to its money, its commodities, its media, and
its tourists. After half a century of aggressive state development, the old order
of territory was hard to discern in everyday social practice. Nepalis who traveled abroad—primarily Gorkha soldiers—had previously had to receive purifi-
catory rites both before and after they crossed the black waters (*kalo pani*) of
the ocean in order to avoid losing caste once home (Sever 1993, 258–59), but
now they were increasingly mobile. As a result, the national border no longer
held ritual significance; indeed, Nepali and Indian citizens could move freely
across the vast southern border and work in either country. Labor migration
and remittances from India and elsewhere played an increasingly important
role in Nepal's economy throughout the latter half of the twentieth century.[11]
Law had also been secularized, with caste abolished in 1962 and freedom of
religion (but not of conversion) guaranteed.

In this context, the only substantial Hindu institution that remained legal in
Nepal was that of the monarchy (Sharma 2002, 22). It was to the figure of the
king, ultimately, that the remnants of an older sacred order still clung. In particular, at this moment of terrible and terrifying news, the king's sacredness emerged
as a prohibition on speech. Journalists experienced this prohibition personally,
emotionally, and as a function of their national identity. Kapil Kafle, an editor in
chief at *Rajdhani*, one of the major national dailies, poignantly recalled,

> For what reason, why [the massacre] happened, how, we still don't know. It's hard
> to believe anything. . . . We weren't eye-witnesses. How can we know? The problem
> was that, after the king had died and we found this out, that he had died, who
> could speak? Could we write simply that the king had died? Who could write this?
> Tell me! "It was said that the king was dead": who can write that?
>
> Q: But the foreign press wrote this, didn't they? They broke the story immediately.
>
> Yes, the BBC said so, but it was easy for them. For those of us citizens inside the
> country, it was very hard. (Interview)

Kafle's response testifies to the immediate and personal difficulty speech posed
to those members of the press "inside the country"—i.e., within the king's

domain itself. Authority, particularly royal authority, had traditionally been expressed through the domination of speech. As Richard Burghart has argued, within a feudal or "lordly" organization of power, the lord alone employs the voice of authority and his subjects must wait for him to speak loudest, longest, and last (1996, 302). Thus it was his inferior relationship to the king—as a citizen who was also a subject—that prevented Kafle from being able to speak what for foreigners it was easy to say. This was not a question, as some have argued, of the press's professional ability (Lal 2001a). It was instead a problem of a political identity which, insofar as it was organized around a sacred center, inevitably conflicted with the demands of the new professional and public world. Sanjib Adhikari, a news editor at Radio Sagarmatha, the first community radio station in Nepal, reflected on the problem of authority and professionalism posed in the wake of the murders:

> *For two or three days we stopped broadcasting news at the station. Why? Because at the time, whoever was at a high level could not make a good decision. Everything played except the news. We should have given follow-up as soon as we heard news of the massacre, no?* (Interview)

The self-recrimination that marks Adhikari's account reveals the profound and seemingly irresolvable challenge that the Narayanhiti incident posed to the identity of the new democratic media as professional, independent, and on a par with the global media. But it points as well to a larger crisis of authority in the aftermath of the killings. The inability of those "at a high level" to make a good decision mirrored the inability of the palace, and to a lesser extent the government, to politically manage what occurred, in large part because of their loyalty to an older model of royal authority that no longer functioned as intended. Indeed, although the older practices of sacred authority reappeared in this terrifying moment of rupture, they proved incapable of actually protecting royal power. The palace's attempt to maintain silence about the royal deaths until the succession had been secured proved to be a tremendous political blunder, producing not security and calm but their opposite. The restriction of information, the suspension of news, and the rushed cremations of the royal family (with Dipendra's in the middle of the night) resulted in intense public anger. Riots broke out in Kathmandu, Hetauda, and Pokhara. The government clamped a curfew on Kathmandu in an attempt to maintain public order, and the army had to be called in to restore calm for the first time since 1990, when, ironically enough, crowds in Kathmandu and Patan had risen in anger against the king they were now mourning. King Gyanendra's statement that the deaths had been caused by a sudden or accidental (*aakasmik*) round of gunfire in particular became a source of both popular outrage and speculation.[12] The new king was ineradicably smeared by the mystery of the murders, his own royal authority in fact undercut by attempts to preserve royal authority.

The crisis of the royal shootings, therefore, produced another crisis: a crisis of representation and, fundamentally connected to this, of authority. The unprecedented, unsettling, and inexplicable deaths of the royal family at the hands, perhaps, of the crown prince resulted in a clampdown on speech and activity that revealed the extent to which royal authority continued to be protected from publicity and, in a sense, distinguished by its unspeakability throughout the democratic era. It revealed, moreover, the extent to which Nepalis continued to equate the welfare of their king's body with the welfare of the country itself, as is described in the classical literature on the Hindu king (Burghart 1996, 223; Dangol 1999, 183) and as was evidenced in the panic and hoarding that occurred in reaction to the news of the tragedy. In this sense, the Narayanhiti *khanda* indeed revealed the continuities of royal authority in Nepal.

But the anger and public disbelief that emerged in response to the palace and press silence exposed the increasing unsustainability of these older practices of royal power within the framework of the modern nation-state and, more specifically, within the context of the modern public sphere. The palace's information blackout only served to cast doubt and shame upon the palace itself and to call into question the authority of the new king. Silence no longer functioned to preserve royal authority, but to desecrate it.[13] As long as the royals continued, even after their death, to be shielded from the bright light of publicity they could not be put to rest, in large part because of the presumption of publicity that now organized political life. After half a century of mass media, the restriction of public information and the censorship of public news had become understood to be illegitimate, even if they were also, as almost everyone acknowledged, omnipresent.

It was in this context that conspiracies delinked the figure of the king from the institution of the palace, in order to preserve the authority of the former while rejecting the censorship of the latter—in order, in other words, to protect the ideal of the nation as imagined in state propaganda from the actual operations of power in Nepal.

The Rumor Raj

By the Sunday after the murders, all the dailies were back in business. After several days, news on Radio Sagarmatha was back on the air, and in the weeks and months to follow a veritable barrage of information and reporting on the massacres made it into print. The mystery of the murders was an unambiguous boon for newspaper sales within Nepal.[14] Newspapers and magazines provided finely detailed narratives of ongoing events related to the murders, including the rioting by crowds and the rushed cremations. But they also published daring editorials which critiqued the palace and demanded further investigation. Most (in)famously, on June 3—only two days after the murders—*Kantipur* (along with its sister publication, the English-language *Kathmandu Post*) published an editorial by Baburam Bhattarai, second in command of the Maoist guerrillas who were currently fighting for state control (and among whose primary demands was the end of the monarchy in Nepal). The editorial blamed

"Indian imperialist and expansionist forces in league with the CIA" for the killings. Bhattarai furthermore implied that the new king, Gyanendra, was acting under foreign direction and ended the editorial by demanding that "all Royal Army officers and soldiers dedicated to 'country and king' (*des ra naresh*), although now unable to protect the king, should be active in a new way in the protection of the country and should support not the puppet of the expansionists born within the palace but the patriotic sons born of Mother Nepal" (Bhattarai 2001). Thus Bhattarai used the deaths of the kings to further a revolutionary project couched in a conventional and state-sponsored vocabulary of nationalism. In Bhattarai's editorial, one can already see the way in which the king was to be repositioned in the aftermath of his death as a figure of deeply ambivalent significance—a figure who somehow represented not the "expansionist palace" but instead the patriotic people. In order to so reposition him, however, Bhattarai had to cast the murders as the outcome of a political struggle between not only the liberal and the imperialist, but also the local and the foreign. In so doing, he neatly equated revolution with a unified national project that could encompass all patriotic sons of Nepal, including royalists, claiming ultimately that "this latest 'Kot Massacre' too, is just one more link in the chain [of foreign aggression]. . . . King Birendra's greatest 'weakness' or 'crime' was that, although a product of the feudal class, he had a relatively patriotic spirit and liberal political character" (Bhattarai 2001).

Bhattarai's qualification of the king's patriotism—only "relatively patriotic" and, of all good things, liberal?—suggests how complicated a stand the Maoists were trying to take: to attack the new inhabitants of the palace as feudal imperialists, while salvaging the old inhabitants of the palace as deep-down patriots. The palace reacted immediately to the publication of his editorial. On June 6, *Kantipur's* editor, publisher, and managing director were arrested in their offices in Kathmandu and charged with sedition and treason. They were kept in jail for eleven days, and only released after international pressure had been brought to bear on the government and a large rally held in Kathmandu in the name of press freedom. Suspicion of the new regime intensified in the context of this overt repression, and the case against the journalists was ultimately dropped in the face of such strong opposition. This backing down only encouraged the publication of further speculation. In many cases, these publications interpreted the palace cover-up itself as proof of conspiracy and foul play, even when they did not propose theories as concrete as those of Baburam Bhattarai. Leading politicians interviewed in the pages of the leftist biweekly *Mulyankan* argued that the failure of the Royal Probe Commission to adequately investigate the murders had only increased their suspicions that what was behind the murders of the royal family was not accident but conspiracy. Politicians freely used the Nepali word *sadyantra*, which means "conspiracy" or "plot," although none specified further details. The accusation of conspiracy emerged from purely negative operations of proof: the palace cover-up, the inconsistencies in the palace story, and the ellipses in the Royal Probe Commission report were all considered suspicious, signs that something was amiss (*Mulyankan*, "Kosle Ke Bhane?" Asar 20, 2059 BS).

The publication and free circulation of these complaints and suspicions reveals the relative media openness that characterized the aftermath of the shutdown of the press on June 2. The press was unprecedentedly candid in its coverage of the palace and the institution of the monarchy during the period of transition and popular outrage in the wake of the murders. The palace and government, after failing at repression, invoked a rhetoric of defense. A large notice signed by the Information Department of the Information and Communication Ministry of His Majesty's Government of Nepal was printed directly against, and in striking contrast to, the angry opinions of political leaders quoted in *Mulyankan*. It reminded the contributors, and the readers, that "only in a country where peace and order is maintained can development occur quickly. Therefore it is the primary duty of all Nepalis to keep peace and order and participate in the work of development with an attitude of unity and national good."[15] The call for unity and national good, as enunciated for example in Gyanendra's coronation address, was the vocabulary in which the government and palace attempted to put the question mark of the murders behind it.

But although the government clearly did not think so, the questioning of the murders did in fact serve to provide unity to a national community. Theories which transformed the murders into an explicitly political crisis of foreign intervention preserved the honor of the dead royals, both the dead father and the dead son. The fate of the royal family could not, it seemed, rest on such a simple and ordinary problem as a marriage dispute. Conspiracy theories such as Baburam Bhattarai's theory of Indian and CIA involvement in the murders, or the rumor (which circulated widely in the Pakistani press) that the Indian intelligence services had played a role in the killings,[16] elided the king's no-longer-political status and, in so doing, effectively recast a familial and generational conflict as a threat to national sovereignty and survival (in the face of which all loyal nationals presumably would and should, as Bhattarai urged, unite).

The emphasis on the patriotism of the old monarch and the monarchy, while most evident in Baburam Bhattarai's editorial, was by no means limited to it. In all commentary, it was Birendra's willingness to allow democracy to emerge in Nepal that was considered his most notable act. An editorial in the *Nepali Times* by C. K. Lal called the king "the sovereign who made us sovereign" (Lal 2001b) without suggesting this was in any sense contradictory. Bipin Adhikari and S. B. Mathe described the monarchy as "a dynasty that defended the country from all imperialist forces throughout its history, which championed national independence and patriotism, which gave Nepal a tradition of sustainable diplomacy, and which had encouragingly learnt to legitimise itself by changing according to the democratic aspirations of the people" (Adhikari and Mathe 2001, 26–27).

This whitewashing of the history of the monarchy in Nepal within a frame of patriotism and nationalism allowed the dead royals to become icons of democracy and of indigeneity, under attack not only by foreign governments but by an imperialist and elitist international order, represented most concretely by the foreign press. Adhikari and Mathe argued that the failure of the international press to give any serious consideration to alternative explanations for the shootings was a sign of an indifference to local realities and indexed the imposition of "the global elite's views" on "the common people of the world's marginalized countries" (Adhikari and Mathe 2001, 46). This view was echoed, with a rather more malevolent intention imputed, in the chants of crowds in the street, who protested in the same moment foreign intervention and false news. The *Kathmandu Post* reported crowds, two days after the shooting, chanting the slogans "Yo sarkar chaindaina, jhuto prachaar chaindaina" (We don't want this government, we don't want false news) and "Bideshi dabab chaindaina, jhuto prajatantra chaindaina" (We don't want foreign pressure, we don't want fake democracy) ("Mourning Nation Seeks Truth," June 4, 2001).

In this context, a rhetoric of national defense and unity emerged around the death of the king not at the palace's behest, but in defiance of both the political and palace leadership, who were considered either sell-outs to a foreign cause or incompetent and undemocratic buffoons (Lal 2001a). It was the local newspapers who became, therefore, the strongest and most vocal advocates of a public united not only in grief but also in anger. They did so by claiming their own voice of political and public authority. In so doing, journalists claimed to speak for and on behalf of the local people, even as they also attempted to discipline and restrain a crowd tending toward what many feared was dangerous excess. Rama Parajuli notes in her analysis of newspaper coverage of the massacre that "at a time when all the political parties were caught in confusion and hence sitting in silence, the newspaper editorials published a range of opinions [*kune na kune bichar prabahit garnu*]. Before the political parties demanded an investigation into the event, the newspapers had already done so. Newspapers also called on the general public [*sarbasadharan*] to maintain a patient attitude, and to be unified at this time of crisis" (Parajuli 2002, 70, my translation).

Indeed, in the dark days after Narayanhiti, when neither the government nor the palace were to be trusted, the press became a stand-in for political authority. By equating silence with wrongdoing and the king's killing with an attack on the nation itself, Nepali journalists could claim to work on behalf of both the monarchy and a free public sphere. Conspiracy theories which blamed foreign governments for the royal deaths occluded the complicated ways in which the media's own silence in the aftermath of the murders emerged out of the sacred nature of the kingship itself. By seeking a middle ground between the palace and the public, the professional press of the democratic period thus ultimately validated a conception of political authority as necessarily public—what Jodi Dean calls "the ideology of publicity" (Dean 2002, 4). This ideology established a qualitative distinction between the dead king, Birendra, remembered now as a democratic and liberal political figure, and the aggressive, repressive, and undemocratic forces of the palace (and by implication the new king).

Journalists actively sought to distinguish the figure of the king from the institution, and administration, of the palace. As an editorial in the *Kathmandu Post* put it, "In a very real sense what happens to the monarchy is too important for the nation to be left to the palace alone" (June 4, 2001). To many journalists, after all, the palace's silence appeared, if not incomprehensible, at the very least a foolish response. Even those initially sympathetic to the new king could not understand why more was not revealed at the time. Yub Raj Ghimire, then editor of *Kantipur* (and one of the men imprisoned for printing Bhattarai's editorial), reflected on a meeting he had with King Gyanendra soon after his coronation:

> I told him . . . that in the long run [more openness] will benefit you also. . . . I said you would always remain a suspect. There will be people coming to write the book [about the murders], coming to make the documentary film, thirty years, forty years later, even after we are gone. So if the proof could have been more open and more detailed . . . it would have been good for him. (Interview)

Ghimire here defends his decision to publish Baburam Bhattarai's editorial by rhetorically mobilizing the endless and inexhaustible energy of a suspicious public. In Ghimire's view, secrecy is impossible, almost self-destructive, in the modern age. He thus claims that royal and press interests will inevitably converge. What would have been good for the public would have been good for the king as well.

But the palace did not agree, and despite its ideology of necessary publicity, there were many things the Nepali press itself could not or would not publish. Local journalists demonstrated little ability, in the aftermath of the murders, to penetrate the palace hierarchy and to get interviews with important eyewitnesses or sources (Parajuli 2002, 67–71), and few besides Bhattarai were willing to publicly implicate the new king in the crimes. Those who did speak became objects themselves of attack and critique—for example, when Colonel Rajiv Shahi, the son-in-law of the king's youngest brother and an eyewitness to the shootings, gave an impromptu press conference before the Royal Probe Commission had come out with its report (which echoed the official narrative), he was roundly criticized for his insolence and his grandstanding. "Politics cashes in on tragedy," as the *Telegraph* put it (June 13, 2001). Meanwhile advertisements mourning the dead royals peppered the pages of the major dailies for weeks after the incident, with the photographs of the dead sometimes including, sometimes excluding, the problematic figure of Dipendra. These advertisements were only slowly replaced by ones congratulating the new king on his coronation. Given the danger and power of the palace, it was far easier to publicly demand more transparency than it was to establish alternative theories of what had occurred.

Doubt was therefore enunciated as just that: a series of questions that could not be answered, and a demand for further action that was not, in the end, taken, in part because of the perduring difficulty of speaking easily of royalty, and in part because of the real risks involved.[17] The fact that, as a result, modern press commitments were expressed via the mobilization and representation of popular disbelief, however, placed in question the professionalism of the democratic press. A sharply worded editorial by Kanak Mani Dixit, again in the *Nepali Times*, attacked what it called "the rumor *raj*," the rule of rumor:

> With no explanation available, the public would be forgiven for thinking the worst of the successors [*sic*] to the throne, former Prince Gyanendra.... But paucity of information hardly explains everything. It is the gullibility that comes with a lack of intellectual curiosity that makes Kathmandu succumb so easily to rumour raj. Vacant minds easily ingest rumour, and this is the case of the Kathmandu intelligentsia, whose members have so little self-respect that they are willing to impute their [own] worst motives to others. Their tendency is always to be certain of a conspiracy when a simpler explanation may suffice. To stick to a straightforward explanation would require too much rationality. (Dixit 2001)

This attack on local Nepali intellectuals emerged in response to the active participation of the modern professional elite—clearly including the press—in a game of second-guessing, one that depended not upon the strict verifiability of fact but upon the compelling resonances of doubt. In so doing, as Dixit suggests, they succeeded in blurring the boundaries between the general public, who could be "forgiven for thinking the worst," and the press and other members of the intellectual elite, who are supposed to know better and to rely, as moderns, upon stricter standards of truth. Unable to find the answers to their questions, the press could only preserve their integrity by making clear, if not their knowledge, then at least their knowledge that they did not know. This preserved the ideal of the public against its actual failure; but also meant the penetration, if only in traces, of the subaltern trope of rumor into the modern public sphere.

The ideology of publicity and the conspiracies that surfaced in the wake of the murders must therefore be understood not as fundamentally incompatible phenomena but instead as mutually necessary and interrelated products of Nepal's modern public sphere. It was not because of a lack of modernity or rationality, as Dixit suggests, that Nepalis turned to rumor and to conspiracy in the wake of the killing of their king. It was rather as a result of the contradictions in the political organization of the monarchy, and of political authority more generally, since the reestablishment of royal power in 1951.

Contradictions between the ideals and the practices of state nationalism had produced a public world saturated by absence and visibly duplicitous; it had produced a public audience self-conscious in its doubts. It was only as a result of his absence from publicity that the king, after his death, could be resurrected, ironically, as an icon of truth in a murky age. It was by claiming to speak in the name of the king that journalists could critique the palace; and it was by uniting around what they did not know that Nepalis could come together as one nation, even if united only by a shared tragedy.

Public Disbelief

The mobilization of conspiracy and of doubt in the defense of the modern ideology of publicity by the local press in the aftermath of the Narayanhiti shootings suggests how centrally the imaginary of the secret functions to support, indeed construct, the modern public sphere in Nepal. Jodi Dean has argued that secrets are vital, even necessary supplements to the preservation of faith in democracy itself, given the perpetual failure of a truly democratic public to emerge. "The secret promises that a democratic public is within reach—as soon as everything is known." Dean writes. "All that is necessary to realize the ideal of the public is to uncover these secrets, to bring them to light" (Dean 2002, 10). Indeed, the public disbelief that emerged in the wake of Narayanhiti functioned, as I have argued above, to render contingent and malevolent otherwise fundamental social and political limits on press freedom in Nepal. In the context of democracy's disappointments and dangers, the blatant visibility of palace censorship in the wake of the royal murders served to unify an otherwise factional audience around a shared sense of disenfranchisement and a collective defense of the public's right to know. A national community thus emerged in the aftermath of Narayanhiti that was, in perhaps more dramatic ways than even Dean imagines, centrally organized around the secret.

Rumor and disbelief have long been primary mechanisms by which individuals in Nepal orient themselves toward the public world. This was in large part a result of the strict control the state wielded over public representation up until 1990. Under the Rana Prime Ministers, who ruled Nepal from 1856 to 1951, repression enforced a "fake medievalism" in Nepal's cities that hid the deepening involvement of the local elite and middle classes with the global economy (Liechty 1997). Via sumptuary laws which restricted who could wear Western clothes or ride in motorcars, for example, the Ranas maintained their absolute distinction from their subjects in their possession of the fruits of the West, while simultaneously upholding the myth of Nepal as a premodern Hindu kingdom whose isolation enabled their absolute authority. Education and the media were tightly controlled and limited to a small circle of elites in the Kathmandu Valley. The Ranas discouraged Nepali nationalism; indeed, the history of Nepal was not taught in the nation's schools. The burgeoning nationalist movement, and its press, emerged only outside of Nepal itself (Onta 1996).

After the triumphant return of King Tribhuvan to power in 1951, however, the government opened Nepal to outside markets, media, and visitors, and solicited the active involvement of foreign governments in development projects. It also actively expanded its investment in media. The state newspaper, the

Gorkhapatra—which, during the Rana period, had been a sporadic publication intended for the very small literate elite in Kathmandu[18]—was turned into a daily publication in 1960 and thereafter distributed to all government offices and to districts throughout the country.[19] In 1965, the *Rising Nepal*, its English sister publication, was founded. The growth in literacy and the expansion of rural bureaucracies meant even those Nepalis far away from the centers of power could learn firsthand the activities of government and could be included in the audience of political speech.

The tagline of the *Gorkhapatra*, *"Bikasko lagi samchar"* (News for the purpose of development), makes clear the paper's didactic and developmentalist agenda. It aimed to educate Nepalis about the necessity of participation in the national project of development. The mission of the newspaper was not the representation of social reality per se but rather the transmission of the goal and viewpoint of the regime. The chief objectives of media laid out in the Communication Plan of 2028 Bikram Sambat (AD 1969) included "(i) to enlist public support for the development efforts; (ii) to strengthen national unity; and (iii) to strengthen the people's confidence in the Panchayat policy" (Verma 1985, 9). Headlines from the *Rising Nepal* illustrate its tone. From July 3, 1966: "A Wave of Enthusiasm Has Gripped the Nepali People for Development." From August 5, 1966: "All Nepalese Engaged in Nation-Building Task." And from January 4, 1978: "Impact of Development Being Felt Everywhere." What is less clear from the titles is that the articles they introduce are composed primarily of reports of speeches and interviews with prominent members of the National Panchayat Council or ministers in the Cabinet. The *Gorkhapatra* thus not only transmitted enthusiasm for development; it transmitted the authorized speaking voices and images of certain important figures in the administration. Chief among these was the king, who stood at the center of Panchayat ideology as the architect of development and as the bridge between the foreign world of modernity and development and the local word of culture and identity (Adams 1998, 34). The transmission of his voice and his image was thus essential to fostering enthusiasm for the project of development among those of his citizens stuck in the backward cultural world of the Nepali village, a place defined in Panchayat and development rhetoric by its absence of development (Pigg 1992).

Older practices of royal ritual were thus translated into a new vocabulary of development which circulated via state media throughout Nepal. Rana-era claims of royal divinity were not replaced but instead layered onto the new Panchayat depictions of the nationalist king.[20] Two photographs suggest the dominant style of the representations of the monarchy in the press during this period. In one, from the *Gorkhapatra* of February 6, 1979, King Birendra greets a welcoming committee of prominent citizens and local panchas in the district capital of Pokhara during one of his periodic tours of the country. The committee is there to felicitate (*abinandhan garnu*) the king, we are told, or in other words to demonstrate and bestow upon him their respect and allegiance and to thank him for his efforts in introducing and encouraging development in the region. In another photograph, from the *Gorkhapatra* of January 12, 1979, a crowd is seen carrying a large image of the first Shah king of Nepal, Prithvi Narayan Shah, through the streets of Kathmandu on the occasion of Unification Day (*Ekikharan Diwas*). In both cases, we see an encounter between a group of citizens and their king which is predicated upon the moment of *darshan*, of receiving the image of the divine. In return, the people are gathered to provide *abindhan*, praise and felicitation. The practice of *darshan* in South Asia has long been a way of mediating the relationship not only between humanity and the divine, but between lower and higher members of the social hierarchy (Burghart 1996, 49).

What is important to note, however, is the recursivity of publishing these images in the newspaper. The king is to view and be felicitated by his people; but, via the photograph, he is at the same time to be viewed by countless others, in a second-order act of seeing that magnifies and extends his visibility throughout the kingdom. This is no longer *darshan*, exactly; the reader is no longer graced simply with the divine image but with an image of others receiving that image. The layering of images reinforces the importance of the event. The mediation of the ritual turns the encounter of *darshan*—predicated on the immediacy of the gaze—into a spectacle of national harmony and progress, one which then reflects upon the energies and the potential of the Nepali people themselves. In this manner, the king became a familiar, although highly ritualized, public figure, an icon of both nationalism and triumphant development, and one who was visible to increasing numbers of Nepalis over the three decades of Panchayat rule.

Nonetheless the failure of the Panchayat system to produce national integration or development as promised undermined the persuasive power of royal ritual and, indeed, the sacred authority of the king. By the time of the People's Movement of 1990, the king was being represented publicly in increasingly disrespectful terms that called into question the fundamental claim of royal propaganda: the unity of the king's and the people's interests. Vincanne Adams quotes Dr. M. D., an organizer of the People's Movement:

> The King and Queen came to stand for the very idea of corruption. "Pampha devi" the protestors yelled.[21] I mean, this was a breakthrough. It had never before occurred in Nepal. . . . In the heat of the moment, they [protestors] were saying to go out of the country. . . . That was the slogan. *Birechor*—Bir is the Birendra, Birechor [*bire chor des chod*] means thief—country thief, leave the country." (Adams 1998, 62)

The inversion of the royal figure—from a sacred gift-giver (Burghart 1996) to a thief—neatly expresses the increasing illegitimacy of the king's political authority during the Panchayat years, and the pervasive sense of disillusionment with the regime and the project of state development. That this slogan in particular was repeated in protests against King Gyanendra, just over ten years later, is no mere coincidence but points to the increasing and perhaps ineradicable politicization, and hence desecration, of the monarch set in motion by the establishment of his visibility in the mass media.

As the decades wore on, the sharp disjuncture between the ideal nation "gripped by enthusiasm for development" and the actual world of continuing caste, ethnic, and gender inequalities produced an intensifying rejection of government media in general. "One treats Governmental speech with some suspicion," Richard Burghart wrote in *The Conditions of Listening*, describing political culture during the Panchayat period, "It is, as a matter of course, something distorted, and the more one claims it to be non-distorted, the more others assume it to be distorted and start reading between the lines" (Burghart 1996, 308). This in no way meant that ordinary Nepalis did not take state media seriously. Quite the contrary; the *Gorkhapatra* required greater attention because of its nontransparency. Much could still be deciphered, but in complicated ways. Rajendra Dahal, editor in 2003 of the newsmagazine *Himal*, remembers reading the *Gorkhapatra* under the Panchayat in search of what it left out:

Q: *Did people use to read Gorkhapatra?*

[It was] compulsory. I have such a habit. I have been reading it for thirty years. Even nowadays, I read Gorkhapatra. It is because it was at the time the only window to see the world.

Q: *Did you believe it?*

No! It didn't give very much information. What was interesting was that . . . no news about strikes [hartals] was given in it. But always the end of strikes were published in it. . . . Once a hartal had been reported to have finished in Gorkhapatra, people knew that there had been a hartal. Also, whatever fertilizer the government sold, or electricity, if there was a price increase, it wouldn't report that, only that there had been a "correction." (Interview)

Dahal's comment reflects the enduring, and often affectionate, disrespect that characterized the relationship between the *Gorkhapatra* and its audience. Never before had Nepalis had so much contact with their government, and their king. Yet this contact also allowed a new kind of distance—what Arvind Rajagopal has called "a critical distance," peculiar to the simultaneous privacy and publicity of the medium (Rajagopal 2001, 6). The new critical distance placed in question not only Panchayat representations, but the public world itself. The widespread perception of pervasive corruption and duplicity produced a world of unstable truth. A well-known poem by the poet Bhupi Sherchan during the 1960s expresses the sense of disillusionment, corruption, and ritual desecration which marked the later Panchayat period. Sherchan writes, in part,

[This is] a country where music competition judges
are deaf people sporting earphones,
and where poetry arbiters have souls
in the process of petrification . . .

where the champions of the youth bear
corrugated wrinkles on their foreheads,
where the "wash and wear crease" of respectability
of even the worst reprobate never crinkles,
where even the most debased whore's face
of synthetic skin never wrinkles . . .

where sugar factories produce not sugar but alcohol . . .

If one were to unearth the foundation of each house here
only hearsay and rumour would be found heaped there
That's why this is a country of hearsay and rumour
This is a country standing on hearsay and rumour
This is a country founded on hearsay and rumour
This is a country of hearsay and rumour (translation in Thapa 2001)

Sherchan's poem conjoins the false promises of development to the circulating rumors of an ungrounded public—rumor and hearsay, as he represents them, are practices which emerge out of and contribute to the reproduction of a system based on lies. Indeed, rumors became central strategies of both the reception and the production of news both in the state news media and in the underground political papers that had emerged by the end of the Panchayat era to contest them. T. Louise Brown comments that "rumour and innuendo were fundamental to the building of an anti-panchayat consensus and were used to undermine the credibility and, hence, the long-term prospects of the Panchayat System" (1996, 120). To counter rumors spread by antigovernment forces, the government would respond with rumors of its own. Brown continues: "Prior to the launch of the Jana Andolan [the 1990 People's Movement], and during its early days, papers carried fabricated reports of prospective cuts in foreign aid. . . . The official government newspapers responded with claims of increased foreign bounty and examples of the successful implementation of aid projects" (1996, 120–21). Insofar as news emerged from within political institutions, it could not be trusted. Indeed, it was the profoundly fractured nature of the public sphere that produced the disillusionment with the system that would catalyze, in a surprisingly short time, the popular uprising of 1990—a movement which extended far beyond the political parties per se to include urban professionals, students, and farmers (Ogura 2001). The movement of 1990 promised in return a restored, transparent, and genuine democracy. The immediacy of the public struggle during the People's Movement—the participation of all ages, genders, and social classes within it—suggested the potential for a new kind of popular agency, one characterized by its unity and its immediacy.[22]

But the wide circulation of Sherchan's poem in the aftermath of the Narayanhiti murders called into question the qualitative distinction between democracy and the Panchayat system which preceded it. Indeed, although the People's Movement was supposed to have brought about a new era of transparency in public life (Adams 1988, 56; Kondos 1992, 274), the new kinds of visibility made possible by the independent press in its wake only served to intensify struggles over representation in the decade after 1990, and further heightened public awareness of the theatricality, or *natakiya*, of politics, and hence, the untrustworthy nature of public representations. The widespread complaints that politicians, for example, held rallies or called for protest campaigns simply for publicity[23] undermined the credibility of the political parties and led to accusations of political bias and censorship when certain papers did or did not report on these events.

Disturbing rumors also circulated about media connections to the crime underworld and to extortion or blackmail rackets.[24] In a world in which publicity was a vital ingredient of power, journalism was both a powerful and a dangerous occupation. In the context of a Maoist civil war, reporters were very much on the front line; they were among the groups most often targeted by both government and Maoist retribution (CEHURDES 2002). Govindra Pokhrel, the editor of a major daily in Kathmandu, described his work as "hiding while writing." "We tell half and we hide half," he told me. "There are things everyone knows but cannot say" (interview).

It was in this context that the legislated absence of the royal family from public life after the 1990 Movement, and then their final absence from the public stage after their deaths, salvaged a once compromised image. "It is a great irony," Aditya Man Shrestha comments, "that King Birendra became more popular in death than in life. He won more hearts when he did the least for the people than when he did the most" (2001, 25). Publicity in the case of the monarch had proven to be, as John Thompson puts it, a "double-edged sword" (1995, 123). Panchayat ideology was not able to convince Nepalis to participate in a system which by its end even its supporters acknowledged was corrupt. But it was able to establish a national imaginary, one which depended upon the symbolism of the kingship.

It was the threat to this imaginary that resulted in the unprecedented demonstration of public grief in the wake of Birendra's death. Nepalis lined up for hours outside the palace in order to see where their royal family had died; shops and businesses closed *en masse* and men lined up in the thousands to have their heads shaved. Shaving one's head is one of the responsibilities of Hindu sons after the death of their father, and its practice in the wake of the king's death links all subjects in a relationship of fictive kinship to their monarch. During the Panchayat period, however, and particularly in the wake of King Mahendra's death in 1972, young men refused to shave their heads and had to be physically forced to do so. But, as Aditya Man Shrestha recounts,

> In 2001, when King Birendra died, not a single case of police using force was heard [of]. On the contrary, hordes of young men volunteered to shave heads of their own volition. The southern district of Siraha outpaced the other districts in the number of those who shaved as a mark of reverence to the departed soul. (2001, 24)

Innovations were also visible in the practice and provenance of mourning. Shrestha continues,

> It was yet another surprise that in the eastern hill district of Ilam, a young woman did the same to express her deep sorrow over the king's death. Hindu custom does not ask the women to shave their heads at the time of their bereavement. Even some Nepalese Muslims shaved their heads to join in the national mourning, although their religion does not require them to do so. The depth of the public sorrow could also be measured on the basis of six suicides that followed the royal tragedy. Nothing of that sort had ever happened in Nepal. (2001, 25)

Public mourning thus made visible the new organization of subjection to the king—one structured not around the hierarchical difference of caste or gender but around the collective equivalence of the nation. Even non-Hindus participated in the explicitly Hindu rituals of mourning, and Panchayat state propaganda, which painted the king as a leader who "love[d] his subjects as his own children" (Kaphley 1967, 11), was echoed in the grief of the crowds. One man was quoted by the *Kathmandu Post* as saying, "I had never imagined that a tragedy of such magnitude could occur. I could have borne the pain of my parents' death, but cannot bear this one" ("Mourning Nation Seeks the Truth," June 5, 2001). Indeed, the paper had reported the day before that another young man had shaved his head in honor of the king's death even though he had not done so after his grandfather died. Grief for the king, in this moment, surpassed even that for one's own family, because of the threat the mysterious death of the king was felt to pose to collective identity itself.

Mourning allowed a direct, intimate relationship between the king and his subjects, outside the desecration and pollution of the public sphere. Fifty years of royal propaganda had established both the sanctity of the monarch and the falseness of his public representations. As an ideal, the king after his death signified everything that Panchayat ideology had represented him to be: the ultimate patriot, the benevolent father, the all-pervasive national presence. This suggests, indeed, the ambivalent power of mass media in Nepal—it can produce a national imaginary via the circulation of texts, but those texts are nonetheless organized around a (perhaps necessary) absence.

The Community of Disbelief

It is through the daily consumption of the newspaper, Benedict Anderson has argued, that the belief in the reality of a national community composed of millions of other familiar yet anonymous national subjects is cultivated. Anderson writes,

> The significance of the mass ceremony [of reading the newspaper] is paradoxical. It is performed in silent privacy, yet each communicant is well aware

that the ceremony he performs is being replicated simultaneously by thousands of others of whose existence he is confident, yet of whose identity he
has not the slightest notion. (1983, 35)

Anderson tacitly supposes that people believe what is represented in the papers,
and that their ability to imagine a community stems from their assumption
that there are millions of unknown others believing the same stories. It is telling, then, that in Nepal the newspaper is not generally read in the privacy of the
home, but on the street or in teashops, with friends, in public and often heated
discussion. In this context, while the newspaper mediates and links strangers,
it does so not by an endlessly equivocal process of mimesis, but in an always
already positioned and far more active engagement of decoding, rebutting, and
ignoring. The horizontally undifferentiated community Anderson invokes, for
all of whose members the text is equally transparent or at least equally strange,
is very different from the community created by the half-speculative text of the
daily broadsheet in Nepal, supplemented by interpenetrating circles of gossip,
rumor, and the perception of secrecy. Indeed, if Anderson sees the national
community as imagined through the positivity of belief, the Narayanhiti incident suggests the power of disbelief to similarly consolidate and construct
national identity.

The murders at Narayanhiti allowed the resurrection of hegemonic state
discourses of the king and Nepali nationalism; they also made newly relevant
the essential mystery of royal authority. Nonetheless, this mystery no longer
served to conserve and protect the social order, but to indict it as a betrayal of
the nation and of the ideology of publicity and transparency which was supposed to structure and unite the nation. The practices of conspiracy, royal mystery, and hence also the obscurely perduring sacred authority of the king were
thus conscripted into the service of the modern social project of the nation. The
press, in the aftermath of Narayanhiti, established its new and growing power
in Nepal: to channel and direct a popular voice, unmarked by political institu-
tionality. In this sense, it indeed represented the new face of the nation. But this
nation was not a positive community but one structured around doubts, and
thus saturated with a new version of royal mystery.

Benedict Anderson concludes the revised edition of *Imagined Communities*
where he begins it, with a discussion of the national dead. In the aftermath of
the disenchantment wrought by the modern world, nationalism functioned as
a kind of secular religion, according to Anderson, to transform "fatality into
continuity, contingency into meaning" (Anderson 1991, 11). In order to do so,
nationalist biographies have to forget, as much as they remember, the deaths
that populate the history of the nation. It is only certain deaths that are remembered. Amidst the millions who die each year, "the nation's biography snatches
... exemplary suicides, poignant martyrdoms, assassinations, executions, wars,
and holocausts. But, to serve the narrative purpose, these violent deaths must
be remembered/forgotten as 'our own'" (Anderson 1991, 206).

In a similar sense, I have been arguing that what the aftermath of the Nara-yanhiti murders reveals is the extent to which a reaffirmation of nationalism required a simultaneous remembrance and forgetting of the king. It was in the name of the martyred and dead king that ordinary Nepalis could authorize their dissent against the hierarchies, including the royal hierarchies, which continued to pervade public and political life. In this way, as well, they could forget significant aspects of the king's authority and imagine, although in the space of impossibility and of grief, another—direct—mode of public engagement with their king and their community.

That nationalism, which was for most of its career a state-centered and state-directed project in Nepal, was in this way turned against those who claimed to represent the nation—the new king and government—is an irony that continues to resonate to this day, given the ongoing decline in the popularity and political power of the monarchy in Nepal and the extent to which a revolutionary group like the Maoists would take up the struggle against Gyanendra in the name of his dead brother. It also suggests, however, the ways in which new forms of mystery and doubt would structure even the democratic public sphere, despite the new transparency of information, in part because of the desire to believe in something beyond the purely political and to come together as a national community, even if united only by a collective exclusion from the truth.

It was indeed this perception of secrecy, this pervasive doubt and exclusion, that would prove the most enduring element of the royal massacre. In late 2007, Nepal's parliament, as part of the end of the Maoist civil war, and in reaction to Gyanendra's increasingly aggressive attempts to monopolize political power, voted to end the institution of the monarchy in Nepal and, in so doing, to transform the kingdom into a democratic republic (*Kathmandu Post*, "Bill Turns Nepal into Federal Republic," December 28, 2007). But even after the rise and fall of the new king's royal authority, the memory of the old king lives on, in the pervasive and undying mystery of his death.

Notes

1. Although it was officially divorced from government under both the Panchayat and democratic regimes, by the time of Birendra's rule the palace was functioning as what T. Louise Brown calls a "shadow government" (Brown 1996, 82). After the restoration of multiparty democracy in 1990 it retained this status, although to a lesser extent after Birendra's general withdrawal from politics. But the palace reduced neither its staff nor the privileges of its employees and, as was visible most starkly after Birendra's death, continued to wield considerable institutional and political power. See the discussion in Dangol 1999, especially chapters 2 and 6.

2. On October 4, 2002, Sher Bahadur Deuba, the elected Prime Minister, asked the king to postpone the upcoming elections for one year because of the difficult security situation caused by the Maoist war. Instead, the king invoked Article 127 of the

Constitution and dismissed Deuba from office on grounds of incompetence. After ruling the country himself for a week, he appointed Lokendra Bahadur Chand Prime Minister on October 11, 2002. Nonetheless, Chand was neither elected nor a representative of his party, and many considered him to be a figurehead, with the king remaining at the helm of the state. On February 1, 2005, the king again took power, but was forced to relinquish it just over a year later, after more than two months of national protests demanding his removal.

3. They did so most notably during the political protests of April–May 2004 (also called the Second Jan Andolan by their participants), during which protestors shouted slogans calling the king and his son, the crown prince Paras, murderers ("Birendrako hatyara: Gyane Paras jyanmara").

4. Jodi Dean, as I describe in more detail below, argues that the modern public is inherently paranoid, and that "publicity holds out the promise of revelation, the lure of the secret. Its pervasive mistrust drives the will to seek out and expose" (Dean 2002, 22). This means that works like Richard Hofstadter's account of American paranoia (1965) must be put in a wider context, rather than resting simply on American exceptionalism.

5. The narrative that follows is based primarily on newspaper reports from the *Kathmandu Post* and *Gorkhapatra* between June 3 and June 15, 2005, as well as selected other reports from local dailies such as *Spacetime Dainik* and *Samacharpatra* and the narratives in Harder 2002, Gregson 2002, and Shrestha 2001.

6. Most notably, these included his continued control over the army and the power to "remove difficulties," granted by Article 127 of the 1990 Constitution. This was the power the king employed on October 4, 2002, to suspend Parliament and install his own government.

7. The two newspapers were *Samacharpatra* and *Spacetime Dainik*.

8. The *Nepali Times*, however, published web bulletins during Saturday, the day after the shootings (as indicated in letters to the editor, *Nepali Times* 46, June 4–16, 2001) and the crowds that congregated around cybercafés point to the growing importance of the Internet as a source of public information much more weakly linked to the territoriality of the nation than the print or radio news. The suspension of e-mail and Internet services in Nepal after the royal coup of February 1, 2005, almost four years after the royal murders, suggests Gyanendra learnt well from this earlier incident how important the Web could be to the spread of undesirable information and opinion.

9. It was not only the Prime Minister who was shut out from the unfolding crisis. As Rama Parajuli notes, while it had been the custom during earlier democratic political crises to call for an all-party meeting to discuss the matter, no such meeting occurred this time, nor did Parliament pass any legislation or debate any issues related to the murders or to the royal succession. All matters remained with the palace (Parajuli 2002, 56).

10. Kaur's chapter in this volume deals with a comparable case of state ambivalence about the relation between political legitimacy and information disclosure.

11. Foreign labor remittances at the time of the royal killings were estimated to make up anywhere between 15 and 20 percent of Nepal's economy. In an article published in 2002, David Seddon, Jagannath Adhikari, and Ganesh Gurung estimated that about one million Nepalis were living and working abroad. See Seddon, Adhikari, and Gurung 2001.

12. In the words of Baburam Bhattarai, "To say that an automatic weapon can let itself into a highly secured room, pick out and kill all the members of one family including the country's national leader and leave all the members of another family untouched, is a gross insult to the basic intelligence of any simple living being, set aside science and logic! One hears that various kinds of robots have been invented in the world, but if anyone has invented such an aware and infallible robot, is it only the throne of Narayanhiti or the thrones of Delhi Palace and the White House as well that must be turned over to him?" (Bhattarai 2001).

13. Agnes Ku makes a similar point when she argues that "openness-secrecy constitutes a sense of democratic codes in public discourse" in which openness is associated with purity and secrecy with pollution (Ku 1998, 179).

14. Yugnath Sharma Poudel, editor of the tabloid *Shree Commander*, estimated that his sales reached 70,000 copies a day during the crisis. On average, his newspaper sold between 9,000 and 12,000 copies each day (interview).

15. The Nepali text reads, "Deshma shanti ra subyabastha kayam hun sakema matra bikasko gati tibra huna saksha. Yasartha samajma shanty, subyabastha kayam rakhi ekta ra rastriya hitko bhavanle bikas karyama sahabhagi hunu sabei nepaliharuko pramukh kartabya ho" (*Mulyankan*, Asar 20, 2059).

16. See "Pak Media Suspects RAW Hand," *Hindustan Times*, June 4, 2001; and "RAW Blamed for Palace Massacre," *Assam Tribune*, June 7, 2001.

17. The Center for Human Rights and Democratic Studies in fact called 2001 a "tragic" year for press freedom in Nepal, largely because of the increasing vigilance of the palace in the wake of Gyanendra's assumption of power (CEHURDES 2002).

18. Yugeshwar Verma writes that the *Gorkhapatra* in this period struggled to sell subscriptions, and at the time of the 1951 revolution it did not have even a thousand subscribers (Verma 1985, 11).

19. Because of distribution difficulties, however, the paper could arrive anywhere from several days to a week late (Verma 1985, 39).

20. Panchayat discourses usually represented the belief in the king's divinity as a function of popular sentiment, separate from the state's promotion of the institution of the kingship. So Kaphley writes, for example, "Right till now the King is looked upon by his subjects as an incarnation of God. [But] unlike in other monarchical states of the world, the King in Nepal has given the Country a new democratic system and, according to the demand of the age, the progressive social and economic reforms" (Kaphley 1967, 49). This simultaneously reproduced tropes of royal divinity while reestablishing the distinction between the backward or innocent Nepali villager and the modern rational state.

21. The name "Pampha devi" referred to the queen, who reportedly had millions of rupees stashed in a Swiss bank account under this pseudonym.

22. Although the movement was primarily a street protest, the mass media allowed those not actively participating in it to feel a part of it. Listening to the FM radio communication of the police during the uprising "provided a way for the otherwise unaffected, nonactivist bourgeois to feel a part of the People's Movement from within the safety of their homes" (Kunreuther 2002, 120).

23. See for example Kavita Sherchan, "Neta ki abhineta?" *Kathmandu Post*, February 25, 1997.

24. The most prominent example of this is the Shrisha Kharki case, in which a film actress committed suicide after a naked photo was published of her in the Nepali weekly *Jan Aastha* after alleged attempts to blackmail her failed. See an account of the controversy in Rai 2002.

References

Interviews (all by author)

Adhikari, Sanjib. 2003. July 15.
Dahal, Rajendra. 2002. September 17.
Ghimire, Yub Raj. 2003. July 11.
Kafle, Kapil. 2003. July 14.
Pokhrel, Govinda. 2002. September 23.
Poudel, Yugnath Sharma. 2002. March 15.

Published Works

Adams, Vincanne. 1998. *Doctors for Democracy: Health Professionals in the Nepal Revolution.* Cambridge: Cambridge University Press.
Adhikari, Bipin, and S. B. Mathe. 2001. "Impact of Information Technology on Developing Countries: The Contextual Perspective of the Assassination of King Birendra of Nepal." *Constitution: A Journal of Constitutional Development* (Centre for Constitutionalism and Demilitarisation, Lagos) 2(1): 24–44.
Anderson, Benedict. 1983. *Imagined Communities: Reflections on the Origin and Spread of Nationalism.* London: Verso.
———. 1991. *Imagined Communities: Reflections on the Origin and Spread of Nationalism.* Revised edition. London: Verso.
Bhattarai, Baburam. 2001. "The New 'Kot Massacre' Should Not Be Accepted." *Kathmandu Post,* June 3.
Brown, T. Louise. 1996. *The Challenge to Democracy in Nepal: A Political History.* London: Routledge.
Burghart, Richard. 1994. "The Political Culture of Panchayat Democracy." In Michael Hutt, ed., *Nepal in the Nineties. Versions of the Past, Visions of the Future.* New Delhi: Oxford University Press.
———. 1996. *The Conditions of Listening.* Ed. C. J. Fuller and Jonathan Spencer. New Delhi: Oxford University Press.
CEHURDES (Center for Human Rights and Democratic Studies). 2002. *Status of Press Freedom and Freedom of Expression: Nepal Report 2002.* Kathmandu, Nepal: Center for Human Rights and Democratic Studies. http://www.cehurdes.org.np/.
———. 2003. *Status of Press Freedom and Freedom of Expression: Nepal Report 2003.* Kathmandu, Nepal: Center for Human Rights and Democratic Studies. http://www.cehurdes.org.np/.
Dangol, Sanu Bhai. 1999. *The Palace in Nepalese Politics: With Special Reference to the Politics of 1951 to 1990.* Kathmandu: Ratna Pustak Bhandar.

Dean, Jodi. 2002. *Publicity's Secret: How Technoculture Capitalizes on Democracy.* Ithaca, N.Y.: Cornell University Press.

De Sales, Anne. 2002. "The Kham Magar Country: Between Ethnic Claims and Maoism." In David N. Gellner, ed., *Resistance and the State: Nepalese Experiences.* New Delhi: Social Science Press.

Dixit, Kunda. 2001. "The Valley of Halla." *Nepali Times* 46. June 6–14. http://www.nepalitimes.com.np/issue/46, accessed September 8, 2008.

Greenwald, Jeff. 2001. "Murder and Intrigue in Kathmandu." *Salon.com,* June 12. http://www.salon.com/news/feature/2001/06/12/nepal/index.html, accessed September 9, 2008.

Gregson, Jonathan. 2002. *Blood against the Snows: The Tragic Story of Nepal's Royal Dynasty.* London: Fourth Estate.

Harder, Ann-Marie. 2002. "The Mourning After." M.A. thesis, University of Chicago.

Hofstadter, Richard. 1965. *The Paranoid Style in American Politics and Other Essays.* Chicago: University of Chicago Press.

Hutt, Michael. 1994. "Drafting the 1990 Constitution." In Michael Hutt, ed., *Nepal in the Nineties: Versions of the Past, Visions of the Future.* New Delhi: Oxford University Press.

Josse, M. R. 2001. "Freedom of Expression and Opinion: Reflections through the Lens of Two Dailies." In P. Kharel, ed., *Media Practices in Nepal.* Kathmandu: Nepal Press Institute with the support of DANIDA.

Kaphley, Indra Prasad. 1967. *Fundamental Bases of Panchayat Democratic System.* Kathmandu: Nepal Press.

Kharel, P. 2001. "Media Situation: Trends and Emerging Issues since 1990." In P. Kharel, ed., *Media Practices in Nepal.* Kathmandu: Nepal Press Institute with the support of DANIDA.

Kondos, Vivienne. 1992. "*Jana-Sakti* (People Power) and the 1990 Revolution in Nepal: Some Theoretical Considerations." In Michael Allen, ed., *Anthropology of Nepal: Peoples, Problems and Processes.* Kathmandu: Mandala Book Point.

Ku, Agnes. 1998. "Boundary Politics in the Public Sphere: Openness, Secrecy and Leak." *Sociological Theory* 16(2): 172–92.

Kunreuther, Laura. 2002. "Domestic Archives: Memory and Home in Kathmandu." Ph.D. diss., University of Michigan.

Lal, C. K. 2001a. "Keep Us Informed." *Nepali Times* 47. June 15–21. http://www.nepalitimes.com.np/issue/47.

———. 2001b. "A Tribute to History." *Nepali Times* 46. June 6–14. http://www.nepalitimes.com.np/issue/46.

Leuchtag, Erica. 1958. *With a King in the Clouds.* London: Hutchinson.

Liechty, Mark. 1997. "Selective Exclusion: Foreigners, Foreign Goods, and Foreignness in Modern Nepali History." *Studies in Nepali History and Society* 2(1): 5–68.

Narayanhiti Rajdarbarko 2058 Jet 19 ko Ghatna Sambandhama Tatthya Jahera Garna Jatit Ucchastariya Samitile Jahera Gareko. 2001 (2058 BS). Antarastriya Manch: Kathmandu.

Ogura, Kiyoko. 2001. *Kathmandu Spring: The People's Movement of 1990.* Kathmandu: Himal.

Onta, Pratyoush. 1996. "Creating a Brave Nepali Nation in British India: The Rhetoric of *Jati* Improvement, Rediscovery of Bhanubhakta and the Writing of Bir History." *Studies in Nepali History and Society* 1(1): 37–76.

_____. 2002. "Critiquing the Media Boom." In Kanak Mani Dixit and Shastri Ramachandran, eds., *State of Nepal*. Kathmandu: Himal.

Parajuli, Rama. 2002 [2059 BS]. "Darbar Hatyakandako Enama Nepali Patrakarita." In Pratyoush Onta, Ramesh Parajuli, and Rama Parajuli, eds., *Midiyako Antarbastu Bibidha Bishleshan*. Kathmandu: Martin Chautari.

Pigg, Stacy. 1992. "Inventing Social Categories through Place: Social Representations and Development in Nepal." *Comparative Studies in Society and History* 34(3): 491–513.

Rai, Hemlata. 2002. "Suicide and the Press." *Himal South Asian*. June.

Raj, Prakash A. 2001. *Kay Gardeko? The Royal Massacre in Nepal*. New Delhi: Rupa.

Rajagopal, Arvind. 2001. *Politics after Television: Hindu Nationalism and the Reshaping of the Public in India*. Cambridge: Cambridge University Press.

Ramprasad, Jyotika, and James D. Kelly. 2003. "Reporting the News from the World's Rooftop: A Survey of Nepalese Journalists." *Gazette: The International Journal for Communication Studies* 65(3): 291–315.

Seddon, David, Jagannath Adhikari, and Ganesh Gurung. 2001. *The New Lahures: Foreign Employment and Remittance Economy of Nepal*. Kathmandu: Nepal Institute of Development Studies.

Sever, Adrian. 1993. *Nepal under the Ranas*. New Delhi: Oxford and IBH Publishing Co.

Sharma, Sudhindra. 2002. "The Hindu State and the State of Hinduism." In Kanak Mani Dixit and Shastri Ramachandran, eds., *State of Nepal*. Kathmandu: Himal.

Shrestha, Aditya Man. 2001. *The Dreadful Night: Carnage at Nepalese Royal Palace*. Kathmandu: Ekta.

Thapa, Manjushree. 2001. "Bhupi Sherchan on Rumor and Hearsay." *Nepali Times* 48. June 22–28.

Thompson, John. 1995. *The Media and Modernity—A Social Theory of the Media*. Cambridge: Polity.

Verma, Yugeshwar P. 1985. *The Development Message of the Gorkhapatra and Some Measures of Its Effectiveness*. Kathmandu: Centre for Nepal and Asian Studies, Tribhuvan University.

Contributors

Asad Ali Ahmed is Assistant Professor of Anthropology at Harvard University.

Angad Chowdhry is a Ph.D. candidate in the Department of Media and Film at the School of Oriental and African Studies, University of London. He is a founding member of the research collective Sacred Media Cow and was guest editor for the South Asian issue of the *International Journal of Zizek Studies*.

Tejaswini Ganti is Assistant Professor in the Department of Anthropology and its Program in Culture and Media at New York University. She is author of *Bollywood: A Guidebook to Popular Hindi Cinema*.

Raminder Kaur is Senior Lecturer in the Department of Anthropology at the University of Sussex. She is author of *Performative Politics and the Cultures of Hinduism* and (with Virinder Kalra and John Hutnyk) *Diaspora and Hybridity*, and co-editor of *Bollyworld: Popular Indian Cinema through a Transnational Lens* and *Travel Worlds: Journeys in Contemporary Cultural Politics*.

Genevieve Lakier is a Ph.D. candidate in the Department of Anthropology at the University of Chicago. Her work focuses on the relationship between protest, violence, and democratization in Nepal.

William Mazzarella is Associate Professor of Anthropology at the University of Chicago. He is author of *Shoveling Smoke: Advertising and Globalization in Contemporary India*.

Christopher Pinney is Visiting Crowe Professor of Art History at Northwestern University and Professor of Anthropology and Visual Culture at University College London. His books include *Camera Indica: The Social Life of Indian Photographs*; *"Photos of the Gods": The Printed Image and Political Struggle in India*; and *The Coming of Photography in India*.

Index

237

Milton Keynes UK
Ingram Content Group UK Ltd.
UKHW032140140224
437844UK00009B/886